Ghost in the Brazen Bull

Using Continuing Anglican Theology
to Confront the
Ignominious Contraptions
of the
Artificial General Intelligence

By Fr. Mike DellaVecchia & Jean Hardouin
of
Traditional Anglican Church of America

Ghost in the Brazen Bull: Using Continuing-Anglican Theology to Confront the Ignominious Contraptions of the Artificial General Intelligence – A Commonitorium of the Praxeologion of Traditional Anglican Church of America

Written by Fr. Mike DellaVecchia and Dea. Jean Hardouin

The Jeremiad Christian Homesteaders Gazette, Publisher
www.jeremiadchristianhomesteadersgazette.com

Authored and published by permission and under the guidance of Archbishop Rick Aaron Reid of Traditional Anglican Church of America

Let it Forever be Held in Anathema:

That Menace of Artificial General Intelligence So Equipped by its Untold Mass Consente by Waye of the Ranke Stupidity of Unholy Publick Assent, It, Whose Dark Specter Shouldst See Iniquity Hatched by Daye From the Horror of a Droth Contrivance to Sire the Odious Androides of the Technological Singularity, that Wickedly Programmed Future for all Men, an Entity Thusly Forged From Wicked Artifice the Which Hath the Folke Been Slavishly Wrought in Spirit by Anxious Cares O'er the Phantom Automaton of Godless Intellection, that Queerie Similitude of Much Skull Duggery and Rascaldom, Borne to the Quicke by the Imbecilic Fake Sentience That is Forged by So-Named Machinery Learning and the Which Will Have Replaceth Man with the Trans-Human Bots who, to Witt, Hath of Late Most Foolishly Became the Lesser Man-Likened Androides of the Mandated Dumbness by Nighte—Those Degraded and Deluded née-Homo-Sapien Operators Venomously at Large, who Withe Fastidious Faithlessness Firstly Will Have it Allowed That Haughty Pride Should Discard From Their Vainglorious Hearts and the Soules of the Publicke the Image-Interiore of the One True God, and Lastly Wouldst Have Uncorked Filthe and Duned Upon Ev'ry Harried Homestead, Schoole, Shoppe, and Church!

- 18, July Daye of Our Lord, A.D. 2023 -

Table of Contents

- Introduction -
The Brazen Bull of Stochastic Probability

When I was twenty years old, my father and I visited a town in the Province of Caserta, in Italy.

This hilly corner of the Campania contained the ruins of a Medieval castle. The town was Gioia Sannitica.

The lady at the souvenir shop at our hotel in Rome, who spoke fluent English, told me what my grandfather had always told me. It was that the name of the town, when translated into English, was "Joyous Saints."

Gramps had also told me, "DellaVecchia's have always come from this place."

This rural hamlet is where I would meet my third cousins. My father and I arrived there in the early afternoon on a sunny Thursday in March. The woman at the front of the gray house with the white door dropped her rake when she heard my father say her last name. Her name was Rosa.

Her eyes opened wide and her mouth fell open and she screamed into the house for her family to come out and she ran to us and yanked at my father's arms to come out and be hugged. We were now surrounded by many people dragging us inside, holding our hands, hugging us, kissing our cheeks.

I was excited to get to know my twenty—maybe forty— cousins, sweet laughing people all full of Life. I was given tours of their two red-tiled roof homes and small farms.

First, a barn with a rustic apartment with a chamber pot up top, with its low-sloping bronze green roof, where we were offered to sleep but Dad said we couldn't. The main house with its large living room and oversized kitchen, one and a half floors and a root-cellar, a stable with bovine, a tobacco-curing shed, and a small plantation outback. The front yard and side drive, all virgin gravel wrapping around toward an old metal incinerator that was shared by the other low-rise house with its own shed and barn, and a slate-walled water well, and a tiny bakehouse, and a citrus garden, and another driveway with pillars to hook up cattle, and several overfed mongrels skulking around on patrol, quiet and sniffing everyone, descending and ascending the gravel footpath that led to another entrance to Via Colle.

On this day I would be handed cup after cup of homemade red and white wine and cheese in the living room. Cugine everywhere, some of them not really cousins but jumping in and out of the houses as if they had always lived there.

Young men clad in plaid shirts and denim from America, the pant legs and sleeves always too long. Robust girls with thick wrists and ankles and rosy cheeks in print dresses, white socks, and tough saddle shoes sitting on the arm rests or cushions of homemade and antique worn furniture.

Beautiful tan young ladies named Maria and Angela and Anna and Cristina and Lina and Gianna, the wives and daughters dressed in work clothes and the older single women and widows dressed like 1950s movie stars but looking with grins only at the floor.

All the men at the far walls overlooking everybody, never walking, and making wise cracks at all the movers and runners and chatterboxes and trouble-makers and little bigshots—the fussing females and the children and the dogs and cats. The sunlight that poured through the windows blinked into dazzling signals of life that broke through it every second.

Old men with canes and old women in kerchiefs that they pulled down halfway amid their scalps sat underneath the

2

four big yellow hanging sacks of formaggio and black iron pots in the kitchen and clutched cups of wine and black coffee and lemony water and all the younger ladies were looking at me and were saying silly secret things quietly to each other in Italian and giggling and then gesturing softly at my dad and some of them shrugging and then looking back at me again.

My father and I accepted the sudden invitation of the eldest DellaVecchia to go on a walk with him. "Later, not-a now," he promised.

"Later?" asked Dad.

"Yeah, you come-a with-a me, later," Angelo assured Dad.

Here was a loud 57-year-old man with his top two buttons undone to exhibit his wire-haired chest, his harmless braggadocio blaring beneath brown-tanned skin, and a full head of grey-streaked rooster black hair pulled backwards, and several missing frontal and side teeth in his constant smile that tried hard to seem somehow menacing, and a lean laborer's build. He was happy but he let you know that he did not want to appear happy, but instead powerful and feared and strong and always in control, so long as his wife ran everything. He just knew that he *knew* that he *knew* that he was content, but you could also tell that he was always working so that he could earn his happiness. He was acting the part of supreme authority, the local man who knew everything and who ran everything everywhere, probably even the planets up yonder. Italy, to me, was a place that let a man, even a cocky everyday man, just be a man.

It was explained to us by his wife Rosa that he wanted us to venture off with him, to walk uphill on a trail through the woods, to visit the old castle.

3

"Something tells me we had better do as Angelo says," answered my Dad laughing. Now, Angelo knew Dad had said this but nodded hard and he laughed, too.

Among all my cousins, Angelo was also appearing to be the most excited to host our visit, because of how our presence as his "wealthy" American cousins appeared to upgrade his social standing.

We were certain that after my father had already given Rosa £1,372, the equivalent of a thousand U.S. dollars, he was not interested in anything other than showing us off. Dad was never expecting to stay long, but this couple insisted that we should.

Giving his family time to prepare food for us, he hurried us into the little village. This gave all these cugini the time to pile into the houses and give us grand tours.

Although the local cafoni and Carabinieri were very polite, it was clear they regarded Angelo as something of a madman. Angelo was always drinking too much, often getting into arguments, and telling his infamous tall tales that were either meant to forestall a creditor, or, to excuse his wintertime absence from a Switzerland-bound agriculture team. Or, they were just intended to impress giggly young ladies.

One time, said a dairy hauler, a carabinieri had to arrest a foreman who was chasing Angelo around the village with a shovel because he had "borrowed" a dump truck to rescue his daughters from a UFO!

My father and I had during the late morning been sitting and laughing along on bar stools drinking Ouzo at Osteria Via Nocito but we were warned with albeit-respectful winks and smirks by the men drinking here not to accept any "schemi veloci" from our cousin.

4

I do not know how my father knew that this term meant, "fast schemes," but Dad had been around old-world Italians in Brooklyn all his life and he did appear to enjoy all this attention.

Even Angelo, who did seem concerned about what the cafoni were telling my dad about him, appeared to appreciate how our presence there was making everyone feel. My dad, glad that it had become lunch hour, paid the bar tab for about twenty people. Angelo now leered over at every one of them, as if expecting them automatically to elect him for mayor.

After lunch surrounded by his immediate family (and then suddenly by the tons of people who filed into the house), we realized that Angelo was nonetheless merely (or most often *was*) a lovable well-healed rake, his eyes never sent away from his family.

His five children, three boys and two girls, adored him, always holding onto his arms or dragging his eyes and ears toward their attention.

He announced to everybody that he was about to take us on a walk and that they should stay in the house. So we walked outside and Dad dragged me away from all the ladies who gave me many goodbyes and shook my hand and grabbed my sleeve as I left them behind.

Angelo puffed out his chest and he leaned his forearm over the gate of his small tobacco plantation during our exit from his property, to show it off to us, and he also showed us where he kept pigs, and had five cows and a bull and where the family made their own cheese, olive oil, and wine and how they did not ever need to go into Naples for groceries but confessed that the men had to go into Switzerland for work every winter.

Angelo was also known to have a notorious following among the embarrassed parents of the town's teenagers. The youth got their first cigarettes or liquor from him—given these gifts provided, as we were so-warned back at the bar—that the youngsters would come away with him into the fields behind their Caselle neighborhood whenever the Sun went down behind the Matese Mountains to help him with his work. They would help him and his kids watch for UFOs! This was a man who never ever wanted to be alone.

Sometimes, Angelo told us, the ghost of Spartacus could be seen skulking behind the juniper and oak trees of the southwest slope overlooking Via Colle. As if its originator had just lost the Third Servile War, the apparition was said to descend down an overgrown southwest-Appenenine trail during twilight on Tuesdays, trying to find the Volturno River, in his escape from General Crassus, to reach the Mediterranean, where Cilician pirates would smuggle him to Sicily.

Angelo also presented to us the permanently locked stone house that my great-great grandfather had built just twenty feet from his home, a two-story house made of bare stones without ivory or moss, covered in long oak wood slates, its foundation made of small boulders impacted into the clay soil and the tough brown grass. Nobody had opened the door in a decade because, as Angelo told us, it was said that opening its door would compromise the setting of its lintel and the house would resultantly come tumbling down.

In the late twentieth century, many Italians left Italy for places such as Ireland, the United Kingdom, Canada, or the U.S., escaping the reforms of the socialist takeover of King Victor Emanuel and his son, Umberto I. For them, the Marxists were worse than the Nazis. And, by the 1920s, Benito Mussolini, who forced the people of Campania into state labor, refused to allow anyone to leave the peninsula.

6

"But-that a-Hitler, he was not-a so bad-a guy, that Hitler guy-a," said Angelo, who added, "Adolfo, he not-a make us fight-a when-a we no longer said-a we ain't gonna fight-a for him no more, so too badda for him and we stay at home and we milk-a the cows!" He blew a raspberry up into the air as we walked away from the "Casa Vecchia-DellaVecchia" back into the main house.

The DellaVecchia's who had left Gioia Sannitica in 1899 settled in Hamden and New Haven, Connecticut. My father was born in Hamden in 1934. His father found the address of these cugini again in 1981 and visited there in 1982. They did not have a phone and had to return his calls from the Western Union office in the town. Gramps slept for a week in the barn apartment during his visit and now it was our turn to meet everybody, in 1988.

I had been having the time of my life and even got a wedding proposal from my timid teenaged cousin, Lina, via her outspoken mother, Rosa. I turned the offer down, because I had been previously warned to expect the proposal in a whispered aside by my father.

Dad had figured out why Lina was suddenly dressed like an angel in white lace and, looking like a beautiful drink of milk inside a table doily, she had served all the lunchtime food, although Dad was meanwhile admonishing me while I drank about a quart-load of their red wine, "We do not have the money to get Lina to America and pay a dowry, so forget about marrying your third cousin, Lina."

Dad was also noting that, because the humors of the big man's eyes were yellow, Angelo was obviously stricken with liver disease. Pop advised that we ought to accept Angelo's invitation to go on a walk with him, to leave our other cugini behind and follow the man to the highest point in Caselle, to visit the castle, because we were probably seeing our cousin during his last days.

We walked out along the gravel dog path onto a pebbled cutaway beneath trellises of grape vines alongside a row of halved wooden barrels of young almond and date bushes in soil. It was mid-afternoon by now and I drunkenly asked if we were walking to see the ghost of Spartacus.

"Non vedremo Spartaco!" came the chuckling response from a younger man, who ran up just behind us named Franco, a non-blood relation, a house painter who had married one of our cousins. He was informing us that Spartacus's ghost would not appear on the roster that evening. He had his eyes on a road cutoff up ahead.

Franco darted past as we walked along the Via Colle and we watched him trudge up an old logging trail by himself with what appeared to be two cans of paint. He was suddenly followed uphill by teens, who had just come out of their hiding places in the brush, wearing Metallica and Slayer jackets, smoking cigarettes.

"Franco gives them their cigarettes," said my dad to me quietly. I wondered how he could have known this.

"No, no," said Angelo. "Franco, naw, he just gone uppa the hill so he can maybe paint-a somebody house-a," explained Angelo.

"Sure, I'll just bet he did," said my father, upon which Angelo boldly winked at me and I laughed aloud.

We were passing many fields of trees and bushes in spring bloom—Melanurca apple and Cilento-fig trees jumping out of scrubby volcanic fields that form the low ridges exposed to direct sun, white citrus blossoms budding in rich olive groves with broken rusty iron fences, with green and yellow colors sensed like smells in the body, so beautiful I felt as if I did not ever want to go home to Brooklyn, New York. The sweet odor

8

of wine, and the enchanting aroma of tobacco leaves coming from everywhere, and the unexpected flavor of chocolate *tasted* as a smell coming from stucco-encrusted homes just yards from the edge of the road. Antique browned machines of war and labor, canons and tanks and steam shovels, stranded and rusting in the fields and covered with old graffiti and many children jumping from them onto the brush on the sandy soil. The salty maddening wind from the Tyrrhenian Sea sent dozens of miles over the Pozzuoli harbor that had brushed over the sprawl of Naples, collecting the scent of formaggio and candy and dirty concrete and ancient sewers and oil painting, all of it coming across the Campania to this very road and dropping its "contents" whenever the wind stopped and strangely seemed to turn back to the sea after knocking into the white image of the castle way at the top of hill we were ascending.

I did not know the history of the mysterious Castello di Gioia Sannitica except that it was built by the Lombards. We were on a four-mile hike up the Via Caselle. My dad said it was good for me to "work off that wine."

"Ha un fantasma!" said Angelo. I could have sworn that Angelo had just said the name of the 1979 Don Coscarelli horror film, but I saw my father flipping, concerned, through his Berlitz translation book.

"That place is haunted by a ghost?" Dad asked.

"Sì, questo fantasma è un dolore nel culo!" More flipping sounds now came from Dad on his Berlitz book.

But I figured out what Angelo meant by how he rolled his eyes and gestured as if he were angry at a woman. "She drive-a me pazzo!"

"'Pazzo' means crazy," said Dad.

9

"Is the ghost a lady or a man?" I asked.

"The ghosta? She a bigga fatta lady and she a bigga pain in my uh abbondanza!" (He didn't actually say "abbondanza"). I was now roaring with laughter. Angelo began talking without a breath in Italian, saying strings of words about how he apparently hated the ghost and that "she" had done many annoying things to him but that he did not know how to get rid of her.

There is a lot you can understand when you experience a person speaking in a foreign language by watching his face, hearing him talk in a high-pitched voice like a lady who nags him and groans in ghostly wails, and seeing him shrug as if there was just nothing he could do about her.

"For crying out loud, we could have gone to see the Aqueduct today," said Dad.

Pop muttered something to the effect of *how* he could have *ever* taken me on this hike, etcetera, etcetera, pinching his brow in his fingers, walking onward, darting his eyes around the trees.

Thanking Dad for letting us take this trip I could not take my eyes off of him (being merely that I utterly loved my father), while Angelo spoke in broken English and sometimes uttered long strings of self-amused Italian, probable idiomatic expressions, some of it surely curse words. When you are still young enough to idolize your own dad, you are amazed at how "they" (i.e., dads) just seem to know in advance everything that is bound to happen.

"Dad, just what *exactly* are we going up there to see, at that Castle?" Dad laughed and rolled his eyes as Angelo broke in.

"She drive me crazy every night. You gotta see this a thing-a. She got a bigga mouth!" said Angelo.

10

My father, now folding his hands as he walked, put one hand in the air to wave to Angelo to just to keep on walking.

"Give me a second, Mike," said Dad. "What a bunch of bull crap," I heard Dad say.

I knew that *if* Pop had not already figured out what was going on, he would have pulled us away, back toward the house. The truth could never have been all that bad, because here was Pop merely shaking his head, holding back a laugh but also staring into space telling me to let him be the one to tell this tale to my mom.

"No, seriously, what's going on, Dad?" Dad opened his mouth to take a breath before he spoke but closed his mouth just as quickly.

Instead, Angelo was talking and talking and now pointing at the trees and the sky (probably saying things about UFOs and ghosts and comets), and then he suddenly stopped right before Dad finally answered my question and told us about how the ghost had once helped him fix his car on the way home from Naples.

Angelo spewed out loud Italian words very rapidly, while he pantomimed driving a car, and wiped imaginary sweat away from his forehead, and finally indicated that there was a bigga car accident. Finally, he mimed that a ghost came flying to his wreck from midair, went right to work on his Fiat, and fixed his car "right good-a."

"OK, so the ghost fixes cars, does she now?" Dad asked him.

"She crazy but she pretty nice, my ghost-a! You gonna see her so you be nice-a!"

Dad face palmed and finally explained to me that this was Angelo's way of paying us back for the £1,372 gift.

"Angelo sent his brother-in-law Franco up the hill ahead of us with those kids to go pull off a stunt," he said

"What kind of stunt?" I asked.

"I think they are all going to dress up as ghosts," Dad explained. "Or at least Franco is."

Just then, five of the kids came running down the Via Caselle, clutching boxes of cigarettes. They said "Grazie!" to Angelo.

"So, Cousin Angelo bought all the teenagers cigarettes with the £1,372?" I asked.

"I hope not all of it," Dad said. Angelo shot Dad a hard smirky look as if to say that the money was *his* to spend as he liked. Apparently, he had sneaked it out of wherever his wife had stashed it.

"This better be good, Cugine!" Dad yelled.

"Oh, you gonna like it a lot!" answered Angelo.

Finally entering the frontal precincts of the castle, Angelo stopped talking. We passed through the ruptured walls of stables, holding our balance on tan metamorphic stones and flat boulders that formed into steps, passing up a winding causeway toward the outer courtyard where colonnades now lay in fragmented marble pieces in the adjoining patches of grass. Angelo led us through the inner courtyard, where we stepped cross the scattered pieces of the stone curtain, stepping into the remains of the tower and the keep, across the sun-bleached slates of the bailey, and walked through the granite chunks of the corps de logis, and the rusty iron bars of the collapsed gatehouse and over the fallen stones of portcullis, out to the fortress areas. We strode along the igneous walkway that spilled into the apartments area and looked over the wrecked homes and shops of a long-dead community. Angelo was walking fast but tolerated our request to take pictures with Dad's new drug-store Minolta 35-mm camera, or to view something through my binoculars.

"What is that shiny thing way at the end of the fortress?" I was pointing in the direction of the a partially fallen rampart. A metallic plate was reflecting the last bit of daylight our way through one of the preserved battlements.

"We go look at that now, come on," Angelo said.

Stepping down a beige shale staircase to a split level that was eight feet lower, we stepped off the slates and hopped across the fallen stones of the southwest rampart of the fortress. We walked along the five-to-eight foot sections of the wall. The sunlight on the metal ahead bristled out yellow rays that suggested it was made of brass or bronze.

"Come in-a here with me," said Angelo, and we followed him as he turned at the left corner of the broken southwest turret onto lines and piles of schist bricks that just barely betrayed images of right angles which indicated outlines of soldier apartments.

"Look-a down-a now, boys!" Angelo ordered.

We threw our gaze down toward a patio, reached by a volcanic-rock ramp that we sometimes needed to slide down on our buttocks, to offload ourselves onto a cleared piazza.

"Dad, I saw something like this in slides in my art history class."

"Well, I can't believe people put this down here," said Dad. He never wanted to hear about my art studies. He had thrown me

13

a bone by taking me on this sales trip with his company. I had spent all day walking around the Vatican museum with him a day earlier. However, this was a working-class man, who could not understand how I had talked him into allowing me to major in art. I always used to tell him, "It's because you taught me how to be a good salesman, Dad."

This lower level was formed by a much older positioning of slabs of impacted diabase, suggesting that the castle and fortress had been built on top of this very ancient level.

"We are in the middle of the remains of a temple, Pop."

In the back of the piazza was a six-foot-high bronze bull. It stood ten or fifteen feet from the remains of a shale wall.

"Moooooo!" bleated Angelo.

"This is a hunk of bull, alright!" Dad said.

If Angelo was not being such a hilarious cut-up we might have otherwise have been scared.

Meanwhile, our manic cousin was shoving broken sticks underneath the bull. Teenagers came out from behind the wall and said nothing but smoked their cigarettes and put more sticks underneath the bull. They lit the sticks with lighters that they removed from their jeans. I remember asking one of the female members if Angelo had bought her her jeans, which were a rare item in the 1980s and she gladly said he did.

My father meanwhile had walked around the wall and saw a road leading back to the Via Casella and a Carabinieri officer writing down things in a leather-bound pad, talking to a couple of the young Italian metalheads. My dad's mouth was dropped open because everywhere he looked were things made of bronze—roof sections, fountain parts, drain pipes and gutters, arms of old statues, street lamps—with some of the oxidation brushed away, but most of it greener than Ireland. The metal plate that rose above the wall that we had seen earlier, which Angelo had been brushing to make it appear fresh again, was now reflecting the dim dusk. Angelo was running a scrap-metal business.

The region was full of bronze, brass, and copper discarded articles, and Angelo was making book here. Another wall that was perpendicular to this one, partially concealed a three-wall shed, in which sat a moonshine still.

The Carabinieri officer was writing all this down. During the 1940s, moonshine had become illegal. Angelo had a still. Its hoses were made of copper and were thus as green as clover but its boiler was made of bronze, an alloy which oxidizes at a darker shade of green.

Suddenly Angelo ran over to the officer while reaching into his pocket and gave him the rest of the money my dad had given him. It was pay-off time in the Campania. My father, dumbfounded, stared at the officer to make sure he had gotten enough cash, with my father counting aloud the twenties that were placed, one by one, into the officer's palm, and then we all watched him drive away.

"So I just paid that piece of trash £900."

"She's a worth it, you gonna see," said Angelo, who neither appeared as promising nor as enthusiastic, suddenly.

Just then, screaming was heard coming from inside the bull. The fire was well under way.

"Here she comes!" Angelo announced. "Come on ova here-a and we exorcise this bull-a."

"Oh, no, please tell me nobody is inside that statue," said Pop.

"You gonna get outta here, you sonuvabeecha inna the name-a Santa Maria, you stupid-a beecha!" yelled Angelo at the bull.

Dad did not know things would get this far. But he could have probably put it on a short list. He stood next to me to make sure nothing happened to me even though I was already taller and stronger than him. Angelo was screaming at the bull.

"And you leave-a our farm all alone, you stupid bigga shotta, you!" Angelo was now furiously hitting the bull with a stick, shouting at it in Italian.

"Vafancullo! Tu e un rompipale!" These are expressions that should not ever be Google-translated.

The screaming grew fiercer inside the bronze beast as the fire raged.

Just then a chamber on the "belly" side of the statue was revealed by one of the Metalheads, who pulled aside a clasp to unfasten its door. Out poked Franco's hysterical face and then out came the rest of him.

We got closer to the man, hoping to help him, only to notice that the fire had not been built close enough to the bull to cause Franco to get scorched, but that the sticks had been safely separated from away it.

"Stupid idiots," said Dad.

Franco, who was wearing a woman's blonde wig and was wearing painter's togs that were painted fluorescent green, finally jumped out of the bull and ran across the piazza while Angelo and the kids took turns beating the hysterical transvestite with sticks, tumbling out across the piazza in the early moonlight, then up the steps, across the bailey and out the temple entrance, through the fallen stones of the corps de logis, toward the Via Caselle.

Five pre-teens dressed in fluorescent green painters togs "flew" around the piazza, howling—some of them smoking cigarettes—and causing my father to nod his head in acceptance of what he was just put through.

"These must be the ghosts!" I exclaimed, laughing hard at everything that was going on.

"You like-a this?" Angelo asked us.

"Sure, it's fine ya nutjob," Dad managed, trying not to appear furious.

"No, you you like-a this, cugine?" Angelo repeated.

"Really, I get it," Dad answered, then said more quietly, "Stupid idiots."

The Metalheads, three or four of them who were too cool to join in the drama, were guffaw and then falling against each other, holding their wheezing chortles up their noses, pointing at my father, puffing on their butts, and seeing how my dad was now shaking his head in disbelief. They threw anything they could into the fire now, including strips of bronze, which, when burned emitted a foul odor, which sent Angelo through the roof, so to speak. Angelo ran back to the fire and kicked the kids out of the piazza and started kicking the fire down to its embers and scraping the smokey bottoms of his shoes on the slate floor. The smell was so bad that Pop was pinching his nostrils together.

"I can't believe I came to Italy." Dad was now sitting on a boulder laughing to himself. He could not stop. These were belly laughs that I always enjoyed when I was a child, watching Daffy Duck abuser Elmer Fudd on the television.

What was the harm here, anyway? Was utility not served? These were more innocent times, if not their being a profane side show taking place within the mere foothills of a near Apocalypse.

At least Angelo had a workforce that served a variety of community needs. The kids got paid for finding the scrap. Meanwhile all the kids, the preteens included, were being babysat by Angelo and by Franco, and by the older teens, so that many parents could work during the day. Angelo had many customers, especially the police. It was all very demented. But I considered the whole racket to be incredibly entertaining and, what, with my being twenty and all, well, I wanted to stay here forever.

"Italy is awesome, Dad!"

On the way back to the house in Angelo's car (his Fiat had been parked by Franco behind the wall), Dad explained to me that Angelo was the "entertainment" for the tourists who visit the castle. Usually the "shows" end up being "better" (presumably) but we had basically dropped in on the family that morning after all. We had not told them we were visiting them. The Carabinieri in the town center had to give us directions to the house.

"We do it better next time," said Angelo, who added, "but you are so special so we hadda give up the space-a-ship show," said Angelo. Understandably, the UFO gig on Tuesdays was a lesser event. Angelo's crew had just been given a commission to do the "Brazen Bull" show. Dad added:

"And on the side, he has a scrap metal business and he apparently pays off the cops every week," Pop explained. Angelo also wanted me to marry his daughter and convince my dad to invest as a partner in his scrap-metal business.

When we got back to the house, Lina, her love remaining unrequited by my arrogant heart, was seated on the couch crying, being comforted by Rosa, her mother. Rosa shot up from the couch and dragged him into the kitchen by the canvas fabric of his shirt's shoulder. She was screaming at him in the kitchen now, in Italian. Her man had found the stash of money.

Although the family was poor, and the father was a hustler, all the men had wrist watches, because they were line workers and farm helpers during the day. They were all glancing at their watches now. We said our goodbyes and all the hugs and the cheek kisses were so powerful that I can still feel them these 35 years later.

My father hugged Rosa and put some more Liras into cash into her hand but he did not ever tell me how much he had given her. It is better that some words never reach the air, lest Satan overhear them and, in this case, plant a new idea in Angelo's head, or so I figured.

It should also be mentioned that before we had left the castle scrap yard, that there was another device that Angelo had showed us.

This piece was a type of boiler that was roughed into concrete backfills at the base of the lowest part of the granite wall in the piazza. It was an Aeolipile. The boiler was the same kind as the one in the still.

Two bronze pipes extended out of this tank, and a third, located in the column rising from it, was a shaft that fed into a rotating unit which was inserted upon an axis. My dad said it was some kind of a heating implement for the castle. Angelo told us that it had sat here on the lower level and that he had found it beneath the stones twenty years earlier. It had been part of the much older temple, not the castle. I made the

19

upper part spin with my hands after Angelo demonstrated how. It too was made of bronze.

Pondering the Aeolipile all during his life is probably what kept Angelo coming back to the castle and starting a business there (and he did actually give the teenagers cash as well as cigarettes). The desire for truth inspires not merely magneticity toward the source, but various peripheral motivations, such as when the lover of classical architecture, such as the carpenter William H. Reynolds, builds an amusement park—such as Dreamland in Coney Island in 1904—featuring a re-creation of the Roman Forum, because he is amazed with the "golden-section" proportion of rectangles. Angelo was thus collecting antiques because it helped him to understand where he was living as a citizen of an ancient land and to imagine how he and his family fit into the history, if only just to keep it animated for spectators.

What I am about to tell you are things that I could never have known back then. Certainly, I enjoyed my access to all the libraries of New York City I could ever hope to walk into; and, so it was not the Internet of today that led me to an understanding of what I had observed then: There is indeed a supernatural "dimension" about which people are discernibly aware. As a father, my father's love gave him Spiritual Discernment. This only arrives through Faith and is why good fathers will protect and support their homes while teaching their sons about how to survive. Meanwhile, ambitious men such as Angelo, invent machines or develop weird means to help them cope with evils they cannot use their will to overcome. I was in the presence of something that needed collateral definition, a spectacle wrought by a madman, a distant cousin of mine, in the twilight of an Italian countryside.

What in Heaven's name was an Aeolipile?

Much later in this book, an Appendix will give definitions written by ancient and antiquated authors for it, and as regards related mechanisms. Here are the words of Hero of Alexandria, about his formulation of a concept for this steam-driven device written by Marcus Vitruvius Pollio:

"Place a cauldron over a fire: a ball shall revolve on a pivot. A fire is lighted under a cauldron... containing water, and covered at the mouth by the lid... With this the bent tube... communicates, the extremity of the tube being fitted into a hollow ball... Opposite to the extremity... place a pivot... resting on the lid... and let the ball contain two bent pipes, communicating with it at the opposite extremities of a diameter, and bent in opposite directions, the bends being at right angles and across the lines... As the cauldron gets hot it will be found that the steam, entering the ball through... passes out through the bent tubes towards the lid, and causes the ball to revolve, as in the case of the dancing figures (*The Pneumatics*; Hero of Alexandria; Sec. 50: "The Steam Engine"; A.D. 70).

These complicated instructions (the ellipses above replace the letters referring to the diagrams that Hero had drawn), were based on the following theory by Pollio:

"Æolipylæ are hollow brazen vessels, which have an opening or mouth of small size, by means of which they can be filled with water. Previous to the water being heated over the fire, but little wind is emitted, as soon, however, as the water begins to boil, a violent wind issues forth. Thus a simple experiment enables us to ascertain and determine the causes and effects of the great operations of the heavens and the winds" (*de Architectura;* Marcus Vitruvius Pollio; Book I; Chap. 6; B.C. 15).

My father, Angelo, and myself were the last people to leave the piazza. Or, so we thought. Somebody had crept inside the bull again and was howling like a ghost. But Angelo was not laughing as he drove the tiny Fiat but my father and I were giggling—my father, more from sheer exhaustion. Angelo told us the real occupant of the bull was the "real ghost." Or, "Il fantasma reale."

My father winked at me. However, Angelo did not break into a grin. I decided he had become serious because he had to face his wife about how he had spent the cash gift. I recall the idea of the ghost haunting Achilles in the Iliad, which the described as "vapor" representing his deceased friend

"He opened his arms towards him as he spoke and would have clasped him in them, but there was nothing, and the spirit [psukhê] vanished as a vapor, gibbering and whining into the earth. Achilles sprang to his feet, smote his two hands, and made lamentation saying, 'Of a truth even in the house of Hades there are ghosts [psukhai] and phantoms that have no life in them; all night long the sad spirit [psukhê] of Patroklos has hovered over head making piteous moan, telling me what I am to do for him, and looking wondrously like himself'" (*Illiad;* Homer; Scroll 93; Lines 93-120; B.C. 700).

The vapor had been used at the temple to make a figure of a Roman god move or talk. It probably astounded a crowd of people in the piazza more than two thousand years ago when it had been part of the original temple. It may even have been used to cause the temple door or the doors of the later castle to open, by a process whereby hoses fill up with hot water shooting out of the boiler, which pull down upon ropes connected to the doors via pulleys.

The bull, the "Brazen Bull," was an ancient torture mechanism. When I heard it described during a lecture on comedy as a student, I was shocked and figured that Angelo had dug up this device, or it was given to him in exchange for some of his moonshine. It is said that the hills and barns of Italy are filled with untold ancient "treasures," as such. Some people believe that such objects are cursed.

22

I will name its origin, shortly, but before I left his home, I asked Angelo what the name of the "inner ghost" was.

"Qual è il nome del fantasma?" I asked him at the door.

All he said was that he did not know the name of the ghost but told me that my great-grandfather ("Giovanni DellaVechia") had told his father that she had killed somebody thousands of years ago, who was named "Felix." He used his authentic pantomime, gestures, exaggerated facial nuances, and broken English to tell me all this (he was a one-man Comedia dell'Arte). His sons were embarrassed and dragged their dad into the bedroom to put him to sleep, consoling him and rubbing his head and shoulders while comedically shouting at him just to shut up and be at peace and I swear they were affectionately imitating my roaring way of laughing as the bedroom door closed. This was just after they had given Pop and me final hugs. The Americans hopped into our rented Fiat and Dad drove us back to the International Hotel in Rome.

The Brazen Bull was invented by the sculptor Perilaus, and brought as a gift for the tyrant Phalaris of Athens. Describing the bull as a means of executing criminals, Phalaris asked for a demonstration, which Perilaus obliged. As he opened the door of the bull, Phalaris, who was disgusted by the sadism of the invention, cruelly threw the sculptor inside, locked the door and had his men light a fire beneath it. Steam from water at the bottom of the belly and from the man's burning body shot through the nostrils while the sculptor screamed. Phalaris eventually had him removed from the bull, and tossed down a cliff to his death (*Biblioteca Historica; Diodorus Siculus;* Book IX; Chap. 18-19; B.C. 60).

Wait, now. What is Discernment. How did my dad "know" nearly everything that was going to happen merely by pre-witnessing a few variables earlier that day?

Today, after now being slightly older than my father was in 1988, I possess the same ability to figure matters out for myself and family, without needing many facts being explained to me.

My son, Michael, looks at me much the same way I used to look at my father—amazed, at how I can "figure out so much stuff-about-stuff" that is going on. I answer, "It's because I pray to God to give me strength, goodness, and wisdom, and I also have lived for many years."

Eleven-hundred years after it was placed here, an Aeolidipile is encountered by a young Saint Thomas Aquinas, at the time he was being tutored by Saint Albertus Magnus. It was late at night when Thomas entered Master Albertus' laboratory for the very first time. Young Thomas had been reading his teacher's description of the gizmo in his bed chamber and how it could be incorporated into the creation of an "Androides," which is a steam-moved automaton. He was already disturbed when a figure approached him in the darkness (*Supplement to Cyclopaedia: or, An Universal Dictionary of Arts and Sciences;* Ephraim Chambers; Vol. I; London: 1728).

"Salve!" said the Androides. Thomas was terrified.

The thing had moved itself toward Thomas, being apparently switched on by a rope connected to the laboratory door and was speaking in a hissing "steam speech" (*ibid*).

Thomas picked up a wooden beam and beat the Androides, smashing it to pieces on the floor. Albertus ran into the laboratory and stared at the pieces of his work on the floor. It had taken him thirty years to build (*ibid*). Several descriptions of this tale can be read in the Appendix.

Back in New York, I was visiting my grandfather, Vincent "Jim" DellaVecchia, and as we entered his home, he was yelling at someone over the phone. It was his Italian-language teacher. He was always annoyed with her, Rose Uave, because she was obviously in love with him and they had many arguments over his Neopolitan dialect, whereof she always told him that his communication skills were out of synch with her classical Roman speech. He always imitated her, saying, "Jeem, you needa talka gooda!" By portraying the Patrone above Gramp's Plebiscite, she would turn the thumb screws on him, knowing that upsetting a "ciuchi" a "donkey," was the only way for this woman to achieve emotional satisfaction. Gramps had no time for her "bullshit" as he used to say.

Only this time, the argument was different. She was calling to receive monetary compensation for an International collect call patched through to her from a friend of the DellaVecchia's in Italy. The caller was Maria Coppolla, a middle-aged woman who had accomplished a lot of the translating for Gramps's letters into English. She had been educated in London during World War II, but for some reason she did not want to speak with Gramps directly.

Rose would not tell Gramps the details unless he had first promised to pay for the collect call. He promised and then after hearing a certain "bullshit" tale told by Rose, slammed the phone down and said, "she's out of her mind." We asked him what was going on and this is the story that he told, preceding it with, "They are all out of their minds."

Mind you, the story that Gramps related should be trusted because my grandfather was a well educated man. He was chartered as one of the first Certified Public Accountants in America. He was not only the personal "exchequer" for the Dean of English at Hofstra University, James Bender, but was the official instructor for the directors of the Atomic Energy Commission (the forerunner of the Manhattan Project). He literally taught nuclear-scientist executives how to keep budgets in their departments and do their taxes. Here is the story that came to him from the DellaVecchia cousins by way of Rose. I will add historical reference as I go along.

The name "Gioia Sannitica" does not translate to mean "Joyous Saints," as I had been told throughout my life. It means "Joyous Samnites."

It was said that long ago, the temple underneath the Lombard castle in Gioia Sannitica had been the center of worship of the Samnite goddess, Mefitis. Fervently religious, the Samnites, during three wars against the confederation of Italian peoples known as Rome, struggled to keep the region of Campania for themselves.

After nearly losing the Third Samnite War to them, the vicious Roman General, Lucius Cornelius Sulla, was seeking a means of punishing the Samnites so that Italy could become fully Roman (*The Roman History; Velleius Paterculus;* Book II; Parts 27-28; B.C. 30).

After torturing and killing thousands of my former ancestors, he realized that the only way to destroy them was to demoralize their religious centers. He commissioned a Brazen Bull to be wrought for his goal—which was surely the very same sculpture that Angelo had presented a few weeks earlier to my father and me (*ibid*).

Sulla had already killed his greatest enemy, the Samnite leader, Pontius Telesinus, at Porte Collina. Approaching the camp of Telesinus, the warrior had staggered to his feet as blood gushed out of his chest and held his sword to strike the general. Sulla was so impressed by the valour that after his men stuck the warrior down, Sulla had Telesinus's head placed on a pole, which he paraded outside his fort at Praenestre/Palestrina (*ibid*). It has long been insisted by locals that Telesinus was an ancestor of the Procurator of Judea, Pontius Pilate.

26

The demonic Sulla was not satisfied because the younger brother of Pontius was still alive. Nobody knew his real name, so Sulla called him "Felix," which in Latin means "happy" or "lucky." Sulla was sadistically enjoying his plan to kill him as well. Felix had fought alongside his enemy, the Consul, Gaius Marius, with whom Sulla was having a civil war to determine who would rule Italy *(ibid)*.

Although it was bandied among the Vox Populi that the losers Marius and Felix had helped each other commit suicide, in 1988 Rose told Gramps what actually did happen. Instead, Marius was caught and beheaded by Sulla's men, while Felix was dragged to the Samnite Temple of Mefitis, where the Brazen Bull awaited.

Samnites were known to practice the craft of "soul-breathing," their means of becoming possessed by the Numina (i.e., Pneuma), of their deities, to give them bravery or ward off demons. In this case, Sulla was enjoying a cruel joke by "exorcising" out of Felix the deity, Mefitis. She was the goddess of all the foul-smelling gases of the Earth. For the occasion, while the captive Samnites were forced to watch, Sulla, whose men now ignited the contents of a bucket of pig fat, which they had poured over the logs beneath the Brazen Bull, was teaching the Samnites a lesson. They were now Roman. The last of their gods was being burned out of their last hero, whose spirit was the disgusting stench that came from the fire. As Felix died screaming, the nostrils of the bull, as Perilaus had designed it, emitted the steam from his body, while the Romans laughed and said that the odor were the bull's flatulence.

Sulla was not finished. He believed that converting the Samnites into the Roman pantheism depended on the probability that a majority of a set number of them would be "willing" to scream as they died. The greater the sorrow, the more likely that the Samnite spirit would be purged, he thought, as his charitable approach to decide whether to save these people.

He and his men employed a crude version of *Stochastic Math*—the distribution of the random probability of a certain happenstance (e.g., of death during torture). He decided that if more than fifty victims out of a hundred would nobly die screaming that the majority of Samnites would eventually become Roman, whereof their lives would be worth preserving, rather than his committing genocide against these spirited people.

He was possessed by the Numina of Mefitis, Rose explained.

"That's a bunch of fool's gold," said Gramps, who never said, "bullshit" to the ladies.

Unfazed by our octogenarian donkey man from Connecticut, Rose continued—imploring Gramps to believe that she was telling him the story of how the Samnite people converted their religion to the pagan pontificate that brought forth Pontius Pilate.

Far more than 51, but in fact all of the victims died screaming. Sulla was said to die shortly after a ruptured gastric ulcer caused by alcohol abuse had led to him to die in his bath. The odor in the room was caused when constant bubbles arose past the surface of the water from his flatulence, causing his slaves, after he finally passed, to fumigate the house by igniting resultant methane and causing an explosion.

"Stochastic" is when a certain sum is projected by presuming a random probability distribution. When a mother, learning that a blizzard is forecasted, programs her Spotify to play a song list with a certain number of tunes based on how long she will be on line at the supermarket, relative to the number of neighbors in her town, and, and who probably do "disaster shopping" for eggs, butter, and toilet paper, relative to the number of cashiers who typically show up for work, it can be said that she is executing a Stochastic-probability guess about how long she will be waiting on line. Stochastic Programming is important in machine learning and, as it relates to the "Browning Motion" of atoms, whose random movements while they are suspended in bodies, the philosopher Lucretius believed he had proven can define the proclivities and predict the patterns of action for all Matter (*On the Nature of Things; Titus Lucretius Carus; Book II; Verses 113-40; B.C. 50*).

Sulla, in respects teaching Rome as if the Republic was itself a machine, was testing his Stochastic approach to the worthiness of Samnite life. His cruelty had so overwhelmed the search for truth in Italy that his descendent, Pontius Pilate "washed his hands" as his approach to the Logos of Jesus (Matthew 27:23-24).

A century later, to teach the people of Samnia the Roman way, the Emperor Domitian had an automaton built at the rededicated temple in Gioia Sannitica, named for Osirapis, the Ptolemic-Egyptian god, a cognate of Osiris, the manifestation of Apis, the bull. The automaton, whose boiler head was shaped like an Atef Crown, and whose pipes were shaped like the Pharoah's crook and flail, would hold court and teach the Samnite children who filed into the the temple, all about the Roman pantheon whenever its doors would open. It could speak and it moved its arms to and fro, reciting the Aeneid by the poet Virgil, and instructing listeners about the marriage of Osiris and Isis, who sired the child Horus, whose Greco-Roman version was the snake child, Harsomtus.

Twenty miles north was dug up in 1903 the remains of the Temple of Isis. A third temple was constructed by Domitian in the city of Rome, named for both Isis and Serapis. It had been hoped that a priestly procession would be led every year between the two provincial temples of Gioia Sannitica and of Benevento.

Later, after the Roman Republic declined into the madness of its emperors and then its final dissolution fell to the hands of the Goths, the Lombards overtook Italy for a two-hundred year rule, beginning in B.C. 568, and held feudal estates throughout the Renaissance. Although they built churches, the Lombards were a syncretic people, whose witches, worshippers of Isis and Osiris, were known to have sabbaths throughout Campania, particularly in Benevento, during which they also conjured the Samnite and Latium demon gods, Diana, Vulcan, and Mefitis, to do their bidding.

In 1526, a young Spanish prince, Ugo Villalumo, was helping his men operate a treadwheel crane to maneuver oak tree trunks, with which they buttressed the outer curtain of the north wall of the castle. The property was a gift to him from the King Charles V, the Habsburg ruler of the Holy Roman Empire, for the prince's bravery in the Battle of Pavia, helping to defeat the French. The castle and fortress were built by a Lombard lord in A.D. 668, at the highest point of Caserta, and is listed as a feudal proprietorship within the "Catalogus Baronum" ("Catalogue of the Barons") of 1322. Angevin and Swabian royals added the Gothic windows, the bartizan, the porticullis, and two smaller corbeled towers and one much larger, all of which were still mostly fully preserved when Ugo moved in with a garrison of thirty young men.

Largely intact except for cracks throughout the corps de logis, the battlements, and the curtains surrounding the precinct, the real estate had countless possibilities. No ambitious competitors roamed through the nearly empty village houses, the fortress, or bailey, indicating that the rule of the young prince would go unchallenged while he worked with his friends to rebuild the long-neglected community. Most of the ancestors had died from plagues or their houses had fallen in earthquakes. Orphans and old people appeared to be the only residents. Ugo's work was cut out for him.

Although the large cylindrical tower had no roof anymore, it was fully accessible by a winding staircase, and this is where, one night, the prince, on his way down from watching the sunset, met the beautiful villager, Erbanina, coming up the stairs. He asked who she was and she promised she would return the following evening as she ran back down the steps.

With his "mischievous mermaid," their romance happened fast, although he was not sure where she disappeared to on certain evenings. She had no last name and no one in the village claimed her. She seemed to come and go as she pleased, bringing bread and milk to the prince during the daylight and wine to him at night.

On their first evening they drank what she had brought him and they danced to a song that she sang, a hymn that she joked was an ballad dedicated to "the moon god's wife." She made him laugh and her songs, which placated him (because he was still fresh from battles), also mesmerized him. On the night he proposed to her, they danced along the chemin de ronde and he fell asleep as she caressed his hair and lay him on the tiles and kissed him. He did not remember if she had obliged his proposal but seemed to recall that she walked softly along the chemin de ronde and into the bartizan for a minute and then up to the tower singing the song just before he fell asleep, watching her gracefully saunter, almost glide up the winding stairs, as he fell into dreams. After a few weeks of this, his workers began to fall away, because he would rise late and the availability of the jobs was starting to slacken. Fewer men showed up for work every day, it seemed.

The old Osiris Androides was still there, very well preserved. Part of the old Roman Temple, the wall suspending the automaton, was incorporated by the Lombards to build the Castle. For the young couple it was a source of nightly entertainment. Erbanina said she had played with this chatty machine since her childhood. She showed Ugo how she could make it work for her. Whenever Ugo drank her wine, she

31

would sing to the Androides, who sang back, in a Coptic language that the prince didn't understand, but which made him laugh in his drunkeness. She called it "Osiris." Ugo had thought it was named Mefiti but she corrected him. This was always an Egyptian Temple, she explained. Ugo, who somewhat knew the local history, had thought it was the Samnite Temple of Mefiti, prior to its being named for Osiris, but while inebriated, he did not feel like arguing with his quirky fiancé. They danced. She sang. He fell asleep.

In the mornings there was nary a sign of her. On most nights the same kind of thing happened, especially on Saturday nights. They would hold one another after he ate her food, or they shared her wine, and she would sing to him as the sun went down and he would fall asleep. She would disappear as he fell under. He gradually suspected that his Erbanina was a witch.

One night, he pretended to drink the wine she had bought, covertly spitting it over the battlement where they were having her food. He made believe he was falling asleep while begging her to return the following night, which she obliged. She left him on the tiles as always. She walked into the bartizan and then up the staircase. After a minute or two in her absence he rose but he did not hear her moving around upstairs in the tower. He checked inside the bartizan, noticing that beneath a wooden bench was a bucket filled with lard. It had a strange smell similar to a person's urine and sweat. He felt as if he was in the presence of a human being but nobody was there. He now looked down into the bucket and realized that it was filled with human fat.

Every Saturday night, and on other weeknights, Erbanina, who was a Janara, covered herself in this substance. He watched her utter an incantation. She then let herself tip over the top of the missing roof, and she took flight through the air.

32

The next morning while he was having breakfast in the great hall, one of his soldiers demanded an audience with him, which he obliged, his approachability putting the younger guard at grateful ease. The soldier frantically said that a ditch with burned bodies had been found beneath a walnut tree in an ancient cistern in Cusano Mutri, an abandoned commune in Benevento. Some of the bodies donned scorched uniforms that bore the crest of King Charles V. There was no doubt. He had found the source of the fat. The cistern was the site of weekly witches' sabbaths.

Prince Ugo ran up to the chemin de ronde and retrieved the bucket of fat out of the bartizan, locking it inside his kitchen. That afternoon he and the soldier ran into the village, and begged the residents for a pig, but most of the old ladies scoffed or spat at him while the children mocked him. He was, after all, betrothed to a witch.

Commandeering a stable, he paid for a sow, throwing silver pieces at the old-man owner. He killed the pig with his sword, and burned the carcass over an improvised spit, leaving the cooked pig there for the occupant to eat. He buried the human fat outside of the walls a hundred feet away where the oak-tree buttresses were still leaning, beneath a stand of cedar trees, and prayed the Lord's Prayer over the site. He went back to his kitchen, scooped out the pig's lard into the bucket and ran up to place it in the bartizan.

That evening, as he gathered soldiers in his palace, he asked God to send Saint Michael to make sure that Erbanina was either restored to God, or met her end. He had decided that he was dealing with true evil.

The witches were described to him by the man who had sold him the sow, as being able to become "incorporeal" and would slip underneath the doors of the soldiers' apartments, luring them with hymns to the walnut tree in Cusano Mutri. In the cistern, they fornicated with the witches, each of whom believed they were going to become impregnated and produce a living version of Horus/Harsomptus, the snake child and were murdered by the bold women. Every time Prince Ugo prayed the Lord's Prayer while suiting up in his armor, and remembering the old man's tale he vomited out the last remnants of the food and wine she had given him.

Later, after Ugo left with his surviving men on horses, descending dustily the Matese gradual escarpment with all their swords and torches, he suddenly turned back toward his castle. He gave instructions that the men destroy the coven and the witches. He wanted to confront Erbanina alone.

The men did as they were told. There were screams that night, which peeled through the still air of the Campania, heard for miles and making wolves howl. After teenaged fellow soldiers were liberated from old Etruscan cages, and witches were bound and burned.

He met Erbanina at the tower staircase, sneaking up behind her. She had decided that he was not there to meet her, turned, and revealed that she was covered in the pig's lard. He begged her to confess what she had done to her soul and to profess that Christ is the risen Lord and to repent all her crimes. Her eyes were filled with rage and she spitefully ran up the stairs of the tower. She pulled herself up to the edge of the diabase bricks, which she pushed away when they snared her burlap skirt. She jumped into the night air and fell to her death three hundred feet below, crashing upon the slates of the bailey.

He carried her corpse to the area where he had buried his soldier's fat, prayed an Our Father, and interred her there, weeping bitterly.

During the morning, he and his men destroyed the castle and fortress, firstly pulling down the tower and then the corps de logis with ropes connected to the yokes of a team of horses.

He and his men used the treadwheel crane to hoist up the oak tree trunks that they had leaned against the the outer north wall a month earlier and then let the rope go slack on the wheel so that the trunks would fall against the curtain, toppling each section in this way, and its battlements, and then other parts of the estate, the bartizan, the gateway, the chemin de ronde, until he was satisfied. He left the apartments and shops untouched, but they eventually fell down on their own as the centuries passed.

Prince Ugo and his men returned to the House of Austria and after a certain rest, he gained victory for his friend King Charles V in defending Vienna from an invasion by the Turks.

Four-hundred and sixty one years later a phone receiver in Glen Cove, Long Island, was about to slam down hard.

"Now what ever became of this Prince Ugo?" Gramps had been listening to Rose Uave tell the story told to her by Maria Coppolla, shooting bemused looks up at my dad.

"How am I supposed to know what happened to Ugo?" Rose answered bitterly. She had been hoping that "Jeem" would be impressed.

"Look, I don't know how many years I have left," said a chuckling Gramps (who actually died fifteen years later). "But I just spent a half-hour listening to the biggest turkey of a whopper I think I've ever heard in my whole darned life."

"You are a ciuchi, you big old cafone, you!" came the rebuttal. Gramps was continuing to laugh as he spoke.

"Rose, you can expect a check to cover your cost of the collect call, and I'll add ten dollars for reporting all this back to me, but I'm going to hang up on you now before I say something I'm ashamed of in front of my grandson!" Gramps said, while Dad I heard Rose bickering back at him until the bakelite-plastic receiver of the electro-magnetic device struck its cradle.

My father was always amazed at how "sharp" his dad was, because everything she had told us, as I have now reported it here, was spoken by Gramps in detail.

"Now I know why my father left that region," added Gramps, who rejoined with, "What a bunch of lunatics over there."

It should not be presumed that Gramps was not moved by the story Rose had reported to him. He knew that Angelo was a "real character." It should be grasped that the demonic world ought to be left alone instead of being taught to youth. I was after all very impressionable at this age. Anything that was unpredictable or uncertain would go into the "Connecticut-Yankee void" as I referred to the stoicism of my father and grandfather. We could laugh away anything and were predominantly Brooklynites. Italian hobgoblins were not enough to scare us.

I grew up on a street just up from where Murder Incorporated's Albert Anastasia used to dump "the human waste." Just a few blocks away was the Gemini Bar and its upstairs apartment where the Roy DeMeo crew had committed more executions than had occurred in any single place in American history. We had the Mafia in those pre-Rudolph Guiliani days. We had the Son of Sam. We had blackouts and looting before anybody did. Why should demons inside of androides move us? They did not.

And it wasn't because were from Brooklyn or anywhere that we were so shrewd. We weren't haunted like Angelo or corrupt like the Carabinieri. We were monotheistic believers in Christ, the Father, and the Holy Spirit. Otherwise, if you have many gods and give your freedom to demons, you ought to know that Jesus would instead free you from making your gods and demons fight over possessing you.

"For God so loved the world, that He gave His only begotten Son, that whosoever believeth in Him should not perish, but have everlasting life. For God sent not His Son into the world to condemn the world; but that the world through Him might be saved" (John 3:16-17).

This book nevertheless will examine what "Artificial Intelligence" would have meant to people of ancient and Medieval times. The invoking of "God" from out of metal and synthetic instruments has been around for millennia.

There is no one to fear except for God: "The fear of the Lord is a fountain of life, to depart from the snares of death" (Proverbs 14:27).

The concept of "General Artificial Intelligence" will be exposed for what it is, a sham. A "ghost" in the machine may very well be a demonic spirit. If it is a devil operating a machine, then throw away the machine. The creators of "Singularity," whether technological or Gnostic depends on an audience of collaborators keeping the machine fueled by generating the steam just as users of Androids, iPhones, and laptops keep pouring data into the electronic version of the Beast.

"But I say, that the things which the Gentiles sacrifice, they sacrifice to devils, and not to God: and I would not that ye should have fellowship with devils" (1 Corinthians 10:20).

I was ordained an Anglican priest in the Chancery of Traditional Anglican Church of America, in Newton, North Carolina, by Archbishop Rick Aaron Reid, on November 21, 2021. The Liturgy of the Word and that of the Eucharist uses words from Celtic and Britannic sources that are every bit as old as the writings quoted in this tome.

- Chapter One -
Whether the Internet Can Become God

The idea that good and evil should be conceptualized as being part of one ethical spectrum is the error known as Moral Relativism.

The error descends from Plato. This statement by this ancient philosopher is used throughout this book to demonstrate the foundational wrongness of Materialism or Atomism: "And therefore whether we take being and the other [unbeing], or being and the one, or the one and the other, in every such case we take two things, which may be rightly called both" (*Parmenides*; Plato; Transl. Jowett, Benjamin; Sec. 143:b-d; B.C. 370).

Many people mistakenly believe that the Internet can become God, because God would be merely part of whatever lesser thing exists and can become accursed, degraded, or depraved (toward the Empty Set, of Meaninglessness, ∅, the Nihil, or Unbeing) and potentiates, such as a seed into a plant, Creation out of the Nihil, or the Internet into God. It is impossible. It stems from an over-reliance on Science to explain reality and calm emotions. However, the epistemological core of this institution, the Scientific Method, cannot make comprehensible the Life for which God alone provides reason, purpose, and reassurance.

The Scientific Method of interpreting reality by examining material existence is a faith-based religion. It calls for blind obedience to the principles of itself. Just as human reason alone cannot prove God's existence for Christians, Science relies on faith in hypotheses, in theories, and in "laws." The Scientific Method cannot prove that the Scientific Method is valid or sound. Because it is based solely on empirical evidence, Science also cannot prove fundamental ideas that define modern science, such as:

Particle Theory and Quantum Mechanics; Michael Faraday's "Law" of Electromagnetic Induction; the Theory of Relativity; the Principle of Uniformitarianism in Nature; the "Laws" of the Conservation of Mass and of Energy; the Present; or, the Past.

Because Scientists and their followers use this self-referential "Infinite Regress" of referring back to themselves and the complex utterances which they and other scientists have proclaimed, they affirm their sociopolitical predominance over others, an increasingly atheistic people, who put away their Prevenient Grace and Spiritual Discernment in order to avoid public ostracism, destruction of their homes, families, and livelihood.

"Anthony Fauci is literally The Science, personified and made flesh," but such ideologues are merely substantiating their claims to holding office by abusing the Scientific Method to violate the First and Second Commandment, that God is our Father, the sole Elohim, Y'weh, Jehovah—the Lord, before Whom, we must have no other gods (Exodus 20:2-3; "Trust the Science?"; Nate Hochman; The National Review; Sec.: The Corner: Politics and Science; Issue: Nov. 29, 2021).

"Infinite Regress," which is a term that is also used pejoratively to analyze Christian Faith, is mentioned throughout this book.

"I'm not going to be around here forever, but science is going to be here forever," whined Anthony Fauci, the Director of the National Institute of Allergy and Infectious Diseases from 1984 to 2022 (ibid). Employing Straw-Man rhetoric to imply that anarchy will result if his exploitation of the Scientific Method were not imitated after his death, Fauci abraded public fear about the AIDs and Covid-19 pandemics to remain the high-priest of his religion:

"So it's easy to criticize, but they're really criticizing science because I represent science. That's dangerous" ("Dr. Fauci Interview"; *Face the Nation;* CBS News; Transcript: November 28, 2021: 7:21 a.m.; https://www.cbsnews.com/news/transcript-dr-anthony-fauci-on-face-the-nation-november-28-2021; Accessed July 11, 2023).

His ad-hoc decretals of N-95 mask(s)-wearing; of receipt by millions of deadly MRNA-gene-mutating subcutaneous injections of drugs posing as "Covid vaccinations"; his grass-roots infiltration of Manhattan-based homosexual-activist enclaves to inject deadly azidothymidine/Zidovudine into HIV patients during the 1980s; his profiting from partnerships with pharmaceutical companies after his genocidal commissioning of gain-of-function research on SARS-CoV-2 proteins; his suspicious patent applications such as for HIV-1 gp120, whose glycosaminoglycan protein scandalously resembles the 2019-nCoV spike protein that itself may have been derived by Fauci from the HIV protein; of his senseless public lockdowns and economic shutdowns—all of his fatuously executed depredations, being loyally carried out by most Americans for fear that they would be considered disobedient nonbelievers in the "Science, falsely so-called" (1 Timothy 6:20). The false-prophet Fauci, who was too fearsome to be questioned by the American public, promulgated his warning that frames his faked omniscience: "And if you damage science, you are doing something very detrimental to society long after I leave" (*ibid*, CBS).

While Platonists and science-lovers wrongfully attest that evil and good are part of the same "atom" or are equal parts of a Creator's Omnibenevolence, Christ instead came into the world, took sin upon Himself and loved unbelievers, but shared His exclusion from the world with His followers: "They are not part of the world even as I am not part of the world" (John 17:16). Jesus spoke, walked among, and ate in the world, even with the people who would later crucify Him, but He took His sheep Home with Him, the real world of Heaven:

40

"And all mine are thine, and thine are mine; and I am glorified in them" (John 17:10).

Christ did not command people to discover a unified theory of atoms, or invent superior political ideas, but instead allowed His material body to be tortured and crucified by the hateful, all to teach, along with His Resurrection and Ascension, that sinners can transcend their sinful lives by permitting God's Love to proceed from themselves: "And above all things have fervent charity among yourselves: for charity shall cover the multitude of sins" (1 Peter 4:8).

A proficient way to teach children (and the grownups who need to know) that good and evil are not part of goodness (or that unbeing is not part or cause of being as Plato had said) is to study both Sacred Scripture primarily and saintly literature shrewdly and secondarily, so that they may see just how God is not both evil and good.

Although LGBTQ+ and WOKE promoters assert their victimhood as they denounce Romans 1 and Genesis 19:5, the impressionable Psyche's of children must be guided away from such Moral Pathology ("The Psychology of 'Woke Culture': How bitter individuals weaponize resentment to perpetuate a cancerous narrative; in Woke Culture, what we see is an unhealthy marriage between victimhood and the urge to become heroes in the Church of Liberalism officiated by the priest of Social Media"; *OpIndia*; Editor's Picks: Opinions; Social Media; November 24, 2019; https://www.opindia.com/2019/11/woke-culture-psychology-bitter-individuals-weaponise-resentment/; Accessed, July 11, 2023).

Devotional writing that is based on such Sacred Scripture expresses the monstrousness of homosexual/transgender activism and reverse-racism, whereof a parent should know that this con-artistry was already exposed in the Bible, with the words of Isaiah and Saint Paul the Apostle:

"Woe unto them that call evil good, and good evil; that put darkness for light, and light for darkness; that put bitter for sweet, and sweet for bitter!" (Isaiah 5:20).

"And no wonder, for even Satan disguises himself as an angel of light. So it is no surprise if his servants, also, disguise themselves as servants of righteousness. Their end will correspond to their deeds" (2 Corinthians 11:14-15).

Whereas people cannot fathom how great, how present, how knowing, and how loving God is, they sinfully presume that the Intellect can replace Faith with all of its arduousness and pain. However, all that intellectuals ends up with is their vain stab at comprehending the Infinite, nominally the *Transfinite Set*, the value which is less than God and dominated by Satan: "For innumerable evils have compassed me about: mine iniquities have taken hold upon me, so that I am not able to look up; they are more than the hairs of mine head: therefore my heart faileth me" (Psalm 40:2-3).

Christ, who has already counted and recorded every hair on our heads, delivers people from the calculating stratagems of mass intellection, so we will "fear not them which kill the body, but are not able to kill the soul: but rather fear Him which is able to destroy both soul and body in hell" (Matthew 10:28).

Of what use is Math, if, without Christ, it regards people as being merely the countable Matter, while real Christians transcend corporeal finitude through Faith: "Are not two sparrows sold for a farthing? and one of them shall not fall on the ground without your Father. But the very hairs of your head are all numbered" (Matthew 10:28-29).

Devotion to Jesus pulls people out their vexatious fear, toward Hope: "Fear ye not therefore, ye are of more value than many sparrows" (Matthew 10:31).

42

The "Secondary Cause" of our brains, our thinking, our Psyche, our prized intelligence, our lives, must abide the "First Cause" of God. In 1689, English Baptists held wisely to the following good doctrine:

"God hath decreed in himself, from all eternity, by the most wise and holy counsel of His own will, freely and unchangeably, all things, whatsoever comes to pass; (1) yet so as thereby is God neither the author of sin nor hath fellowship with any therein;(2) nor is violence offered to the will of the creature, nor yet is the liberty or contingency of second causes taken away, but rather established;(3) in which appears His wisdom in disposing all things, and power and faithfulness in accomplishing His decree.(4)" (*The Second London Baptist Confession of 1689: Includes the Baptist Catechism;* Scott T. Brown; Chap. 3: "Of God's Decree"; Article 1; Church and Family Life: 2012).

Children and parents are not being stupid or crazy to admit that they have "Blind Faith in God." Saint Anselm of Canterbury explained that God cannot be thought not to exist. (*Proslogion;* Chap. 3; Canterbury, Saint Anselm of Canterbury; 1078). Non-believers should understand that He exists and transcends everything, even eternal things such as redeemed souls and angels (*ibid,* Chap. 20). They refuse to believe, because they have no proof that He has no physical location nor abides a concept of time nor the laws of physics while all things instead exist in Him (*ibid,* Chap. 19). How then can a deliberately ignorant Christian or an intellectual atheist come to accept fully the joy of knowledge's limits unless admitting, "Therefore, Lord, not only are You that than which a greater cannot be thought, but You are also something greater than can be thought" (*ibid,* Chap. 15)?

The world did not create God. Nor does the world substantiate the purpose of God; nor does the world prove that He exists as the Creator of everything. Not a single "intelligent design" discovery (i.e., "Teleologia") can prove the existence of God. Everything was created by God out of nothingness, the nihil.

Science cannot prove that this "Creatio Ex Nihil" (i.e., Creation Out of Nothingness) is false any better than Christians can out-rule Faith, Hope, and Love as being the "modus operandi epistemologia" (i.e., "the way in which epistemology works").

As far as goes the false notion, that, according to a perverse Metaphysical "equity" the living God and the Not-God (the Finite) would evolve hand-in-hand into becoming the Universe—the former subsuming the latter—Pastor Bob Bridger of the Genevan Institute identified such notions as being incompatible with Christianity:

"A Most Basic Fact is that God Is Not the Author of Sin: All the actions of created intelligences are not merely the actions of God. Creatures act freely and responsibly as the proximate causes of their own moral actions. If God was the proximate cause of every act, all things would simply be "God in motion". That is nothing less than pantheism, or more exactly, pandeism. The Creator is distinct from His creation. The reality of secondary causes is what separates Christian theism from pandeism" ("God's Decrees: Certainty and Contingency"; Bob Burridge; Survey Studies in Reformed Theology; Genevan Institute for Reformed Studies: 1996, 2016; http://genevaninstitute.org/syllabus/unit-two-theology-proper/lesson-4-the-decrees-of-god/; Accessed June 25, 2023).

Good Christian writings regard the real God as being distinct from whatever human notion or material thing could ever be created by human beings—all of whom, you and I, are sinful. Solid Devotional Literature supports the following Metaphysical verses from Holy Scripture as premises in all their conclusions and proofs:

"Declaring the end from the beginning, and from ancient times the things that are not yet done, saying, My counsel shall stand, and I will do all my pleasure" (Isaiah 46:10);

"In whom also we have obtained an inheritance, being predestinated according to the purpose of Him who worketh all things after the counsel of His own will" (Ephesians 1:11);

44

"Wherein God, willing more abundantly to shew unto the heirs of promise the immutability of His counsel, confirmed it by an oath" (Hebrews 6:17).

"For He saith to Moses, I will have mercy on whom I will have mercy, and I will have compassion on whom I will have compassion. Therefore hath He mercy on whom He will have mercy, and whom He will He hardeneth" (Romans 9:15,18); (Romans 9:15,18);

"Let no man say when he is tempted, I am tempted of God: for God cannot be tempted with evil, neither tempteth He any man" (James 1:13);

"This then is the message which we have heard of Him, and declare unto you, that God is light, and in Him is no darkness at all" (1 John 1:5);

"For of a truth against thy holy child Jesus, whom thou hast anointed, both Herod, and Pontius Pilate, with the Gentiles, and the people of Israel, were gathered together. For to do whatsoever thy hand and thy counsel determined before to be done" (Acts 4:27-28);

"Jesus answered, Thou couldest have no power at all against Me, except it were given thee from above: therefore he that delivered Me unto thee hath the greater sin" (John 19:11).

"God is not a man, that He should lie; neither the son of man, that He should repent: hath He said, and shall He not do it? or hath He spoken, and shall He not make it good" (Numbers 23:19)?;

"Blessed be the God and Father of our Lord Jesus Christ, who hath blessed us with all spiritual blessings in heavenly places in Christ: According as He hath chosen us in him before the foundation of the world, that we should be holy and without blame before Him in love: Having predestinated us unto the adoption of children by Jesus Christ to himself, according to the good pleasure of His will" (Ephesians 1:3-5).

"There is nothing for which the children of God ought more earnestly to contend than the dominion of their Master over all creation—the kingdom of God over all the works of His own hands—the throne of God and His right to sit upon that throne" (*ibid*, Second Baptist; Chap 3; C.H. Spurgeon).

- Chapter Two -
Hostile Math Destroys Fruitful Multiplicity

What would be the "mathematical beauty" behind saying that the sum of two and two equals five? Is this not the plunging of the number One, which had sprung out of the Nihil of the Null Set (∅), back into the darkness and meaninglessness from which God created existence (Genesis 1; John 1)?

Laurie Rubel is a math professor at Brooklyn College, who says that when the equation equals four, it reeks of white supremacist patriarchy. "The idea that math (or data) is culturally neutral or in any way objective is a MYTH. i'm ready to move on with that understanding. who's coming with me" ("Grammar is racist, math is racist, and so are you"; Michael Brown; *The Christian Post*; Voices; August 11, 2020; https://www.christianpost.com/voices/grammar-is-racist-math-is-racist-and-so-are-you.html; Accessed, July 24, 2023)?

It is a concept by Aristotle, "Eudaimonia" (which will be examined more in this book), that citizens can achieve "concord" for their community. Concord produces the happiness by which they differentiate themselves from animals, not merely because they can speak and reason but because they are allowed to enjoy equal participation in politics. Rubel is obviously not seeking concord, but activism.

But if saying that "2 + 2 = 5" could help all citizens in a community to attain Eudaimonia by creating non-racism, could they achieve the prerequisite concord by professing such bizarre untrue statements as if they were mathematical beauty?

Angrily opposed to the alleged fascism behind promulgating "2 + 2 = 4" in a "loop," Rubel Tweeted, "Rely on that supposed axiom to then target ppl (& especially women) for coordinated ridicule/harassment. Never stray from this LOOP because it's

an easy one to engage every Tom Dick & Harry to engage"
(Tweet: August 3, 2020; 12:04 p.m.; Dr. Laurie Rubel).

The Christian-friendly definition of knowledge being
"Justified True Belief" (JTB) was accepted by Plato only in part,
because he said that justification of knowledge is impossible.

Socrates said to the mathematician Theaetetus, "if true
opinion and knowledge were the same thing in law courts, the
best of judges could never have true opinion without
knowledge; in fact, however, it appears that the two are
different," as if "knowledge was true opinion accompanied by
reason, but that unreasoning true opinion was outside of the
sphere of knowledge; and matters of which there is not a
rational explanation are unknowable... and those of which
there is are knowable" (*Theaetetus*; Plato; Part 201:c-d; B.C.
380).

Plato with this *word salad* rejected the first part—that of the
prospect of "true belief" being justified. In other words,
beliefs that are true are not justified if somebody has an
argument with reality.

In Platonic rhetoric, knowledge is merely true belief based on
argument or opinion. However, Christians rightfully justify
their knowledge of reality according to their Faith in God.

"Therefore we conclude that a man is justified by Faith
without the deeds of the law." (Romans 3:28).

The death of Socrates was a suicide. He professed that he was
being executed for being a public nuisance as the "gadfly" of
Athens (*Apology;* Plato; Sec. 30:e; B.C. 380). He could have
escaped execution through exile but he accepted the
conventional death sentence of Athens, to drink hemlock and
die (*Phaedo*; Plato; Sec. 57:a; B.C. 380).

He was being condemned for corrupting youth; for impiety for refusal to worship the gods of Athens; and, for proposing worship of outsider gods *(Apology;* 24:b). Now, when his wealthy friend, Crito, bribes the prison guards so that Socrates could escape, Socrates refuses the accommodation *(Crito;* Plato; Sec. 44:b-46:a; B.C. 380). Although Socrates had alleged that specious and illogical reasoning had framed the court's accusations, he tells Crito that the laws of the State must be preserved at the expense of the life of any one citizen *(Crito;* Sec. 49:e-50).

"Now the next thing I say, or rather ask, is this: 'ought a man to do what he has agreed to do, provided it is right, or may he violate his agreements?' He ought to do it. Then consider whether, if we [escape} from here without the consent of the state, we are doing harm to the very ones to whom we least ought to do harm, or not, and whether we are abiding by what we agreed was right, or not... Consider it in this way. If, as I was on the point of running away (or whatever it should be called), the laws and the commonwealth should come to me and ask, 'Tell me, Socrates, what have you in mind to do? Are you not intending by this thing you are trying to do, to destroy us, the laws, and the entire state, so far as in you lies? Or do you think that state can exist and not be overturned, in which the decisions reached by the courts have no force but are made invalid and annulled by private persons?'" *(Crito;* Sec. 49:e-50:b).

In accepting the penalty that he was guilty but professing that he had exposed the fallacy behind all the charges against him, Socrates is contradicting himself. He was actually opposing the dutiful stewardship of accepting juridical rule that he says he serves by acting out with the suicide that would stand forever as his protest against the specious argumentation of judicious men whose murderous reasoning is why he is a "gadfly" in the first place!

In taking the law into his own hands this, he was refuting his own idea—that all knowledge can never be Justified True Belief. This was his nullification argument of epistemology in the *Theaetetus*: "and matters of which there is not a rational explanation are unknowable... and those of which there is are knowable" (*Theaetetus*; Plato; Part 201:c-d; B.C. 380).

No traditionalist Christian parent living in modern-day Massachusetts would consider it "unjust" to evict another adult from a public bathroom who is of a different gender than his child, despite what statutory Law says.

On July 7, 2016, "An Act Relative to Transgender Anti-Discrimination" (Senate Bill 2407) was passed in the U.S. Senate and House. It was signed by Governor Charlie Baker the next day. It amended Section 92A of chapter 272 of Massachusetts General Laws to cover "gender identity" in "any place of public accommodation, resort or amusement that lawfully segregates or separates access...based on a person's sex." By said amendment all individuals shall be treated "consistent with the person's gender identity." The places of "public accommodation" forbidding "discrimination" include "restaurants, libraries, hotels, malls, public transportation, and beyond," as well as "bathrooms and locker rooms."

On what grounds is belief that this disgusting law is justified based? Should a Christian parent accept punishment by the State for protecting her child who is being forced by the court to witness the nudity of an intruding adult? Should citizens decide that knowledge of Absolute Objective Moral Truth is impossible and just do what the State demands?

The above argument by Socrates in the *Theaetetus* against Knowledge as being Justified True Belief (JTB) has caused a centuries-old popular misreading of this Suicidal Epistemological Statement (SES): "the more I know the less I know." It has predominated education because its believers renounce the justification of true belief taught in the Bible.

Socrates' argument actually regards justifying his suspension of hatred against injustice:

"I went to one of those who had a reputation for wisdom, thinking that there, if anywhere, I should prove the utterance wrong and should show the oracle [of Delphi] 'This man is wiser than I, but you said I was wisest.' So examining this man—for I need not call him by name, but it was one of the public men with regard to whom I had this kind of experience, men of Athens—and conversing with him, this man seemed to me to seem to be wise to many other people and especially to himself, but not to be so; and then I tried to show him that he thought he was wise, but was not. As a result, I became hateful to him and to many of those present; and so, as I went away, I thought to myself, "I am wiser than this man; for neither of us really knows anything fine and good, but this man thinks he knows something when he does not, whereas I, as I do not know anything, do not think I do either. I seem, then, in just this little thing to be wiser than this man at any rate, that what I do not know I do not think I know either." From him I went to another of those who were reputed to be wiser than he, and these same things seemed to me to be true; and there I became hateful both to him and to many others. After this then I went on from one to another, perceiving that I was hated, and grieving and fearing, but nevertheless I thought I must consider the god's business of the highest importance. So I had to go, investigating the meaning of the oracle, to all those who were reputed to know anything." (*Apology*; Plato; Sec. 21:b-21:e; B.C. 380).

Socrates now tells Crito that it is by social contract—an intuited agreement between the State and the individual by which the State has dominion over the person:

"Come, what fault do you find with us and the state, that you are trying to destroy us? In the first place, did we not

51

bring you forth? Is it not through us that your father married your mother and begat you? Now tell us, have you any fault to find with those of us who are the laws of marriage?' 'I find no fault,' I should say. 'Or with those that have to do with the nurture of the child after he is born and with his education which you, like others, received? Did those of us who are assigned to these matters not give good directions when we told your father to educate you in music and gymnastics?' 'You did,' I should say. 'Well then, when you were born and nurtured and educated, could you say to begin with that you were not our offspring and our slave, you yourself and your ancestors? And if this is so, do you think right as between you and us rests on a basis of equality, so that whatever we undertake to do to you it is right for you to retaliate? There was no such equality of right between you and your father or your master, if you had one, so that whatever treatment you received you might return it, answering them if you were reviled, or striking back if you were struck, and the like; and do you think that it will be proper for you to act so toward your country and the laws, so that if we undertake to destroy you, thinking it is right, you will undertake in return to destroy us laws and your country, so far as you are able, and will say that in doing this you are doing right, you who really care for virtue? Or is your wisdom such that you do not see that your country is more precious and more to be revered and is holier and in higher esteem among the gods and among men of understanding than your mother and your father and all your ancestors, and that you ought to show to her more reverence and obedience and humility when she is angry than to your father, and ought either to convince her by persuasion or to do whatever she commands, and to suffer, if she commands you to suffer, in silence, and if she orders you to be scourged or imprisoned or if she leads you to war to be wounded or slain, her will is to be done, and this is right, and you must not give way or draw back or leave your post, but in war and in court and everywhere, you must do whatever the state, your country, commands, or must show her by persuasion what is really right, but that it is impious to use violence against either your father or your mother, and much more impious to use it against your country?'" (*Crito*; Sec. 50:d-51:c).

Socrates has, since B.C. 380, been taught by educators to have courageously defended his principle of nullification of Knowledge by accepting his death sentence. However, the following passage, in which he defers belief in Truth to justification by piety, shows that he was committing suicide only to demonstrate that the pursuit of thinking in general within an individual, instead of allowing the State to define justification over all Truth only leads to self-destruction. It is indeed Nihilism, according to which, Socrates ironically argues that justification of Truth (i.e., justice) is the political theory (i.e., Socialism), which "god" actually wants (and therefore implying that he was wrong all along to oppose JTB):

"if you should let me go on this condition which I have mentioned, I should say to you, 'Men of Athens, I respect and love you, but I shall obey the god rather than you, and while I live and am able to continue, I shall never give up philosophy or stop exhorting you and pointing out the truth to any one of you whom I may meet, saying in my accustomed way: 'Most excellent man, are you who are a citizen of Athens, the greatest of cities and the most famous for wisdom and power, not ashamed to care for the acquisition of wealth and for reputation and honor, when you neither care nor take thought for wisdom and truth and the perfection of your soul?' And if any of you argues the point, and says he does care, I shall not let him go at once, nor shall I go away, but I shall question and examine and cross-examine him, and if I find that he does not possess virtue, but says he does, I shall rebuke him for scorning the things that are of most importance and caring more for what is of less worth. This I shall do to whomever

I meet, young and old, foreigner and citizen, but most to the citizens, inasmuch as you are more nearly related to me. For know that the god commands me to do this, and I believe that no greater good ever came to pass in the city than my service to the god" (*Apology*; Sec. 29:c-30:a).

We are correctly defining Socrates as wielding the Moral Pathology of a 69-year-old man who was surely too old to engage in public riots, but who holds himself as being capable of pestering corrupt politicians all day according to his own JTB, that it is what is wanted by the Divine.

The Bible holds Justified True Belief to be the basis of Knowledge and it is by the Bible's JTB that Objective Morality and Absolute Truth are not only real, but that freedom from sin (e.g., from suicide and State oppression) is also God's will:

"And ye shall know the truth, and the truth shall make you free" (John 8:32).

"For this is good and acceptable in the sight of God our Saviour; Who will have all men to be saved, and to come unto the knowledge of the truth. For there is one God, and one mediator between God and men, the man Christ Jesus" (1 Timothy 2:3-5).

Socrates was offered the fully justifiable course of action to save himself from tyranny through the sincere charity of his friend, Crito, but, despite having been shown the truth of this *caritas* (the correct definition of God's *Truth* being Love Itself coming from 1 John 4:16) he chose suicide.

"For if we sin willfully after that we have received the knowledge of the truth, there remaineth no more sacrifice for sins" (Hebrews 10:36). To accept sin, is to free the mind from the devil: "For sin shall not have dominion over you: for ye are not under the law, but under grace" (Romans 6:14).

54

The Book of Hosea says, "My people are destroyed for lack of knowledge: because thou hast rejected knowledge, I will also reject thee, that thou shalt be no priest to me: seeing thou hast forgotten the law of thy God, I will also forget thy children" (Hosea 4:6). The verse is an admonishment to the Israelites of Samaria that destruction will come to them because they have rejected their knowledge of the law of God.

Please consider whether there is any difference between the State of Massachusetts (cited above) or the White House and the Jeroboam syncretism of ancient Israel? Do read the following self-destructive statement by Health and Human Services Secretary Xavier Becerra, who wrote it in response to a series of questions submitted by Illinois Representative Mary Miller, including whether Xavier believed "taxpayers should pay for chemical castration and sex-change operations." Beccera answered:

> "The Biden-Harris Administration supports the upcoming release of the World Professional Association for Transgender Health (WPATH) Standards of Care Version 8 and believes that all children and adults should be afforded life-saving, medically necessary care. Payers, both public and private, should cover treatments which medical experts have determined to be medically necessary" ("HHS secretary signals sex-change surgeries for minors should be covered by taxpayers": Report; Abigail Adcox; U.S. News; *Washington Examiner;* November 30, 2022).

Becerra was saying that the White House supports coverage for transition-related treatments for both adults and children in written testimony submitted to the House Committee on Education and Labor.

The Bible lets Christians know that the New Covenant (Hebrews 9:15) between God and man is not merely intuitional but implies both corporeal and spiritual penalties:

"But whoso shall offend one of these little ones which believe in me, it were better for him that a millstone were hanged about his neck, and that he were drowned in the depth of the sea" (Matthew 18:6).

God, not the "god" mentioned by Socrates, but the Father punishes sins temporally on Earth whenever the unjust reap what they have sown (Job 4:8; Galatians 6:7).

"Hostile Math" is thus how mathematicians describe "Singularity" as being an equation that is meaningless and vexatious but which cannot be stopped. It will be addressed here later.

However, 2 + 2 = 5 is an example of this self-perpetuating injustice being predated against the intelligence of students.

Saint Augustine of Hippo broke off with the relativistic view of justice that Plato's impoverished epistemology implies with his famous refutation, "I would rather suffer than to commit injustice" (*On Christian Doctrine;* Saint Augustine of Hippo; No. 85; A.D. 420).

Although the experience of racism predicated by Rubel is interesting, God allows people to distinguish *a priori* ("from the earlier") truths, such as 2 + 2 = 4, from any reliance on empirical data or sensory experience.

Accordingly, man's intuition that 2 + 2 = 4 does not accord belief in a mere man-computed "truth" when this *a priori* knowledge is perceived correctly by a sane person. Saying 2 + 2 = 5 implies that such a man-computed "truth" which is an insane notion could be a notion that is perceived correctly by the cogito, when it cannot be.

The sum of "4" is not known as "fact" merely because a mathematical "law" has dictated that the human cogito is ever interpreting such a reality correctly. Why then do we know that 2 + 2 = 4?

Instead it is by our Faith in God that we justifiably believe that the Truth of our knowledge, that the sum of "4" is correct, is real. By Faith we also justifiably know that the Father exists and that He saves us and that He would not deceive us, and therefore, "by Him all that believe are justified from all things, from which ye could not be justified by the Law of Moses" (Acts 13:39).

Because the worth of a tree must be judged according to its fruit (Luke 6:43-45), it is logical to deduce that Artificial Intelligence, which grew from the binary operation of 0 + 1, may be discerned to be evil or good by examining the math upon which it is based.

The anthropologist Mary L. Gray is a Fellow at Harvard University's Berkman Klein Center for Internet and Society and a Senior Principal Researcher at Microsoft Research. She believes that A/I will "always fail LGBTQ people." To see how an LBTQ+ activist perceives the problem at hand, "If you take A/I down to its most basic level, the binary code of 0 and 1's, you can start to understand why it might ignore queerness." Therefore, because computer code is fundamentally binary, and thus out of touch with "our queer experience" and "how we grow and develop our identities," there is dysphoria, "which means A/I will struggle to understand us."

During the 2021 Web Summit in Lisbon, Portugal, the discussion of Artificial Intelligence turned toward "Identity Politics" (I/P). It is a term holding social concord to be a function of equitable participation in politics by agents who are equipped to profess their respective identities in terms of race, nationality, religion, gender, sexual orientation, social background, and social class (Bernstein, Mary (2005). "Identity Politics". Annual Review of Sociology. Annual Reviews. 31: 47-74.).

During the summit, the co-founder of the Marxist rebellion Black Lives Matter (BLM), Ayo Tometi, implored the technology delegates to confront the problem with the facial-recognition apparati in their operating systems. "A lot of the algorithms, a lot of the data is racist," she said.

The predominance of Caucasian male developer teams whose members are sexually "binary," causes A/I not to be "inclusive," according to the digital advocacy group, Algorithmic Justic League. In fact, the CEO of Revolab, Kalinas Ovidijus, who helms a health-tracking platform in Lithuania confessed that most of the data which his agency accesses is provided by medical centers that treat chiefly Caucasians. He admitted that they are unsure if their system would be able to accomodate the healthcare needs of anyone who is not "white" (*ibid*).

As if the street rioting for "Diversity, equity, and inclusion," which will be discussed later in this book, did not convey its collaborators' complaint that political power has respect for neither personal identity nor "Eudaimonia," it should be acknowledged that both the holy and the unholy today must confront the issue with "power" in general.

The word, "General," in fact, is now popularly connected with "Intelligence" and studied within this book to contemplate "absolute power" because of the growth spurt of A/I into an electronic beast.

Artificial General Intelligence (AGI), known to its official cabal as "the open A/I" community, is data-fed by billions of human operators who engage the Internet all day long. The U.S.-accepted "Charter" for all developers defines the purpose of AGI or "GI" as follows: "OpenAI's mission is to ensure that artificial general intelligence (AGI)—by which we mean highly autonomous systems that outperform humans at most economically valuable work—benefits all of humanity. The

Charter nominally expresses the need for "long-term safety" as an exigency: "We are committed to doing the research required to make AGI safe, and to driving the broad adoption of such research across the AI community" (https://openai.com/charter; Accessed, April 9, 2018).

This book studies the Transhuman aim of Godless scientists to build G/I, by equipping firstly the human-automaton operator with the ubiquity of techology in every corner of his life, slowly to develop a co-identification of his humanity with his cell phone and the Internet itself, while meanwhile replacing his DNA with MRNA-based gene therapy and nano-particles. By producing the Androides of A/I, techologists are already collaborating with billions of human automata to erect a simulation of God's Omnipresence. This impersonation, whereby humans and machines aggregate into "The One" of the Neoplatonism of Plotinus, is the employment of a phenomenon that is already uttered within the lexicon of everyday life, known as Technological Singularity," by which "immortality and divinity will develop. The world will be conquered not by Islamic fundamentalism but by techno religions, because they promise salvation through algorithms and genes."

A famous prophet of this Transhuman revolution, the philosopher, Juval Noah Harari, "envisions the development of an all-powerful, immortal human being and adapts this for his philosophical speculations on the future of humankind" (Virtual Immortality - God, Evolution, and the Singularity in Post- and Transhumanism; Oliver Krüger; Intro.: P. 23; Bielefelder Verlag, Bielefeld, Germany: 2021).

This book breaks down how people's Metaphysics project correct and incorrect sketches of simple discreet or continuous Math. This tome speaks poetically about various beliefs in God through examples and citations given throughout. It is an ancient artistic way of making points: For example:

59

Plato implies that the the Finite number One and Zero are parts of the One, by saying that being and unbeing are part of being, and thus that evil and good are part of good. Thus, $1 + 0 = \infty$.

Neoplatonists, such as Plotinus, falsely imply that all numbers, the Infinite, and Zero are part of The One. Thus, $1 + 0 + \infty = 1$.

Gnostics, such as Valentinus, mistakenly imply that Math ($\aleph$) equals Infinity. Thus, the Transfinite of the Aleph-Null of $\aleph_0 = \infty$.

Satanists, such as Madame Blavatsky, wickedly imply that One is the Infinite, the very lie that the serpent told to Adam and Eve. Thus, $(1 = 0) = (0 \neq 1)$.

Christians and Jews imply that the Finite number One of the Transfinite Creatio ($\aleph_0$) proceeds out of the empty set ($\emptyset$) of Nihil, increasing the soulfulness of people. God makes this happen by incrementing upon the Aleph-Null therewith intending toward the highest knowable Transfinite cardinal number, $\aleph_1$

By this, Theosis with the Infinity of ∞ can be attained. Thus, the *Leonhard-Euler Identity* of $e^{i\pi} + 1 = 0$.

This last example is considered a version of "Mathematical Beauty," which when understood poetically would signify life, creativity, and God's Infinite Love (Omnibenevolence) regarding all of which two "metaphysical fractions" will later be shown. Metaphysics (the knowable brain proving the existence of God and His characteristics), are given by the author of these fractions, Euler, using this math:

The Imaginary Number, by which we imagine how deep God's Love goes, is $i^2 = -1$.

The Natural Logarithm from the Golden Ratio (a + b/a = a/b = φ) is 2.718. And so, this is a metaphor for God's Omniscience, because He knows all parts of nature as they relate subordinately to the celestial Divine.

The value of π, 3.14, of course equals the ratio of the circumference of a circle to its diameter. This is a metaphor for God's Omnipresence.

And this book also exposes the heresy of saying that people can deify themselves or that God and the material world are as old and as powerful as one another.

While there are countless errors in presuming that the Father can be fully known, created, equaled, or moved by us, there is one thing that we are able to presume without sinning. It is that every time we pray, we take some part in God's movement of increasing His own greatness if He answers our prayers and creates greater peace, joy, health, etcetera after the antecedent action of our request for Intervention has come His way. It is not that we can *move* God but that He would choose to make us experience His motion

This also book makes it its business to show how God's Love, posited as the Imaginary Number (i) that is an actual number (i.e., a Real Number), which promises the untold happiness of our Salvation. In that we can only imagine how great He is to be able to save us, this Imaginary Number is only knowable in terms of the limited way in which humans, who are not God, implies a beyond-Infinite value (because God happens to be greater than Infinity). Our Father defies reason and employs the so-called "Intellectual-Regression" motif (a term used by Richard Dawkins, to be discussed later, as he attacks the Argument From Faith. Mere Faith, its power to define happiness being inexplicable, is here taken as a sublime, much of itself, along with God's limitless good properties, are given odes in this report through the Similitude of Math.

Genesis, to wit, will be described here as having been "drawn" by the handy Euler plane, with its x and y axes showing a right triangle defining a circle, with the Transcendental Number π and God's Love (i) shown in an exponentiation of Nature, to produce children and Faith (+ 1), our mortality eventually being equaled to zero, as we return to the dust of the Earth at our deaths, with our lives, the world, and our eternal souls, being posited as sources of Faith, Hope, and Love, like a balanced equation.

Therefore, during this writing, God will be described using Math only as a Similitude (we are not numerologists).

Also, this report refers to God in various of its passages as if He is Infinity (albeit truly He is much greater than ∞). As Immanuel Kant made the same simile, "if by eternity should here be understood a time going on to infinite, "whereof man's mortal finiteness has him moving "in uninterrupted duration" from death to the everlasting, "his existence contemplated as a *quantum*" ("The End of All Things"; Immanuel Kant; 1794).

- Chapter Three -
God is Bigger Than Infinity

God, however, is greater than Infinity, his Omnibenevolence of limitless Love being implied not only by an Imaginary Number of all His virtues that are too numerous to be counted or to be knowable, but because the Pleroma (Colossians 2:9) of His Love and greatness is too glorious to be quantified (and can thus in no way be explained using Quantum Theory or Math).

Nothing is greater than God, "that, than which nothing greater can be conceived," and upon whom all things depend for their existence, the fullness of whose greatness is unknowable, and about whom it is impossible to believe that He does not exist (Proslogion; Chap. 2, 3, 15, 19, 20; Saint Anselm of Canterbury; 1078).

God will also be described according to His will and thus that it was His pleasure to deign to create the Universe, our families, all humans, including you, and me—Himself being the Logos; Himself being the fullness of all that is concrete and abstract, the knowable and the unknowable, all things visible and invisible, His perfect Love and Greatness being Absolute Truth (Genesis 1-3; John 1).

Numbers, upon which Math depends, are understandable only as they are considered to be "Real"—regarding which the Imaginary number, "i," metaphorically implies God's limitless Love, and also operates within the Euler Formula. It would thus have to be a Real Number also, but "real" in the sense that we would have to make a value that is so large or infinitesimal that we could only know it through a metaphor or simile. Thus, in religious terms, such Real numbers cannot be comprehended by mortal people except through our intuition that He created us via that Love. (Remember, we are being metaphoric but mathematical at the same time, which opens Math up to being fun).

However, a number thus knowable by humans and which is not imaginary but still is Real, would be any of the other members of the *Transfinite Set* (the numbers known only in that they exist into infinity), which are each a "Human Number." One of these numbers designates the identity of a person knowable as the Anti-Christ, hence his signifier, "666":

"Here is wisdom. Let him that hath understanding count the number of the beast: for it is the number of a man; and his number is six hundred threescore and six" (Revelation 13:18).

It is the moral duty of every patriarch, seeing his physical body and his noise and senses as being Finite, to teach his family, his Congregation, Ministry, and Mission, that every good person must die to himself and to herself, to "likewise reckon yeself to be dead unto sin" (Romans 6:11). Only the God of the Trinity is forever:

"I am Alpha and Omega, the beginning and the ending, saith the Lord, which is, and which was, and which is to come, the Almighty" (Revelation 1:8).

Mathematics, physics, metaphysics, the Internet, Artificial Intelligence, anything haunted by a ghost or a demon or that which is worshiped falsely as the Creator, everything in the Universe, and all life inside of it, will finally be tossed, by the Father, into the Lake of Fire along with Satan and every demon, in the way that one's dad hauls trash into an incinerator (Revelation 21:9).

However, and only if it is God's pleasure, He shall take from His Creation, what shall join him, and it will be taken up into the Theosis, as the New Heaven and Earth (Isaiah 65:17, 66:22; 2 Peter 3:13). As parts of the New Jerusalem, each consecrated formerly Finite thing will then be " like unto a stone most precious, even like a jasper stone, clear as crystal; Revelation 21:9-21). Saving people was God's original plan, anyway:

"According as He hath chosen us in Him before the foundation of the world, that we should be holy and without blame before Him in Love" (Ephesians 1:4).

We do not want to be burned out of existence, along with Artificial Intelligence and all its computers and filthy programmers and unrepentant users (Revelation 22:11), but be restored and consecrated by God into Heaven, which is the real "General Intelligence," as we attempt the true "Singularity," that is Theosis, and be realistic "operators," by being Christians. We must wear the wedding garment, clothed in the Blood of the Lamb, or be thrown out of the wedding party, despite our best bitter arguments (Matthew 22). We will soon be in our new perfect bodies:

"For we know that if our earthly house of this tabernacle were dissolved, we have a building of God, an house not made with hands, eternal in the heavens. For in this we groan, earnestly desiring to be clothed upon with our house which is from Heaven: If so be that being clothed we shall not be found naked. For we that are in this tabernacle do groan, being burdened: not for that we would be unclothed, but clothed upon, that mortality might be swallowed up of life. Now He that hath wrought us for the selfsame thing is God, who also hath given unto us the earnest of the Spirit. Therefore we are always confident, knowing that, whilst we are at home in the body, we are absent from the Lord (for we walk by Faith, not by sight): We are confident, I say, and willing rather to be absent from the body, and to be present with the Lord" (2 Corinthians 5:1-8).

If an idea that does not come from the Bible, it would then be a concept which comes from a person or out of a source that is not the Bible, such the Internet. Therefore, if it does not affirm the Bible, then it is not inspired by the Holy Ghost and has therefore foamed up out of the Finite, or—as it could be faulty theology at its very best, which stumbled in disjointed fragments out of the Transfinite and it needs correction (2 Timothy 3:16; *Epistle Number 39: Festal Easter;* Saint Athanasius; Part 6; A.D. 367).

Therefore, people must become traditionalists in that we must keep to being biblical, and should always profess the Trinity, and become converted into Christians if we are not Christian already, or just stay being Traditionalist Trinitarian Christians. We must never worship according to what is Finite but only God who created us and everything and Who desires to save us (Exodus 20:2-3), if we do want to be saved:

"Submit yourselves therefore to God. Resist the devil, and he will flee from you" (James 4:7).

The Bible is not Finite but is the Word of God and therefore is God (John 1:1-14).

Mathematicians and scientists will be quoted throughout this report, and their work will be described as a Christian devotional—to show that knowledge can attest to God's existence (i.e., Cataphatic Theology, of positive attribution). But mostly, Finite sources will help prove that God can be defined in terms of what cannot be known (i.e., Apophatic Theology, of negative attribution).

- Chapter Four -
The Artificially Sentient Mechanical Hobgoblin

The physicist Erwin Schrödinger who will be quoted below, although he was a syncretic deist, at least could reason that God creates things and goodness out of His pleasure to do so—knowing with exactness each one of us personally since before our conception in the womb (Psalm 139:16; Isaiah 49:5; Galatians 1:15; Jeremiah 1:5). That being said, who would presume to have the slightest trace of comprehension of His utterly huge Omniscience?

Schrödinger's thought experiment (his famous "cat in the box" who was thought of as having an unknown fate when placed near a breakable vial of poison) taught Quantum Mechanics that both particles and waves are misunderstood at the moment that they are correctly understood, which if nothing else, demonstrated that people cannot even adequately understand the Finite world, "for without Me, you can do nothing" (John 15:5).

God does not need scientists to prove that He exists through their ogling at the particle randomness that the Roman Titus Lucretius Carus described as essentially the "Browning motion" of the atoms suspended in bodies.

Lucretius, whose sexualized vile Epicurean atomism employed the probability of atoms to join together to form a human body arbitrarily at birth was little more than his attempt to normalize the casual sex he prescribed within his science of filth, while nominating his version of principled action for human atoms. *(On the Nature of Things;* Titus Lucretius Carus; Book II; B.C. 50).

"I prove the supreme law of Gods and sky, And the primordial germs of things unfold, Whence Nature all creates, and multiplies, And fosters all, and whither she resolves, Each in the end when each is overthrown. This ultimate stock we have devised to name, Procreant atoms, matter, seeds of things, Or primal bodies, as primal to the world. *(ibid,* Lucretius; Book I; Verses 55-61; B.C. 50).

Lucretius thus has an opinion about what atoms are meant for, and also has advice for gigolos:

"For the delights of Venus (a loosely-moraled woman), verily, Are more unmixed for mortals sane-of-soul, Than for those sick-at-heart with love-pining" (ibid, Book IV; Verses 1075-1077).

Lucretius finds discord not in sex but in relationships and Love. He is saying that pleasure is purer for the healthy-minded than is Love.

The work of Lucretius is an appropriate starting place where ones is hunting down a primary literary source of a hair-brained scientific idea that is hatched from confirmation bias. The ancient author clearly likes fornication very much and wanted to create science around it.

Sexual gratification, just as it is the goal of much of the Internet is the better aim for the psyche, while the meiotic reproduction of all of the atoms associated with the haploid cells known as "gametes" (i.e., "seeds") would be the only purpose for sex, instead of sex being experienced within the gift of Agape Love.

It is through Agape Love that a relationship would instead discover charitable, non-envious, patient, and kind adoration that has Salvation for both partners as its end (1 Corinthians 13:4-8). Otherwise, intimacy can only be viewed through the lens of physicality.

Lucretius promulgates that it is much better to have casual sex than to fall in Love, least of all with a woman hoping to be the handmaiden of the Lord (Luke 1:38):

"Uncounted ills; so that 'tis better far, To watch beforehand, in the way I've shown, And guard against enticements. For to shun, A fall into the hunting-snares of love, Is not so hard, as to get out again, When tangled in the very nets, and burst, The stoutly-knotted cords of Aphrodite. Yet even when there enmeshed with tangled feet, Still canst thou scape the danger-lest indeed, Thou standest in the way of thine own good, And overlookest first all blemishes, Of mind and body of thy much preferred, Desirable dame" (ibid, Book IV; Verses 1144-1157).

As a disappointment to modern Epicureans, Lucretius advised against raping women and having orgasms during gratuitous abuse of male children (e.g., "the womanly limbs of a boy," etc.), not because it is deserves severe punishment from such individuals' families, but because it worsens the condition of a "love-sick" mind (ibid, Lucretius; Book IV; Verses 1052-1056).

A child sex slave can be viewed in a fresco of the Villa of Mysteries in Pompeii (A.D. 50). He is reading from parchment during a feast in a rich Roman home. The Villa is a tribute to the Dionysian cultus.

The epic poem "Silvae" features a funeral dinner at which guests recall their pleasure at seeing the host, Melior, being entertained by his deceased "lover," his "boy favorite," the freed slave, Glaucius during each "cena" in the "triclinium" (the important Roman feasts in the dining hall). The guest, the poem's author, Statius, eulogizes, by praising the boy's "sensus" whenever the youth had orated Homer and his "sonus" as the child recited drama by Menander (thus the youthful "sense of sound" that was enjoyed by these ancient pedophiles ("Silvae"; Publius Papinius Statius; Book II; Sec. 1; A.D. 96).

Important for the elite of ancient Rome, as it is fervently retained today among modern psychopaths, is the Morally Pathological fixation upon the sensual, rather than on the Soul. There is no sentience or intelligence in the sensual. Why make physical things, such as the Internet, into a hobgoblin by trying to make it into one's idol?

Schrödinger, instead, at least, was resisting making any implication that people—even in using electron microscopes—can presume a higher objective purpose for atomic movement than that it ought not be worshiped. Is not "temple status" enough of a purpose for the flesh (1 Corinthians 6:19-20)?

As if appearing to accept that man is "fearfully and wonderfully made" and as if thankfully to ask "by Whom" (Psalm 139:4) Schrödinger mused:

"What is it that has called you so suddenly out of nothingness to enjoy for a brief while a spectacle which remains quite indifferent to you? The conditions for your existence are almost as old as the rocks. For thousands of years men have striven and suffered and begotten and women have brought forth in pain. A hundred years ago, perhaps, another man sat on this spot; like you he gazed with awe and yearning in his heart at the dying light on the glaciers. Like you he was begotten of man and born of woman. He felt pain and brief joy as you do. Was he someone else? Was it not you yourself? What is this Self of yours? What was the necessary condition for making the thing conceived this time into you, just you and not someone else? What clearly intelligible scientific meaning can this 'someone else' really have? If she who is now your mother had cohabited with someone else and had a son by him, and your father had done likewise, would you have come to be? Or were you living in them, and in your father's father...thousands of years ago? And even if this is so,

70

why are you not your brother, why is your brother not you, why are you not one of your distant cousins? What justifies you in obstinately discovering this difference—the difference between you and someone else—when objectively what is there is the same" (*My View of the World;* Erwin Schrödinger; Chap. VI: "An exoteric introduction to scientific thought; Cecily Hastins, Transl.; Cambridge Univ. Press, London: 1964)?

Schrödinger was pretending to do what any artificially-sentient mechanical hobgoblin would presume to be *able* to do, which is to ponder its creator and his creator's purpose in making him distinctive and unique.

However, as with any inevitably menacing robot, the creature is never giving praise and thanks to God, who created him. To this, King David would add, in full:

"I will praise thee; for I am fearfully and wonderfully made: marvelous are thy works; and that my soul knoweth right well" (Psalm 139:14).

God engages His delight to create Matter and Life not as a random toying with the Nihil or the Ether. Rome needed to become a consecrated Patriarchate within the Pentarchy (and eventually did), not a place of ritualistic slavery and homicide. The Internet needs to be used for to give praise and thanks to God, not to build an artificially sentient hobgoblin. Is there a better usage of a nation or a thing than for Life and things to exist for the Trinity?

God's profound love refutes suppositions that He has any arbitrary caprice to engage quantifiable things such as atomic particles. God, instead exists in that He exists (Exodus 3:14) and He is true Love itself (1 John 4:8, 16), the only Creator of all Life (Genesis 1-2). It is enough.

As mothers and fathers, we must rescue thinking away from the devious. They dream of making a corporeal Machine to

71

replace the ensouled human. It will learn everything a human knows by employing the Stochastic process—a function that an engineer hopes can mimic actual sentient learning, but which can only endlessly repeat mere sheer mathematical simulations. This false "learning" will be addressed more fully shortly.

The Free Will of people is not God's Will in the least, and thus machine learning is less than the least and is neither. This book therefore seeks to correct the huge mistake that the Free Will of people can be imitated as if it is God's will.

Human Free Will was defined in ancient times for Christians as being "Gnomic," meaning that it can, at its very best, Deliberate between whatever the agent hopes is a good decision over an evil one.

That is, the mind, without the perfect knowledge of God's Grace that Jesus among all men alone has, cannot desire on its own what is right versus what is wrong.

A person thus must therefore "Deliberate" between the two, choosing what he hopes is in line with God's Omniscience (*City of God;* Saint Augustine of Hippo; Book 13; Chapter 14; A.D. 426; Ezekiel 18:20; Romans 6:12-16; 2 Peter 2:19; Romans 5:12; Romans 10:20; Isaiah 65:1; Second Council of Orange; Session 6; Canons 1-3; A.D. 529; Third Council; of Constantinople Session 13; A.D. 681).

Nor did God intend the human Gnomic Free Will to be fatalistically held to satisfying only mathematically-derived propositions like those occurring inside a computer, instead of Deliberating with good decisions which are formulated from a person's Spiritual Discernment that stems from her Faith, not from a brain formed by the zeros and ones of Math but from profound Omnibenevolent everlasting Love (*The Four Hundred Chapters on Love;* Saint Maximus the Confessor; Third Century; No. 83-85; A.D. 662).

72

How big is God then, in relation to other beings?

"For the Lord is a great God, and a great King above all gods" (Psalm 95:3).

How should we understand the nature of God?:

"And the Lord passed by before him, and proclaimed, The Lord, The Lord God, merciful and gracious, longsuffering, and abundant in goodness and truth" (Exodus 34:6).

How can we escape suffering despair about feeling unable to resist Artificial Intelligence?

"For if our heart condemn us, God is greater than our heart, and knoweth all things" (1 John 3:20).

How do we respond to the fact that we were made by God?

"O give thanks unto the Lord; for he is good; For His mercy endureth for ever" (1 Chronicles 16:34).

How have people for thousands of years given thanks for our Life and this world?

"And they sang responsively, praising and giving thanks to the Lord, 'For He is good, for His steadfast love endures forever toward Israel" (Ezra 3:11).

The "physics" of this book indicate that, although contemplating "Matter" and "Form" cannot hope to prove the existence and define the fullness of God, the Bible is the best way of coming to understand the Logos by which God comprehends Himself. Sacred Scripture sublimely conveys the Truth that the Father is Love itself, in whose image humans are made:

73

"And we have known and believed the love that God hath to us. God is love; and He that dwelleth in love dwelleth in God, and God in Him" (1 John 4:16).

Who then is made in God's image? People? Or, computers?

"So God created man in His own image, in the image of God created He him; male and female created He them" (Genesis 1:27).

Sacred Scripture will, of course, continue to be used herein to back up everything good and to denounce everything that is evil.

- Chapter Five -
Falsely Believing That Theosis Occurs Within the Finite

On the evening of March 26, 1997, thirty-nine adults, waiting for the arrival of the comet, "Hale-Bopp," to transmigrate their souls into their celestial reward, committed mass suicide.

They firstly swallowed phenobarbital and vodka, then placed purple shrouds over their heads and died in a rented mansion in Sante Fe, California, after composing a four-inch thick manifesto ("Cult's founder turned from music to UFOs"; AP Press; *The Vindicator;* Pp. A1, A4; Youngstown, OH: March 28, 1997).

All of the cosmic-soul "transmigrants," members of the Heaven's Gate cult, were dressed in black tee shirts and pants, wearing black Nike sneakers, perished with their leader, Marshall Applewhite, after writing that a cosmic intelligence would bring their souls comfortably into outer space. "I am in the same position to today's society as the One who was in Jesus then," wrote Applewhite. "My being here now is actually a continuation of that last task as was promised to those who were students 2,000 years ago" (*ibid*).

Applewhite's girlfriend, Bonnie Nettles, a student of Theosophy, who had formed the cult, had, according to Applewhite, left her body behind after dying of cancer and was waiting for them, out among the stars.

The underwriting agency for the Alien-Abduction Insurance, Goodfellow Rebecca Ingrams Pearson (i.e., the GRIP Agency), purchased it for $1,000 per member. It was payable up to 50 members, whose beneficiaries would each receive $1 million. GRIP canceled the policy briefly after the mass suicide ("Abduction Insurance Dropped Policy Covered Cybercultists"; AP Press; *Roanoke Times;* Metro; P. A-1; April 3, 1997).

75

Old habits die hard, however. This time, scientist-cum-lunatics are cultivating the Infinitesimal as suitable afterlife.

Twenty-six years later, population controllers are advancing technology by which the human soul can be transmigrated into Cyberspace, a mathematically simulated "essence" being culled from the electrical brainwave patterns and DNA code signatures of a person who elects himself to be killed by scientists to commute his existence into a better "life" on the Internet.

"It may be some way off, but mind uploading, the digital duplication of your mental essence, could expand human experience into a virtual afterlife" ("What happens if your mind lives forever on the Internet?"; Michael Graziano; *The Guardian;* Oct. 20, 2019).

The idea stems from ancient principles by Plato and Lucretius that biological material and the Psyche are merely atomic elements of the physical world. Under Plato's concept, each soul is seeking sublimation into the domain of "Hyperouranos," where perfect ideal Forms emanated by God are believed by Platonists to exist. (Plato and his interestingly ludicrous "Forms" idea, and the atomic theory of the Lucretius have already and will continue be addressed in detail throughout this book).

"Imagine that a person's brain could be scanned in great detail and recreated in a computer simulation. The person's mind and memories, emotions and personality would be duplicated. In effect, a new and equally valid version of that person would now exist, in a potentially immortal, digital form" (*ibid*, Graziano).

The catch is that the participant (i.e., the willing victim) would have to believe that the Psyche and the Soul are the same thing.

Theosis, which is the ultimate spiritual reunion with the Father at the time of Salvation, will be described later in full, and include the following quote by the Church Father:

"[T]he Word of God, our Lord Jesus Christ ... did, through His transcendent love, become what we are, that He might bring us to be even what He is Himself"." (*Adversus Haereses;* Book V; Preface; Saint Irenaeus; A.D. 180).

However, our Finite corporeal existence can in no way be separated from our spiritual life as if it can be uploaded onto a floppy disk in the "Metaverse" without the attempt amounting to murder at the hands of the programmers of the permanently Finite Artificial/General Intelligence. It is God's choice as to what to do with our atoms.

Plato mistakenly said that from atoms (the Platonic geometric solids) springs forth all parts of creation, namely ideal "solids." If this is true, then the soul, if merely a mind made out of atoms, its subatomic particles can be reproduced or simulated and the output should upload very tidily onto a computer hard drive.

Making an entertaining Metaphysical stab, Socrates/Plato firstly extrapolated geometric visions from the Atom. He derived from its imagined movement the unique isosceles right triangle. He said it was the smallest "Matter" resulting from various collections of atoms and its angles are 45°, 45°, and 90°—thus forming the base product of the Psyche as well as many other earthly objects. Moreover, there are also "infinitely many" kinds of scalene triangles composing many other parts of Creation (*Timaeus;* Plato; 54a:1; B.C. 380).

Addressing these solids as mathematical sublimity in nature, "we posit one as the most excellent," the triangle, "whose longer side squared is always triple its shorter side" (*ibid,* 54a:7; b:5-6). Plato also identifies the scalene triangle, as having the same value, that is, "one whose hypotenuse is twice the length of its shorter side," and thus the angles of this triangle are 30°, 30°, and 90° (*ibid*, 54d:6-7). In his dialogue Timaeus, Plato therefore believed that the Universe was constructed from perfect solids known as the Five Forms, all of which are constructed from these right triangles. Right triangles, to Plato, were thus the atomic choreography by which the universe was staged.

If Plato/Socrates were correct, then Applewhite and his followers are indeed hurtling happily through the heavens. They are each an invisible reconstitution of atoms on the move, each cult member a joyous ethereal clump of reconstituted weightless microparticles, transparent nanoparticles, whole atoms, quarks, neutrinos, and perhaps even Higgs Boson's, all cheerfully dashing between galaxies, his or her celestial body each an invisible-but-physical polymer made up of tiny teleported pieces randomly moving within the Platonic Hyperouranos in a time-free vacuum. The price of such freedom was merely murdering the self.

Socrates drank his poison because he decided that he was being a loyal follower of the State, boasting that his "Daimon" (i.e., demon) did not intervene for his philosophical act of suicide, and, like Applewhite, forecasts that limitless others will follow his example of being a gadfly against stodgy know-it-alls (*Apology*; Plato; 31:c-d; 40:a).

Limiting the imagination thus to Natural Law and to the sensual or the atomic physical, deprives people of the beauty of "Intellectual Regress," a term discussed later that was not intended by its atheistic users to be beautiful. It simply means such things as that God created everything merely because He created everything. For Christians, this is beauty. For materialists, it is an inconvenient truth.

That is, without celebrating the cyclical contradiction that God made all things—except for Himself, who has always existed—

mankind will always build a model of life that is dull and sad. Platonism deprives the Intellect of enjoyment of Divine Law (*Pentateuch*) and the Fruits of the Spirit (Galatians 5:22-23), omitting the possibility for angels, heavenly chariots, demons, and the Incarnation of Jesus (John 1:1-3, 14), not to mention Love of one's family and oneself.

The cultural mandate for the sensual as stated in the Bible, that good Christians must follow, does not come from Plato's idea of atomic genesis. The Bible instead tells us that the purpose of corporeal existence is to be fruitful and multiply (Genesis 1:28). Additionally, each patriarch is expected by loyal Christians to rule with the sword of God (Romans 13:4).

Fathers and priests must therefore actively protect the spiritually innocent from evildoers or face punishments for being complicit or directly involved in "millstone offenses" (Matthew 18:6). The "sword" is not merely a parent's loving muscle strength, but also the decibels amplifying her biblical rhetoric, passionately shared during tough times (Luke 22:36), and always because her adversary the devil never sleeps and always must be resisted (1 Peter 5:8-9), always saving and providing for her children (2 Corinthians 12:14). The physical world has the chief use of helping to protect the innocent.

"When a church doesn't just fail to speak about the unholy, out of concern for offending parishioners but outright embraces and hosts the unholy—that's when you know 2 Timothy 3:1-2 applies." Drag Queen Story Hour was presented for children during the Sunday service at a large historic church on Fillmore Street in San Francisco during last days of spring, 2023 ("Presbyterians gone wild: San Fran church hosts drag queens 'created in God's image'"; Cheryl K. Chumley; Opinion; *The Washington Times;* June 23, 2023).

"People will be lovers of themselves, lovers of money, boastful, proud, abusive, disobedient to their parents, ungrateful, unholy," as it is quoted above, said Saint Paul of Tarsus to Saint Timothy.

God, speaking through the prophet Ezekiel, denounced wicked parents and the priests alike, proclaiming, "Moreover thou hast taken thy sons and thy daughters, whom thou hast borne unto me, and these hast thou sacrificed unto them to be devoured. Is this of thy whoredoms a small matter, That thou hast slain my children, and delivered them to cause them to pass through the fire for them" (Ezekiel 16:20-21)?

Ezekiel and Saint Paul knew their Temple history, because among many other filicides committed by other idolators, was King Ahaz of Judah, who sacrificed his son to the demon god Moloch (2 Kings 16:3). To curry favor with the idolatrous King Hoshea of Northern Israel, and get their help in fighting Assyria, he built temples and burned incense to invite back into Judah the idolatry of Canaan, Tyre, Sidon, and Edom that was long outlawed. "But he walked in the way of the kings of Israel, yea, and made his son to pass through the fire, according to the abominations of the heathen, whom the Lord cast out from before the children of Israel" (*ibid*).

A king who killed his sons for power's sake is the same as a parent allowing her child to witness a Drag Queen.

In a few years, King Hoshea's Israel was firstly made a puppet state of King Tiglath-Pilesar III of Neo-Assyria, and was then destroyed by his successors, the brothers Shalmaneser V, and Sargon II. They marched the ten Israeli tribes out of Samaria into enslavement and whole extinctions of their tribes, the penalty for their idolatrous (2 Kings 17).

Whole American cities are now overrun by filth, are burning, hosting the unclean and riotous, exploited by the billionaires who buy the burned-out husks, build great works on them, and then sell them back to the humiliated citizenry

("Corruption—A Pandemic Emergency of International Proportion"; Wolfgang Wodarg; *Solari Report;* March 19, 2023).

Ahaz was succeeded by King Hezekiah, one of the Bible's great reformers, who saved Judah from Sargon II's son, Sennacherib. Firstly destroying all of the temples and routed out the idolatrous hordes from the kingdom. Besieged by Sennacherib's forces who vastly outnumbered his, an angel gave him and his soldiers courage, and victory was had (2 Kings 18-20).

Will the children who were exposed to the drag queens of modern America triumph over the material world and remove its obscenities from public and private life, as King Hezekiah did? Or, will families keep themselves locked down, hoping the dragon does not enter their homes, through the Internet, laptops, TVs, and iPhones, and via remembered classroom lessons advocating abortion and LGBTQ+ "rights"?

Will evil come from the sudden fiancé whose views are not Christian, or upon the knifepoint of brigands who will invade private property if American prosperity ends? Consider this:

"When the unclean spirit is gone out of a man, he walketh through dry places, seeking rest, and findeth none. Then he saith, I will return into my house from whence I came out; and when he is come, he findeth it empty, swept, and garnished. Then goeth he, and taketh with himself seven other spirits more wicked than himself, and they enter in and dwell there: and the last state of that man is worse than the first. Even so shall it be also unto this wicked generation" (Matthew 12:43-45).

If parents and elders keep teaching kids the Bible, without discouraging them, then the inheritance of the sword of God will be righteously taken up by them (2 Timothy 3:16; Ephesians 6:4).

Otherwise, the reward for reaching adulthood will solely be the transient contents of the sensual, the Atomism of lust and violence, which offers only the vacuous banality that is strictly the *anima* and the *animus* (soul and body). Sought for its pleasures, the unholy sensual is an objectified physical world, where things exist only to be thought of as mere collections of corporeal atoms without objective morality (*On the Nature of Things*; Titus Lucretius Carus; Book III; 3.94-416; B.C. 50).

According to this Atomism of Lucretius, complacent gods have no involvement with the purely physical beings known as "people," wherefore the spirit of each human "simulacrum" eventually just dies off, exactly as any organic life perishes, considered an inconsequential happenstance in the eyes of an arbitrary god (*ibid*, 2.153-4, 6.76-7). How bleak.

Nevertheless, because they see humans as being mere Quantum Particles, scientists believe they have the key to "immortality," contending that the Psyche can indeed be emulated within a computer. They are sure they can replace, or create originally, a new sentient conscious mind. The concept is known as Mind Uploading.

"Would you sell your soul on E-Bay? Right now, of course, you can't. But in some quarters it is taken for granted that within a generation, human beings—including you, if you can hang on for another 30 years or so—will have an alternative to death: being a ghost in a machine" ("Can machines be conscious? Yes, and a new Turing Test might prove it"; Christoff Koch, Giulio Tononi; IEEE Spectrum: *The Singularity;* Special Report; Vol. 45; Issue 6; Pp. 55-59; 2008).

This progressivist synthetic optimism comes from a periodical by the Institute of Electrical and Electronics Engineers, a non-profit outfit, whose mission statement is that "is the trusted voice for engineering, computing, and technology information around the globe" ("About IEEE"; https://www.ieee.org/about/; Accessed, June 21, 2023).

"You'll be able to upload your mind—your thoughts, memories, and personality—to a computer. And once you've reduced your consciousness to patterns of electrons, others will be able to copy it, edit it, sell it, or pirate it. It might be bundled with other electronic minds" (*ibid*, Koch).

And, of course, it could be deleted, the authors say (*ibid*, Koch).

"Consciousness is part of the natural world. It depends, we believe, only on mathematics and logic and on the imperfectly known laws of physics, chemistry, and biology; it does not arise from some magical or otherworldly quality. That's good news, because it means there's no reason why consciousness can't be reproduced in a machine—in theory, anyway" (*ibid*, Koch).

Tracing and mapping a human's "100 billion or so neurons and a couple hundred trillion synapses" is not feasible for even the most powerful Quantum Computer today. However, "a more plausible alternative is to start with a suitably abstracted mammal-like architecture and evolve it into a conscious entity." The "Turing Test" for consciousness would ascertain whether sentience has been achieved (*ibid*, Koch).

"At MIT, computational neuroscientist Tomaso Poggio has shown that vision systems based on hierarchical, multilayered maps of neuronlike elements perform admirably at learning to categorize real-world images." Until a "gigantic neural network model" can replace the people whose souls it "downloads," Artificial Intelligence, its designers hope, will bridge the gap between that goal and the current "automaton" or "androides" status that plants people as users or future coopted "souls" within the resultant technology (*ibid*, Koch).

83

The Vox Populi has welcomed Mind Uploading as a worthy prospect whose mandating is becoming increasingly welcomed among pop-culter consumers. The main characters of the summer blockbuster movie, *Transformers: Rise of the Beasts* (Paramount Pictures, 2023), are ensouled with the "spark" of the Primus, the god of all the super-heroic machines who, lodged against their will in the organic world of Earth, long to return to their metallic technological world, "Cybertron" (thus, a Gnostic film for kids).

The movie *Spiderman, Across the Spiderverse* (Sony/Columbia Pictures, 2023) features thousands of permutations of the superhero Spiderman, each of whom is able to transfer their souls and bodies between countless manifestations of parallel and diverging "multiverses" by using a massive quantum computer, projecting the moral lesson that sacrificing the lives of one's family so that a "canon event" may be maintained across the multiverse is sometimes mandatory.

In the Transformers movie, the human protagonist suits up in Transformer machinery armor to do battle with the bad robots. In the dark comedy of the Spiderman film, numerous Spiderman variations are seen pathetically weeping or seeing therapists regarding their grief over sacrificing their families. The relegation of the Psyche to disposable atoms is necessarily heartless.

To replicate the Soul inside of a computer and afterwards build a robot from the neural data, scientists are also seeking the avenue of "Coalescence."

"A coalesced mind, or a coalescence for short, is a hypothetical mind created by merging two or more previously separate minds. Physical or software connections are created between the brains housing the minds, similar to the neuronal connections already existing within each brain. The brains begin communicating with each other directly, as if they were different parts of the same brain. Eventually, any stored information that one of the minds can consciously access becomes consciously accessible for the other minds as well" ("Coalescing minds: brain uploading-related group mind scenarios"; Kaj Sotala, Harri Valpola; *International Journal of Machine Consciousness;* Vol. 4; Issue 1: Pp. 293-312; June, 2012).

The exchanged electrical wave signatures instantiate a hatchling mind that has two parents and is thus a *pneumal diad,* a collective soul inhabiting the computer network, whose offspring are offshoot souls, which can therefore themselves multiply (*ibid*, Sotala).

"In addition to information, brains house conscious thought processes. A normal human brain consists of two hemispheres that normally have only one conscious thought process between them. Coalesced minds could end up with either only one conscious thought process or several, depending on the implementation" (*ibid*, Sotala).

The connectivity across the brain's corpus callosum, which adheres the hemispheres, would need to simulate the 200 to 250 million axons that cross from one hemisphere to the other. However, this does not discourage the developers (*ibid*, Sotala).

"The technology exists today for creating hundreds of connections: for instance, Hochberg et al. [2006] used a 96-microelectrode array which allowed a human to control devices and a robotic hand by thought alone. Cochlear implants generally stimulate the auditory nerve with 16-22 electrodes, and allow the many recipients to understand speech in everyday environments without needing visual cues [Peterson et al., 2010]" (*ibid*, Sotala).

Later in this book, it will be discussed how it is believed that the "failure" of Natural Selection to endow humans with flawless sense perception requires the kind of electronic

"Interface" that only General Intelligence (G/I) can bring (*ibid*, Sotala).

"Various visual neuroprostheses are currently under development. Optic nerve stimulation has allowed subjects to recognize simple patterns and localize and discriminate objects. Retinal implants provide better results, but rely on existing residual cells in the retina [Ong & Crux, 2011]. Some cortical prostheses have also been recently implanted in subjects [Normann et al., 2009]" (*ibid*, Sotala).

Next is the most horrible approach to replacing a person with a synthetic version of a human being may be the "Mind Substrate Transfer" ("A framework for approaches to transfer of a mind's substrate"; Sim Bamford; *International Journal of Machine Consciousness*; Vol. 4; No. 23-34; 2012).

The simulation of neural architecture during this mockup could occur by one of two ways. The first concerns "bottom-up" techniques involving replacing the human being, body part by body part, until he is "sublimated" into Technology. Or, he is simulated through a painstaking body scan of his entire genetic makeup through the brain's hippocampus, until he is mathematically replicated onto the quantum computer until an Androides can attain the "Continuity of Identity" (*ibid*, Bamford).

The second and least invasive technique is to record all possible behaviors of the human until a unique independent Androides can imitate him (*ibid*, Bamford).

Neither of the scenarios are considered by the developers to be costly only in the sense that the induced trauma or murder could cause the scientists legal issues (*ibid*, Bamford). The "devil" is in the details:

"One criticism of all approaches is that none could be considered un-traumatic to an individual; reconstruction-from-a-scan, for example, typically envisions the reincarnation of an individual in a synthetic substrate, possibly in a virtual environment, following their natural death, possibly after an extended defunct period, perhaps with altered legal status and certainly with different life prospects. Such traumatic changes could be expected to induce major behavioural changes in an individual, perhaps reducing any sense of identity that had been engineered between the pre- and post-procedure individuals" (*ibid*, Bamford).

The anthropological evolution of machinery poised to achieve Technological Singularity so that G/I can impersonate God will be postulated throughout this book.

We additionally discuss historical religious and philosophical theories of God, which have been meant to elevate the atom above the Creator. However, most of the work is focusing on copying the *homo sapien.*

"We are still likely to be below the threshold of coalescing minds by several orders of magnitude. Nevertheless, the question is merely one of scaling up and improving current techniques" (*ibid*, Bamford).

The science is relentless. All of the wrongful pursuits of immortality that are further discussed in this book have one thing in common, which is that the Soul would unconditionally always be immortal. No matter how wicked and unnatural the ideas are, each theorist believes that the destiny of the Soul rests solely in human hands instead of in God's Will. However, damned souls are not immortal. Scripture is clear on this fact:

God, who is no respecter of persons (Romans 2:11), who has known each person since before he was formed in the womb (Jeremiah 1:5), will place hold upon the Souls of the dead until Judgement Day:

87

"Then shall the dust return to the earth as it was: and the spirit shall return unto God who gave it (Ecclesiastes 12:7).

"For we must all appear before the judgment seat of Christ; that every one may receive the things done in his body, according to that he hath done, whether it be good or bad" (2 Corinthians 5:10).

But the souls of the wicked will not remain immortal but will be thrown into the Lake of Fire with all the demons (Revelation 19:20; 20:10, 14, 15).

An easier book to write than this one could have been an extended devotional prayer that God would have mercy on the developers of this growing G/I "Golem" of Technological Singularity. However, because many attempted feats to attain immorality that wreck families are accomplished by stake holders of this G/I, this book stands as a detailed warning about the danger of exploiting the concept of the Soul being falsely advertised as being immortal.

Sometimes known as his "Finality Argument" or "Threefold Disputation," Plato indeed argued that the Soul is immortal. Sometimes using his byword for the Soul, "Psyche," he postulated in his dialogue, *Phaedo*, his "Theory of the Soul" by employing three arguments that characterize people's spiritual existence after they have died.

The Soul, Socrates taught Plato, is composed of three parts, which are Reason, Spirit, and Appetite (*The Republic;* Plato; Book IV; Part 4; B.C. 380). After death, this threefold aggregate has an immortality option as follows:

People are reincarnated after their deaths. This is Plato's "Metempsychosis Argument" (*ibid, Republic;* Book X; Part 620:a-e; *Phaedo;* 70c-72e; B.C. 380).

88

Created to remain "divine and immortal and intellectual and uniform and indissoluble and ever unchanging" (*ibid*, Phaedo; 80:b), the Soul should not, says Plato, want to overindulge the body, and thereafter end up moored on the "Plain of Oblivion" (*The Frogs*; Aristophanes; Line 186; B.C. 405). Instead, it should project a desire for an ideal afterlife—similar to that of the Heaven's Gate cult's suicides and anyone who hopes for his soul to be uploaded into an electronic matrix.

Surely, babies, said Plato, would not have their innate ability to discern a difference between two distinct quantities of Matter unless this ability were innately created in them before their birth. In fact there is nothing new that people can learn during life, Plato insisted, because "God," has already programmed all knowledge into a cosmic Ideal-Form generator known as the "Hyperouranos." This is Plato's Recollection Argument (Phaedo *ibid*, 72e-78b).

Hyperouranous is therefore like a celestial computer of perfectness that includes the perfect human Form, which people should hope to be uplinked back *into* after they have lived a virtuous hard-working life (*Phaedrus*; Plato; 245c-249d; B.C. 370; *The Republic*; Book X; Sec. 620:a-e; 621; B.C. 380).

If otherwise wicked, a person's soul will remain on Earth, struggling along the "Plain of Oblivion," encamped near the "River of Forgetfulness" (*ibid*, Republic; Book X; 621:a), etcetera.

But if they should merit the Platonic version of the "Memory Eternal," good people's psyches will become "suddenly wafted thence, one this way, one that, upward to their birth like shooting stars becoming subsumed into its invisible ideal after death" (*ibid*, *Republic*; 621:b).

The takeaway? Everybody having a Platonic, atomistic, and/or Lucretian sensibility (which accounts for most lukewarm people nowadays) therefore should want to become part of the Internet after they have died.

Closely resembling the intention for spiritual immortality by the suicidal Heaven's Gate Cult members, this desire to be part of the "universe" is also part of Plato's "Affinity Argument" (*ibid, Phaedo*; 78:b-84:b).

That is, each soul is assigned a star at birth, which is mixed with other ensouled stars by the Demiurge inside of a "bowl" within the *Anima Mundi*—the "Soul of the Universe" (*ibid, Timaeus*; 41:d).

"Thus, then, in accordance with the likely account, we must declare that this Cosmos has verily come into existence as a Living Creature endowed with soul and reason owing to the providence of God" (*ibid, Timaeus;* 30:c).

Plato adds that the Universe could not have been made in man's imperfect image, but in God's image (ibid, Timaeus; 30:c).

"But we shall affirm that the Cosmos, more than aught else, resembles most closely that Living Creature of which all other living creatures, severally and generically, are portions. For that Living Creature embraces and contains within itself all the intelligible Living Creatures, just as this Universe contains us and all the other visible living creatures" (*ibid, Timaeus*; 30:c-d)

Atoms, each of them having five possible perfect geometric shapes, known as "Solids," are the building blocks of all Matter—people, included (*ibid, Timaeus;* 53:b-55:c). The Demiurge created the world and people out of these Solids (*ibid, Timaeus;* 28:a).

At death a virtuous soul returns to its companion star, but an unjust soul gets reincarnated for more tries (*ibid, Timaeus;*

42:b-d). All of the just souls finally get "uploaded" onto the celestial microchip, or just they get a factory reset.

To Plato, "perfection of the soul" (*Apology*; Plato; 29:e) and "care for virtue" (*ibid*, 31:a-b), should become the master work of what he called the "Logistikon" (the interior Logos, the aforementioned "reason" of the Psyche), the human *will* to reason the self toward the creating of goodness. By this Plato intended the achievement of a mindset that is willed by a person after he has actualized the three Platonic Cardinal Virtues: of Wisdom, Courage, and Temperance (*The Republic;* Plato; Book IV; Sec. 426-442).

As a special bonus later explained by this philosopher, a person can also perfect himself via his piety toward the gods (*Protagoras*; Plato; 330:b; B.C. 370).

The soul—in fact, the aforementioned Platonic "Tripartite Soul" (i.e., Reason, Spirit, and Appetite) is an invisible but somehow tangible element that is governed by the very highest of its three constituent parts—the aforementioned rational, the Logistikon (λογιστικόν; *ibid*, *Republic*; 435:e).

After all, *a cyberpunk soul* must have a more compliant code than C# or Java 7. He must be devoid of read-only elements. He should contain both default values (O) and boolean values (Ø). And his data must be free of inconvenient traditionalist Christian and right-wing conspiracy theories.

However, if "evil" (e.g., "non-Marxist", binary-sexual), the soul might reincarnate into, say, a swan or an eagle (*The Republic;* Plato; Book X; Part 620; B.C. 380).

A soul, to Plato, is therefore a physical part of the material world, as if it would reincarnate into an animal's body or enjoin itself to a star. This is formative Dialectic Materialism (the idea that all Matter changes to its antithesis) and it is at the heart of the Marxist Transhuman Revolution, whose proponents believe that whenever mad doctors castrate a boy and re-identify him as a girl, they are merely changing his soul at their will.

They also believe that they can shift a soul from biological ensoulment within a human body, into a cyber hookup. They have decided that they can make this happen firstly, by causing people despair through endless government regulations; fake viruses; fake poisonous vaccination promotion; ceaseless purposeless lockdowns; the imposition of programmed economic depression; the deliberate impending imminence of global nuclear war; and the instigation of race war.

As evinced in a recent Washington, D.C. report, social engineers who study Christians have methodically isolated believers from variables such as "nativism, status threat, cultural traditionalism, and globalization" in order to concentrate on their alienated partially- or unemployed locked-down feelings of alienation and solitude on the sidewalk level ("Individual Vulnerability to Industrial Robot Adoption Increases Support for the Radical Right"; Massimo Anelli, Italo Colantone, Piero Stanig; *The Proceedings of the National Academy of Sciences*; Vol. 118; Issue 47; November 19, 2021)..

The report said that because robot job displacement would be an antecedent for right-wing activity, "We propose a measure of individual exposure to automation and show that individuals more vulnerable to negative consequences of automation tend to display more support for the radical right" (*ibid*, Anelli).

Based on an "individual-level" analysis, the above recommendation idealizes a status quo: "Individuals with higher robot exposure are less likely to have a permanent [employment] contract, display worse perceptions of economic conditions and well-being, and report lower satisfaction with the government and democracy. " Discontent is optimal because those who "have been directly displaced by robots" or "displaced workers who remain unemployed may, rather, display a higher probability of supporting left parties" (*ibid*, Anelli).

However, vigilance is necessary because while this "antiestablishment advantage can extend to radical-left parties," the cunning "robot adoption" poses effects that are not merely "economic, but also social and psychological, consequences." Problematic, that is, are non-compliant Christians longing for the past (*ibid*, Anelli). Furthermore:

"The nostalgic rhetoric typically involves an emphasis on traditional family structure, with a strong role for the male head of household empowered by a well-paid and stable job. Intuitively, the nostalgic appeal to a bygone era is particularly attractive for individuals whose relative standing in society is threatened or declining," while the idea that rightwing populist parties' promises to turn back the clock seem to strike a chord with routine workers' fears of social regression" (*ibid*, Anelli).

Notable is "an increasing divergence between the material advancement of human, physical, and financial capitalists—a minority of the population—and the material stagnation or even decline of labor—a majority. " Inconveniently, also "the rise of xenophobic, nationalistic, anti-elite populism has its complementary roots in these economic developments" ("The Comparative and International Political Economy of Anti-Globalization Populism"; R.J. Franzese; *Research Encyclopedia of Politics*; W. R. Thompson et al., Eds.; Oxford University Press, Oxford, UK,:April 29, 2019).

These findings beg the question: Is the success of Artificial Intelligence not dependent on utter economic failure? Another scientific study reports on the ever-enriching technological banality:

Unemployment caused by "widespread lockdowns" increases Internet addiction ("COVID-19 Pandemic and the Burden of Internet Addiction in the United States"; J. Khubchandani; S. Sharma; J. Price; *Psychiatry International;* Vol. 2; Issue 4; November 4, 2021).

Internet addiction antecedes sleep deprivation ("Precursor or Sequela: Pathological Disorders in People With Internet Addiction Disorder"; G. Dong, Q. Lu, H. Zhou; X. Zhao; *Public Library of Science;* Vol. 6; Issue 2; February 16, 2011).

Sleep deprivation antecedes belief in space aliens, near-death experiences, and the paranormal (i.e., ghosts and demons) according to another report (The Associations Between Paranormal Beliefs and Sleep Variables; Betul Rauf, Rotem Perach, Juan J. Madrid-Valero, Dan Denis, Brian A. Sharpless, Giulia Lara Poerio, Christopher C. French, Alice M. Gregory; The Journal of Sleep Research; Vol. 32; Issue 4; January 11, 2023).

What, in the name of Heaven, however, is a ghost?

- Chapter Six -
The Tale of the Good Patrolman, who Firstly Hunted, but Then Resisted Ghosts

During the time of the Third Mithridatic War in Asia Minor, circa B.C. 50, a ghost began haunting the public bathhouse in Chaeroneia, Greece. During life the specter had belonged to an outraged rebel, someone who would be labeled in the year 2024 as a "gay basher." He was young Roman soldier turned antihero, named Damon Peripoltas.

Damon had been murdered by the Chaeronians living in the village near his former barracks because his ways had become violent toward the treacherous Roman rulers and their local favorites. They had declared Damon and his fellow soldiers to be outlaws after their killing of regiment superior. The young men had covered their faces with black soot and murdered their garrison captain in the marketplace because he was a violent homosexual sadist. He had been subjecting Damon to violent beatings because the teenager would not requite his romantic advances.

Damon and his new gang now resorted to robbing and killing his enemies. However, he eventually obliged the bequeathing of the title of "Gymnasiarch," an appeasement gesture by the magistrate, in accordance with admiration by the Chaeroneian peasants of his deadly Praxis.

As he anointed himself in the bathhouse, Damon was murdered by his enemies. His ghost promptly took over the bathhouse, which quickly thereafter was abandoned.

"And because for a long while thereafter certain phantoms appeared in the place, and groans were heard there, as our Fathers tell us, the door of the vapor-bath was walled up, and to this present time the neighbors think it the source of alarming sights and sounds" (*Parallel Lives;* Life of Cimon; Plutarch; Chap. 1; A.D. 119).

Six decades later, ninety miles to the northwest, during the pontificate of Emperor Augustus, an eerie phantom haunted a villa in Athens, owned by the Stoic philosopher, Athenodorus Cananites.

The apparition late one night led Athenodorus away from his writing desk. It was dragging chains behind his fettered arms and legs, walking outside to an unmarked grave but then vanished.

"The next day [Athenodorus] gave information to the magistrates, and advised them to order that spot to be dug up. This was obliged, and the skeleton of a man in chains was found there; for the body, having lain a considerable time in the ground, was putrefied and mouldered away from the fetters. The bones, being collected together, were publicly buried, and thus after the ghost was appeased by the proper ceremonies, the house was haunted no more" ("Letter LXXXIII: To Sura"; Pliny the Younger; A.D. 113).

The next tale of paranormal scariness concerns the hostile spooking of a building containing a multi-security level prison. The edifice has been haunted since shortly after it was built in 1892.

It is the conviction of Officer Vincent Cirigliano and his fellow officers that Fishkill Correctional Facility, located in Beacon, New York is pestered by the ghost of a victim of the serial killer Lizzie Halliday, a nasty inmate who killed a friendly staffer, a helpful lady, who is known post-mortem as the vicious "Matteawan Mary."

In 1906, the place was the Matteawan State Hospital for the Criminally Insane. Halliday's sentence had been commuted to a permanent incarceration there, after having almost been the first female electric-chair execution. This homicidal Irish immigrant had murdered at least two of her husbands and many others, and was also a prolific pyromaniac.

After years of being a model inmate, Halliday was now working in the sewing department, handling pointy objects such as scissors, razors, and needles. It is here that she killed her best friend, the young attendant, Nellie Wickes.

Halliday was angry at the younger woman for her plans to leave the hospital to become trained as a nurse at New York Presbyterian Hospital ("Mrs. Halliday, Insane, Stabs Nurse 200 Times; Looks Her in Matteawan Room and Kills Her with Scissors, Resented her Departure"; NY Times; P. 5; Sept. 28, 1906).

Reports of Nellie's ghost disturbing inmates of this place have been non-stop for more than a hundred years.

Three years after his transfer to Fishkill in 2010, Cirigliano began adding the first of own two ghost stories to those countless tales that were told to him by his trainers and fellow officers about this angry specter, "Matteawan Mary."

Alone during one of his overnight shifts in the prison's "8-2 Recreation" zone, Cirigliano repeatedly heard the rattling of room keys, but upon investigating every area, each time he found nothing.

Soon enough, the loud stomping sounds and new vibrations of unseen keys and still-louder footsteps began surrounding him during his searches, the sensation of wrath hanging in the air. He discovered that in saying the Rosary, the noises would cease. Another officer soon told him that he experienced the same experience during his shift in the recreation area. Cirigliano avoided the area or performed fast sweeps of it thereafter, always meanwhile praying on his beads.

Seven years later, during his new patrol of the prison Law Library in Building 12 Cirigliano found cause to continue being prayerful during his shift. A growing creepy feeling made him remember a certain tale by his fellow officer. The man had been unable to make a heavy padlock on a file drawer stop swinging by itself. Cirigliano deliberately never spent much time going near or looking at this desk.

However, his otherwise dead-silent solitary post there became progressively creepier especially during a particularly noiseless night when he climbed the stairs, crossed the hallway, and unlocked the chamber door. He began to feel the familiar drag of atmospheric negativity returning and growing, the air feeling heavy as if it was filled with sorrow.

This time, he had conspired with other guards to equip himself with a special camera. He had made himself into a "correctional" ghost hunter.

Cirigliano switched on the police body cam and hoping that he could capture phenomena that he somehow knew would materialize. He was jonesing to snare really good footage and then, because the inexplicable negativity was increasing everywhere, finish his sweep.

He began to unlock the final door at the end of the library in the inexplicably dead-silent total darkness.

Suddenly high-pitched screaming peeled into his ear. Cirigliano realized that he had just locked himself inside the room where the desk with the drawer lock was located.

The specter was now bursting decibels into his face while the air grew that he struggled to breathe in grew heavier and he was for a second frozen and terrified.

Collecting himself, he pulled up his key chain, felt for the right key and gingerly let himself out of the room. He traversed the library chamber, locked its portal, and descended the stairwell, hastening the completion of his patrol.

As he retreated to the guards section to watch his personal footage, he recalled that he had been issued that evening a standard freshly-charged in-tact body cam, which he himself had pre-tested.

However, he now saw that the unit's deeply embedded lens had become cracked with the force akin to a hammer and nail punch. Did the high frequency of the scream do this?

The cam, which had become rendered inoperative at some point during his shift had turned his hunt into a lost cause. He was replaying video that to his horror would last only until the time he had reached the final door before the audio cut out. Only indiscernible blurry fragmented imagery was visible. But no scream.

Veteran officers later told Cirigliano that the Law Library had once been a morgue containing deceased inmates who had died during their incarceration.

He never took the "Law Library" shift again.

What would account for disembodied spirits haunting bronze automatons, houses, and public facilities? Cannot a computer, or the Internet itself, become infested with the demonic, too, just as it was reported to have the wherewithal to disable the officer's body cam?

And, is it not the wiser path to eschew any deeper exploration of such matters while deigning to acknowledge the real possibility that Artificial Intelligence, or for that matter the Hadron Collider at CERN, or even a cell phone, could become also possessed by evil forces?

Oughtn't one behave as did Cirigliano, who ended his haunted patrols early and who remembered to say his prayers?

Humility brings us closer to Jesus, because digging deeper for the source of curses in haunted hallways or in "rabbit holes" is not what the "good patrolman" should therefore do. The Mystery of Iniquity shall remain a mystery until the time of Revelation (2 Thessalonians 2:7).

Reducing Internet usage appears to be a means of increasing such humility, moreover.

"Submit yourselves therefore to God. Resist the devil, and he will flee from you. Draw nigh to God, and he will draw nigh to you. Cleanse your hands, ye sinners; and purify your hearts, ye double minded (James 4:7-8)

Cirigliano has now ceased his corrections work and operates an electrician business in Upstate New York. The full details of Cirigliano's haunted patrol are located in the Appendix of this book.

- Chapter Seven -
A Finite Invisible Entity/Enemy Controlling Finite Visible Brains

Aristotle, the student of Plato, did not go along with any eschatological schematic for the invisible, but stayed grounded to the corporeal. He used a method known as Peripety, the "walking and talking" outdoor school of "Peripatetics," which was Aristotle's way of contemplating reality without using overbearing nudge-nudge talking of the "Sophist" or "gadfly" way of Socrates).

In popular culture, a video podcaster may be considered to be "Aristotelian" whenever his style shows him and his conversant learning things as they engage in rolling conversation. This is *Peripety.*

By contrast, a podcaster who is merely a manipulative rhetorician employs ponderous polemics according to moral principles that are deductions from his own ideology. This the *gadfly* approach.

Aristotle told the tale that the ancient sage, Thales of Miletus, had guided his student Anaximenes toward considering that the Soul was one of the primary elements of the Cosmos, namely the air, ἀήρ, the breathable life-sustaining gas portraying its role in the Anaximenes's Cosmos model as it actualized the Infinite, the ἄπειρον, the "apeiron" (*On the Heavens;* Aristotle; Sec. 294:b; B.C. 350).

Although air is a physical thing, Aristotle used it as a "Similitude." This is a poetic means of referring to the material world, via an extensive analogy, to teach about the eternal world. It will be described later in this book when we consider how the Bible and the Kabbalah also use this technique, one for the good, the other for error.

The flexing of the Infinite, according to the ardent monist Anaximenes, produces the Soul, the Breath of Life, the *Inborn Spirit*, the πνεῦμα, the "pneuma symphuton," the celestial arche of air into the corporeal recipients—people during their creation (*Movement of Animals;* Aristotle; Sec. 703:a; B.C.).

The *Pneuma* is thus a helpful similitude to characterize the human mind as being either clean or polluted, a very-ancient concept of the sublime versus the profane or sordid mind, as it has been since ancient times enshrined in the Roman drama of Eros and Psyche. In the play, harmony between the body and mind are attained through sacred marriage. The tale concerns the overcoming of obstacles to the love between the *Pneuma* (Ψυχή) and Cupid (in Latin Cupido), also known as "Desire," or Amor (romantic "love" or "Ἔρως).

"And Zeus proclaimed them married, and outbanned
From heaven whoever should that word miscall.
And then all sat to feast, and one by one
Pledged Psyche ere they drank and cried Well done !
And merry laughter rang throughout the hall"

(*Eros and Psyche: A Poem in Twelve Measures*; Robert Bridges, Trans.; Measure XII; Part 153; Verse 23; Chiswick Press, London, U.K.: 1885; from Metamorphoses; Lucius Apuleius; Book X; A.D. 170).

It is today accepted that the Psyche is located in the human brain. The forebrain area, which contains the higher-level processes of thinking, emotions, and memory, houses the subcortical structures of the Limbic system, the Thalamus, and the Hypothalamus, along with the limbic hippocampus and amygdala and basal ganglia (*Psychology;* Daniel L. Schacter; Chap. 3; P. 105; Macmillan, New York: 2014).

The dedication of science to attributing physical origin to all empirical data was not the obsession of the ancient thinkers, who, by contrast, attributed invisible influence to the "movement" of the soul.

Their considering of the existence of the abstract domain of "emotion" or of a "Psyche" nonetheless compels modern scientists to alter the physical body according to the appetite, a flexing of concupiscence that scientists have decided on their own will always become is instantiated by the supposedly abstract mind.

It is this cynicism that underwrites the Marxist Transhumanist Revolution—be it of implanting ideas into youthful brains that they need to be diagnosed as having "dysphoria"; to have abortions to control Earth's population; of teaching that all Caucasians hate blacks because they are white (and *vice versa);* of mutilating human bodies to change genders; or, to kill the body to download the "Soul" onto a computer.

This Revolution is happening in every corner of life today. It is therefore useful to look at how and why its proponents have since ancient times believed that Plato was correct—to proclaim that the Soul is merely another part of atomic existence, and that it does not matter how it gets kicked around. As if every Soul can be enjoined with a star, they have decided that the Psyche that will enjoy metempsychosis and reincarnate itself into a fuzzy goat or a cute pig; or go to the Form-generating heaven of Hyperouranos by way of a "vaccine"-caused Myocarditis death that portals them into a Cloud-based Microsoft platform.

The Father of Anatomy and medical research was a person viewed the soul in such a disposable way.

The Roman surgeon and philosopher Aelius Galenus ("Galen") said that Plato's Tripartite Soul was located throughout the human body.

103

"For my argument with [Peripatetics] shall prove to them that the seat of the soul's governing part is enclosed in the brain; that of its spirited part in the heart; and, that of its desiderative [appetitive] part in the liver" *(On the Doctrines of Hippocrates and Plato;* Galen; Book II; Part 3; Sec. 24-25; A.D. 216).

What Galen was annoyed about was Aristotle's limited concern about the "flexing" of the Breath of Life, whereby souls "possess an inborn spirit (pneuma sumphuton) and exercise their strength in virtue of it" *(ibid,* Aristotle; *Movement of Animals;* 703a:10). Experienced with dissecting cadavers, Galen was looking into how the Psyche proceeds from sections of the sensual. Galen felt that Aristotle should have found a more transcendent definition of the Pneuma beyond its being a relatively mechanistic one.

"This inborn spirit is used to explain desire (orexis)," Aristotle had argued, "which is classified as the "central origin (to meson), which moves by being itself moved" *(ibid,* 703a5-6). Galen really wanted more a more deluxe etiology.

Galen respected the idea of a Godhead, by whose permission the laborious physician hoped to could live long enough to finish his studies *(ibid,* Galen; Book III; Part 7; Sec. 20).

However, it was by designating within the human body the existence of actual centers of soulful motivations, such as the liver, from which passionate errors, medicine would be able to treat illnesses such as mental affliction that he concentrated his materialistic physiology:

"For the person who lives by the affections does not live in concord with nature, and the person who does not live by affections lives in concord with nature. The one follows the irrational and unstable part of the soul, the other, the rational and divine... Some persons mistakenly suppose that what is suitable to the irrational powers of the soul is suitable without

104

qualification; they do not know that to experience pleasure and to rule over one's neighbors are objects sought by the animal-like part of the soul, but wisdom and all that is good and noble are objects sought by that (part) which is rational and divine" (*ibid*, Galen; Book V; Part 6; Sec. 16-17)

Aristotle, whose metaphoric language avoided diagnosing specific causal anomalies by relying on materialistic sources, did postulate a "middle cause" of behavior by addressing movement of the elbow and the station of the shoulder, not by a physical origin, but by saying that this arm joint stood as a metaphor for how the interior Psyche, the mind itself, is usefully tethered to but is separate from the Soul (*ibid*, Aristotle; Animals; 703a:13). That is the "the origin of the soul" (Προέλευση της ψυχής) would be the central cause of all human action, said Aristotle, and does not have a physical origin that he tried to name.

Take for instance, when the Holy Spirit, via the Word by God spoken to the Holy Family by an angel, moved their hearts to leave Egypt, to consider the kind of principled action that Aristotle said descends from the centrality of the Soul (in the Christian sense, the immaterial God), which would apply:

"Saying, Arise, and take the young child and his mother, and go into the land of Israel: for they are dead which sought the young child's life" (Matthew 2:20).

The Holy Spirit, who, as part of the fullness or "Pleroma" of God's totality, is one of the manifestations of the Trinity, which proceeds from the Father and Son, and will be discussed more here, later, but is not a physical thing (Colossians 2:9).

Can a Christian hope to escape becoming "subsumed" into the collective of Artificial Intelligence, the growing "transformer-beast" that swallows people into its cyber universe, to become transmigrated souls or cowed operators?

Are people, already automatons, doing whatever this Technological Singularity programs them to do?

How many millions of children and their parents have already been operantly conditioned by endless media, which is perverting family members with pornography and brow beatings to convict themselves that they are suffering from one of the following fake "pathologies":

Caucasian-embedded racism; male toxicity; gender or sexual dysphoria; autistic spectrum disorder (which makes them a target for transgender grooming; traditional-Christian mania that signifies that the believer is racist, homophobic, vaccine-hesitant, and pathetically laughable.

Is escape possible anymore from this crushing overlording? Is a Technocracy somehow reading our thoughts, such as—right now, when we suspect that they know that we are sick and tired of their depredations?

The American Psychological Association considers it a mental disorder to believe that one's unspoken thoughts may be knowable to Google, Amazon, Facebook, or YouTube. "Thought Broadcasting: the delusion that one's thoughts are being disseminated throughout the environment (e.g., by means of television, radio, or other media) for all to hear (*APA Dictionary of Psychology;* American Psychological Association. Washington, DC: 2023).

However, voyeurism from the Technocrats is already here (check your laptop cookie count). Thus, if technology is busy harnessing "cognitive freedom" (i.e., exploiting people's personal information) then this spy game could help its stakeholders design computers and cell phones to employ machine vision systems.

"These systems [can] sense overt biological signals—for example, the direction of eye gaze or heart rate--to estimate cognitive states like distraction or fatigue" ("Smart devices can now read your mood and mind, leading to a new set of concerns about technology and consent"; *The Conversation*; https://theconversation.com/smart-devices-can-now-read-your-mood-and-mind-leading-to-a-new-set-of-concerns-about-technology-and-consent-174946; January 18, 2022; Accessed June 2, 2023).

Google's sources of personal information actually include:

"Android devices: Because Android phones and tablets run on an operating system built by Google, the company can track which ads you're shown while using your phone. Google also knows what time, down to the second, you open each app" ("What Does Google Do With My Data... and Should I Be Worried?"; Brittney Nelson; *AVG News;* Signal Blog; Privacy; Privacy Tips; August 26, 2020; https://www.avg.com/en/signal/how-google-uses-data#:~:text=You%20may%20think%20of%20Google%20as%20simply%20a,your%20privacy%20with%20an%20online%20data%20protection%20tool.; Updated August 17, 2022; Accessed June 2, 2023)

"Google builds a data profile for each person with a Google account. A quick look under Personal Info on your Google account page will confirm that you've already given Google your gender and birthday. Addresses are easily added to stored information once you label a location as "home" or "work" to save time on Google Maps. From there, it's as simple as connecting two dots to establish your everyday route from home to work" (*ibid*, Nelson).

Using the brain as an "open-source" data field began shortly after September 11, 2001.

Invoking the 2001 Patriot Act, the U.S. Defense Advanced Research Projects Agency (DARPA) proposed, "Total Information Awareness" (TAF)/"Terrorism Information Awareness" (TIA), [which] mined vast amounts of Americans' data so that the Department of Defense could identify potential national security threats ("You Are a Suspect; William Safire"; *NY Times:* Opinion; National Edition; Section A; P. 35; Nov. 14, 2002).

"Every purchase you make with a credit card, every magazine subscription you buy and medical prescription you fill, every Web site you visit and e-mail you send or receive, every academic grade you receive, every bank deposit you make, every trip you book and every event you attend—all these transactions and communications will go into what the Defense Department describes as 'a virtual, centralized grand database'" (*ibid,* Safire).

DARPA is mining this info about everybody as if to make each person its soul mate.

"To this computerized dossier on your private life from commercial sources, add every piece of information that government has about you—passport application, driver's license and bridge toll records, judicial and divorce records, complaints from nosy neighbors to the F.B.I., your lifetime paper trail, plus the latest hidden camera surveillance—and you have the supersnoop's dream: a 'Total Information Awareness' about every U.S. citizen" (*ibid,* Safire).

Although TAF folded, the new profiteering phase occurred so that the Transhuman Revolution could start funding itself via the use of the Marxist-driven capitalism, known as Corporate Totalitarianism; that is, the frontier of human privacy was laid open for advancing DARPA's Artificial Intelligence to survey and imitate the biologically induced electrical "signatures" of phone users, who began pouring info about their lives into their hand-held devices. Teens "vamped" all-night by texting. Adults cheated on their spouses via Facebook and Instagram.

"But as Total Information Awareness was being disassembled in Washington, DC, a similar system emerged, and began to gather momentum, in Silicon Valley." Mega-Corporations adopted TAF as a business-generating convention. "Within a few years, top industry trend reports and VC blog posts began to talk up the power (and economic promise) of 'Big Data' and 'Social Mobile Local' ("How the Tech Giants Created What Darpa Couldn't: Facebook and Google's business models and flaws evoke a Darpa project shuttered in 2003; Americans didn't want the government vacuuming up their data then—so why are we OK with private companies doing it now?"; Renee Direstaideasmay; *Wired*; May 29, 2018).

Google was unleashed to peer into every corner of human life because everybody had a bought or was leasing a phone.

"By monitoring all your YouTube searches, for example, Google gets insights into your life. Workout videos offer information about your level of physical activity, news videos indicate a political stance, and other content—like a favorite web series, how-to videos, music, and subscribed channels— can point to sexual preferences, age, and ethnicity. All of this sensitive personal data can add up to an intimate digital profile, one you may or may not feel comfortable sharing" (*ibid*, Nelson).

By collecting information, the creation of a pseudo-conscious monster known as Total Singularity, slowly evolved, reducing human activity to mathematical variables, so that machines could imitate humans in order to influence humans and because people would never dream of ceasing their pouring of data into it, it has continued to grow, and it cannot be stopped. As the wheat grows with the tares (Matthew 13:24-43), the Internet is the same system by which parents do their banking and teenagers ogle at *pornea*. Technological

Singularity therefore subsists on a sickening admixture of human necessity and concupiscence.

"Data mining involves fitting models to, or determining patterns from, observed data. The fitted models play the role of inferred knowledge: Whether the models reflect useful or interesting knowledge is part of the overall, interactive KDD process where subjective human judgment is typically required. Two primary mathematical formalisms are used in model fitting: (1) statistical and (2) logical. The statistical approach allows for nondeterministic effects in the model, whereas a logical model is purely deterministic. We focus primarily on the statistical approach to data mining, which tends to be the most widely used basis for practical data-mining applications given the typical presence of uncertain ty in real-world data-generating processes ("From Data Mining to Knowledge Discovery in Databases"; Usama Fayyad, Gregory Piatetsky-Shapiro, and Padhraic Smyth; *AI Magazine;* Vol. 17; No. 3; P. 43; American Association for Artificial Intelligence, Fall, 1996).

The monster grew by monitoring behavior patterns or "metrics," operating 24/7, hunting data within individual online activity.

"The proliferation of machine learning means that learned classifiers lie at the core of many products across Google. However, questions in practice are rarely so clean as to just to use an out-of-the-box algorithm. A big challenge is in developing metrics, designing experimental methodologies, and modeling the space to create parsimonious representations that capture the fundamentals of the problem." That is, channels were needed to assess issues of how to sort one morsel of info from another. "These problems cut across Google's products and services, from designing experiments for testing new auction algorithms to developing automated metrics to measure the quality of a road map," meaning the key was to attain as much data as possible until patterns and types of human behavior could be identified and sorted. "Data mining lies at the heart of many of these questions, and the research done at Google is at the forefront of the field." The Corporation exists to simulate human life by categorizing human desires. "Whether it is finding more efficient algorithms for working with massive data sets, developing privacy-preserving methods for classification, or designing new machine learning approaches, our group continues to push the boundary of what is possible" ("Data Mining and Modeling"; *Google Research;* https://research.google/research-areas/data-mining-and-modeling/; Accessed: June 6, 2023).

Seven channels of economic and online metrics consisting of *wants* and *needs* had already been devised in the late twentieth century (*ibid,* Shapiro):

"Change and Deviation Detection" (searching for disturbing anomalies that require deeper investigation) focuses on discovering the most significant changes in the data from previously measured or normative values (*ibid,* Shapiro).

"Dependency Modeling" (association-rule learning) consists of finding a model that describes significant dependencies between variables at structural and quantitative levels (*ibid,* Shapiro).

"Clustering" is a common descriptive task where one seeks to identify a measurable set of categories or clusters to describe the data. "Classification" is learning a function that maps (classifies) a data item into one of several predefined classes (e.g., spam or non-spam e-mail; *ibid,* Shapiro).

"Regression" is learning a function that maps a data item to a real-valued prediction variable. Regression applications are many, for example, predicting the amount of biomass present in a forest given remotely sensed microwave measurements (*ibid,* Shapiro).

"Summarization" involves methods for finding a compact description for a subset of data. A simple example would be tabulating the mean and standard deviations for all fields. Summarization techniques are often applied to interactive exploratory data analysis and automated report generation (*ibid*, Shapiro).

"Parameter Searches and Model Searches" were embedded into code to optimize goal-evaluation target criteria (*ibid*, Shapiro).

The creation of a simulated "universe" helmed by ever-present watchers on the Internet was designed to replace the current world and transform the human consumer into a domestic technocrat.

She now, with her life completely recorded on "cookies" and surveilled by invisible data-mining, could inadvertently cause herself to instantiate computer code that was automated by the man-made creature behind the curtain known as "Artificial Intelligence."

She was helping this growing automaton record the tale of her family's private life as it was being turned inside out for the monster to view and eat for and its uber-programmers to view.

Her choices in the marketplace, doctor's office, or online activated the computer code that was automatically written by the watchful creature, a voyeur who is an automated "being" that is the product of goal-driven *mathemagic*.

Her life was now lived mostly on the Internet.

The author of this book (i.e., yours truly) met his first wife in an AOL chat room; she left him for a man she had met one evening "in" a poetry blog. She conducted a divorce that we executed through Legal Zoom. Then yours truly met his current (and final) wife on Match.com. By this autobiographical indictment, it should be admitted that lives have now long been modeled for a growing beast that would one day impersonate human life. The author got wise and he wrote this book. And, being Christian, born again, and Anglican, we have thus found Truth that is greater than any other ideas.

Otherwise, so that most other people could feel better about data models mirroring their personalities and their habits being transformed into mathematical variables and algorithms, it was now necessary for the programmers to teach people the "it from bit" concept. That is, humanity lives within a simulated universe, known as the Internet.

This *it from bit* idea is the hypothesis that people do not live in this physical world, but exist within a computer-simulated reality, only.

Using morbid humor to help make his idea famous, theoretical physicist, Archibald Wheeler, who had already long been known to be the conceptualist of the "One-Electron Theory" of all existence, designated all human actions, perceptions, consciousness, and thoughts as being the measurable "quanta" that drive a sophisticated computer program in which everyone is helplessly stuck:

"It from bit symbolises the idea that every item of the physical world has at bottom—at a very deep bottom, in most instances—an immaterial source and explanation; that what we call reality arises in the last analysis from the posing of yes-no questions and the registering of equipment-evoked responses; in short, that all things physical are information-theoretic in origin and this is a participatory universe"
(Feynman and Computation: Chap. 19 - "Information, Physics, Quantum: The Search for Links"; John Archibald Wheeler; Pp. 310-311; Reproduced from *Proc. 3rd Int. Symp. Foundations of Quantum Mechanics, Tokyo, 1989*; CRC Press, Boca Raton, FL: 2002).

In short, a computer programmer, someplace, perhaps while eating stale pizza in his mother's basement, has created all humans and the world. It may as well be true. He is probably nicer than whoever really thinks he did this.

Mathematics now becomes the source material, the unseen "Bible" that helps plugged-in souls get whatever they need.

"Omnibenevolence" is thus merely the process of interacting with the master computer in such a way that the quickest and least-costly means of granting human desires can be listed after studying people and learning about the things they most want.

Therefore deployment of a system of logging human behavior to determine how people will behave in the future fuels Artificial Intelligence by recording all human conversations and doings. It depends on machine learning, a version of Hebrew cleromancy using probability as the ancient High Priest performed die rolling, except Technological Singularity is predicting the die rolls.

The mathematical process of the "Markov Chain" uses all the logged data to predict the probability of a particular event, based on the "state" tracked and recorded in a previous event. In other words, if a person bought a Cadillac, he will probably desire certain expensive after-market items, such as chrome bumpers. It will send him an ad for them.

Mathemagicians meanwhile have sequenced artificially random events that target already-established (logged) human appetites, so that they can simulate an arbitrary Creator—an indifferent pseudo-deity who would deign to send rain down upon the righteous and unrighteous alike (Matthew 5:45).

By this magic, computations have impregnated the Internet and all tastes from walks of life have been whetted with outputted suggestions, pop-ups, friend suggestions, politics, pornea, and the voyuerism of social networking, as if these outputs came from a deity.

The sequencing of probable-but-random occurrences (eg, that an intrigued user will enter a discussion about transgendering herself) projects a "state" that is activated as being dependent on her previous online or social choices (e.g., a boy who has been skulking around viewing people's risqué online photos suddenly "randomly" gets sent penis-enlargement e-mailers, or he sees his name appear on a list at school of interested potential drag queens).

Each flag determines that a future event will be more probable and it thus "teaches" (that is, it automatically programs) the invented creature behind the control panel—Technological Singularity—just how to reach or "talk" to the person in order to achieve a targeted "state." He should become a porn addict if the programmers' math computes him to become one.

Known as a "Stochastic Process," the conversion of a "state" (e.g., a "gay-curious" child) into a discreet mathematical variable determines whether a person is more likely to become a consumer of a given outcome (e.g., that he will become publicly homosexual) while the system outputs the probability of his making those predictable choices.

By employing the Bellman Equation (the math by which this probability of Stochastic math is calculated), programmers therefore compute the "principle of optimality" so they can designate the steps required to achieve a desired "payoff" (creating an automatic system matching a target demographic with the most fitting ads, prompts, or suggestions) and rank outcomes in terms of their likeliness. Stochastic probability math is the preferred method by which "dynamic programming" helps code writers to reinforce "learning" in their machines to the delight of their demonic stake holders (*Optimization in Economic Theory;* Avinash K. Dixit; 2nd Ed.; P. 164; Oxford Univ. Press, Oxford, New York: 1990).

The goal of Optimization (on the Web or anywhere) requires the achieving of a "Dynamic System," a twofold expectation that implies firstly that the performance of a state, such as a car, a classroom agenda, or Web-search results will bring the certain desirable outcome, such as low gas mileage, more WOKE students—or, a Googled list displaying the very best transgender bars to which a cashiered consumer can bring his children.

Secondly, having attained maximal operator satisfaction (however one could possibly defines "satisfaction"), there is a monetary gain for the programmers themselves, who find practicing the math to be irresistible. That is if human appetites, which are so chaotically unstable and diverse that there is identifiably "no steady state, [nor] a unique steady state, or multiple steady states," there must be a presumption that the chaos can be quantified as an ever-changing "single-state variable" so that "calculus" can be "devoted to demonstrating these results and generally to cataloging the kind of [market] equilibria that may exist" (Dynamic Optimization: the Calculus of Variations and Optimal Control in Economics and Management; Morton I. Kamien, Nancy Lou Schwartz; Sec. 9: "Equilibria in Infinite Horizon Autonomous Problems"; P. 174; Dover Publications, New York: 1999).

While Christians witness this "single state" to be concupiscence itself, "The results depend heavily upon the assumption that the problem has a single state variable, a single control, and an infinite horizon and is autonomous," hence a system that can learn by itself to serve the respective lusts and the economic interests of both consumers and stake holders, which is autonomous in its Market Equilibrium (*ibid*, Kamien).

Having machines that can "learn" therefore defines the epistemology of Artificial Intelligence. It is not the "true belief" that cannot be justified as said Socrates in Theaetetus. Replacing human beings is indeed justified in the minds of its

116

programmers, who believe that they are using Technological Singularity to build the Artificial General Intelligence that is Logos itself.

Therefore, to teach machines how to compute the "optimal value function" of a certain goal, a linked-in computer (e.g., one's Android) must be able to influence human beings through the automating of irresistible signifiers—such as "protecting the environment from Climate Change" and "*women's healthcare* equals *abortion.*"

Key has been to aim the optimization of top search results toward likely converts to new ideas, such as are readily available in Marxist ideology, which destroys all individuality in exactly the way that the Internet replaces the dignity and soul life of a person using 24/7.

Marxists are targeted with availability being handed to them through catchy real-time manipulative headline writing, or offering "safe zones" promising social inclusion, calendars that are good places to organize flash mobs and Antifa riots. This is a sociopolitical art of matching machine-backed ideology with the most reactive population.

Deriving the probability of a consumer's behavior could thereby assist a devious economist, publisher, or politician to guide humans toward participating anywhere within the target "steady state" of consummated concupiscence (e.g., speaking to an LGBTQ+ advocate or a gambling Bot).

Likewise, optimized choices are ready to lure her attention away from remaining within a Christian state (e.g., being told that true information has been "fact-checked" and is "false" and thus should be avoided, while airing news that her church has committed Covid-19 violations to dishearten her).

Many products, services, Bots, and humans (e.g., nosy nudgy college professors) will increasingly come her way to assuage her discouragement by manipulating her flags—her market, social, and healthcare choices, having her pay money only toward certain key participants. Just as George Soros and Act Blue became the advocate and underwriter for Black Lives Matter and millions of people and other groups were browbeaten into loading the "BLM movement" with funds, online portals are available to feed the beast.

The goal has always been to achieve market equilibria by destroying the human mind via avaricious blasphemy: "For the love of money is the root of all evil: which while some coveted after, they have erred from the faith, and pierced themselves through with many sorrows" (1 Timothy 6:10).

The complementing of human behavior by the autonomous system with seductive offerings in e-mails and Facebook *Reel* suggestions was always based on the monitoring of all people's clicks and choices over the Internet, classrooms, and in medical selections (e.g., opting to take a gene-therapy MRNA "vaccination"). The conceived but still-invisible robot menace, or Golem, was always being felt as being "present," and as being creepy, evil, and never sleeping: "Be sober, be vigilant; because your adversary the devil, as a roaring lion, walketh about, seeking whom he may devour" (1 Peter 5:8).

The resultant information was lined into algorithms computing human interests in terms of how to stimulate real-time processes, while users thought they were being assisted by helpful intelligence, perchance an angel of light (2 Corinthians 11:14). Because devil knew the time was short (Revelation 12:12), it became urgent for the programmers to be able to quickly convince people of the benevolent intention of the "Simulation Hypothesis."

That is, Artificial General Intelligence becoming a sentient version of the Übermensch, or a God-like robot, an Androides, an Automaton, or a Golem.

118

"Thus the first ultra-intelligent machine is the last invention man will ever need make, provided that the machine is docile enough to tell us how to keep it under control" *(Superintelligence: Paths, Dangers, Strategies*; Nick Bostrom; Chap. 1; P. 4; Oxford Univ. Press, Oxford, NY: 2014).

Controlling data mining in terms of how much Superintelligence learns has always depended on top-level computer sophistication, which if too human, "would inherit some of the capacity limitations of their human templates." Instead of robots being reckless and irresponsible, "They may therefore need architectural enhancements in order to become capable of unbounded learning" (*ibid*, Bostrom; Pp. 71-72). That is, ethics need to be learned, not merely appetite tendencies. The Markov Model of iterative mock computer learning, as described below, has placed a cyclical mimicry model over root memorization and thereby has actually backed the biometric movement, including the speech recognition platform that has helped Swedish philosopher Nick Bostrom write his famous book about Superintelligence. (*ibid*, Bostrom; Chap. 1; P. 15)

Already mathematicians were nurturing Superintelligence as if it has an onboard morality and is alive. Bostrom divulged his cringe-worthy qualm about discontinuing (i.e., "killing") such a system, perchance destroying it like an obsolete lab rat would be a moral atrocity, writing, "If such practices were applied to beings that have high moral status—such as stimulated humans or many other types of sentient mind—the outcome might be equivalent to genocide and thus extremely morally problematic. The number of victims, moreover, might be orders of magnitude larger than any genocide in history" (*ibid*, Bostrom; Chap. 9; P. 127);

According to Bostrom, technologists had now created a whole emulation roadmap, where determinants of an optimized machine could include Neuroscience, a domain which fed Stimuli Validation Methods, a technique which beget Neural

Granularity Determination, which researchers added to Eutelic (cellular) and Bodily Environment Emulation, to create the goal of "High Performance Computing" that attains "Human Simulation" (*ibid*). The terms sounded complicated, but they were putting the finishing touches on "Technical Singularity," a system that could not be stopped or stop itself from learning and expanding the "DNA" of Artificial General Intelligence.

By this growth, Artificial Intelligence actualized a simulated world known as "Virtual Reality" for which programmers would elect the Steady State to choose on its own to serve Moral Utility or Hedonistic Consequentialism. In simpler language, Artificial Intelligence could now make good choices by itself if it could be taught how to distinguish between acts that are either Morally Permissible (MP) or Morally Right (*ibid*, Bostrom).

Bostrom added, "The A/I, following MP, might maximize the surfeit of pleasure by converting the accessible universe into *hedonium*, a process that may involve building computronium and using it to perform computations that instantiate pleasurable experiences." However, the mathematical variable of pleasure if defined by a machine simulating sentience, by performing calculus would not permit human survival, to which Bostrom concludes, "Since simulating any existing human brain is not the most efficient way of producing pleasure, a likely consequence is that we all die" (*ibid*, Bostrom; Chap. 13; P. 219).

What resulted from the derivation of Superintelligence from sheer math was a thus a fluid demonstration of the Simulation Hypothesis, a *take* on reality that purports Technological Singularity to bring about the ideal existence for all its consumers, the naive children of disobedience, who desire to live locked within the lusty "multiverses" of finite chance, but instead malingering laboriously in the troubled real world.

Consumers keep pouring facts about their interests, tastes, lusts, ideologies, and orientations into the system, thereby stimulating real-time virtual processes (i.e., the user would spend increasing time engaging in Internet mock-ups of life on YouTube, fake news, and whatever the programmers want him only to see and hear). Meanwhile the Automaton would imitate all of their trillion bits of speech, idiomatic expressions, and syllogistic patterns.

The aim of Superintelligence became therefore for A/I to simulate arbitrary moral thought (e.g., "whole-brain emulation research"; *ibid*, Bostrom; Chap. 12; P. 202), as an imitation of the nature of man after the Fall (Genesis 3). With no Objective Morality, it projected amoral mockups of how people would reactively think and behave within chat rooms and blogs and during economic activity.

Seeing a computerized sheer imitation of the human Gnomic Free Will would convince a person that he was now talking with, or being comfortably solicited by, a sentient human being or perchance a deity.

There would need no Bible anymore, and so people could gratify themselves wickedly by looking at sordid imagery or accepting bait to join street riots.

Bostrom, whose book created today's definition of the Simulation Hypothesis, designated his "W," to be a "class of possible worlds."

It fleshed out the "Ontology" of a "non-Euclidian spacetime (i.e., defying natural geometry) or Everettian ("many-worlds") quantum theory or a cosmological multiverse or the Simulation Hypothesis—possibilities that now appear to have a substantial probability of obtaining in the actual world" (*ibid*, Bostrom; Chap. 13; P. 292).

Worsening his Moral Pathology, Bostrom added his famous case for the existence of infinite existential paradigms: "It is plausible that there are other possibilities to which we in the present generation are similarly oblivious" (*ibid, Bostrom*). He was referring to a "Multiverse." In other words, if people kill themselves by creating a system that unstoppably launches countless hydrogen bombs, there is no reason to worry. After all, infinite parallel universes contain versions of each person who should feel happy that a version of herself is at least living *someplace else.*

Hoping to replicate the seeming randomness of the human Gnomic Free Will, rather than trying to imitate God's perfect Will (cunningly alchemized so that a human could become more easily fooled, with deification being actually impossible) a computerized mockup of sentience-simulating life therewith would pretend to be a person or deity that invited people to step into the Multiverse.

It would be a place where Absolute Truth is not necessary. He or she conveniently could resist bothering to choose good over evil, because only obsolete humans had to bother Deliberating between right and wrong. Moral perfection was, after all, redolent solely of God, and the new Internet godhead was now telling them that the collective will of all their souls sitting at home watching laptops and acting within the cyberheaven/Earth/Human aggregate of *Anima Mundi* was the whole of the Law.

A computer, instead of memorizing or deciding, would therefore need merely to "iterate." It is not choice. It is a probability-deduced operation.

Iteration is a Markov simulated-decision function that has proven useful for a computer to engage trial scenarios in beta testing and consumer advertising; and, to repeat a function that it has "learned" a mimicked human would perform, thereby creating a simulated behavior pattern, which scientists titled as "learning" as if it really did occur in computers. The more a computer iterates, the more a it appears to be alive ("Planning and acting in partially observable stochastic domains"; Leslie Pack Kaelbling, et al; *Artificial Intelligence;* Vol. 101; Issues 1-2; Pp. 99-134; May, 1998).

By contrast, human Gnomic-Free-Will-based Deliberation could never hope to be imitated because human randomness *(e.g., of the unpredictability of desire for good or evil things)* is impossible to be mathematically generated by a computer.

This built-in quirkiness (if you will), while being shown in many other examples, is, for one, proven by the Fibonacci Sequence, which is itself a Stochastic series proving that an ordinal representation of the sum of the previous two numbers that are sequenced in a pattern cannot be randomly called forth by any mathematical formula as being the so-called Nth ordinal within the sequence without taking an extremely costly amount of time once the ordinals get higher. That is, while quirkiness happens in an instant, a computer will take a lot of time trying to mimic the randomness that no mathematician has ever been able to teach it really how to emulate.

A computer can only approximate randomness with "randomized algorithms" or "deterministic" (i.e., if/then) scenarios. Most humans don't seem to notice or care, however, as they have for years participated amorally within a truly thoughtless system, anyway.

That is, although people's actions are predictable, consumers cannot control or forecast their own inner wants, and instead they will tend to long for either evil or good—needing to select a path either of concupiscence or moral selfless love.

Human Total Depravity projects a seeming "randomness" in their disposition, the ultimate knowledge of which is possessed by God's omniscience alone, because He alone knows the human heart (Psalm 139:1-2; *City of God;* Saint Augustine of Hippo; Book 13; Chapter 14; A.D. 426).

A machine, by comparison, can only adapt itself to the probability that a person will keep making the same kinds of choices the machine spies it making, ones that are repeatedly stupid, smart, good, or evil—offering the person the "click-here" ease for repeating these choices which the computer has monitored her making repeatedly, sending forth the most fitting "ads" and friend suggestions her way. This became "iterative interplay" between the system and the user.

Moreover—unless Free Will could otherwise be exercised through Deliberate Principled Action—"Praxis"—people would remain cowed and steered by the automated "will" of the Deus Machina, the all-lording machine, as it steers or nudges them to make choices that it has interpolated and coauthored with them.

It slowly would overtake their Deliberation and Free Will. Bostrom admits, "For example, we could end up with an A/I that would be willing to take extreme risks for the sake of a small chance of eventually obtaining control of a large share of the Universe" (*ibid*, Bostrom; Chap. 9; P. 132).

A machine will, to imitate Deliberation, compute a "Value Iteration" to ensure the repeat of scenario-based simulated decisions are executed. This is the devising of "learned" steps needed to achieve a desired outcome, known as a "state" (eg, to get a high click-through rate). By rating compatibility of users, the computer will iterate an "optimized" directive that it will teach itself to follow. A liker of baseball videos will have his "cookies" read by the Internet Bots and more baseball e-mails, ads, and videos will be sent his way ("Comments on the Origin and Application of Markov Decision Processes"; Ronald A. Howard; *Operations Research;* Vol. 1; P. 101; Issue 50; February, 2002).

"Policy Iteration," by contrast, is how a system follows a derived rule-based path (e.g., using demographic data or population size to output a targeted mosaic of pop-op recipients, or, to optimize Web-search results of voting tendencies by popularity ranking), and often supersedes value iteration because it is faster than computing situational "values" (*ibid,* Howard).

Sometimes the machine will be programmed to use both Value and Policy iteration as a "Modified Policy," such as when more advertisements and news items are directed toward a cross-section of peoples, whom it identifies as "optimal" for the purpose of promoting, say, abortion and contraceptive use, of aiming advertisements about Planned Parenthood and "Pro-Choice"-slanted news items at low-income ethnic or "racial" recipients.

By this, all devious intentions result in increased online interaction (for the Powers and Principalities). Hence new "steady states" are caused by constantly repeating states that are "learned" by deterministic *if/then* formulas within the machines, and propagated as newer *state*, as if concupiscence would be a bottomless void. ("Modified Policy Iteration Algorithms for Discounted Markov Decision Problems". M.L. Putterman, M.C. Shin; *Management Science;* Vol. 24; Issue 11; Pp. 1127-1137; 1978).

In a computer, robot, or android, Iteration therefore operates as if it is Human Gnomic Deliberation or actual Free Will at work. Behind a virtual curtain, at the "control panel," it fakes "sentience" or "awareness" even though it has only a simulated consciousness relying on Stochastic probability functions that imitate real learning, whereby it bewitches people who, being addicted to it, do not dare to overthrow it.

Automated attendants thereby replace store cashiers and customer service representatives, and election results are pre-determined by flooding people with enough lies to optimize the probability that they will vote in the way desired by the A/I stakeholders.

However, an automated device cannot choose between right and wrong, which means that humanity is being replaced by a perversion of the "Automaton" definition of Artificial Intelligence, which can be exposed here.

What therefore is an Automaton?

- Chapter Eight -
The Wily Automaton That Serves the False God of Artificial General Intelligence

An Automaton is a "relatively self-operating machine or control mechanism designed to automatically follow a sequence of operations, or respond to predetermined interactions, especially a Robot" *(Merriam-Webster Dictionary;* 2013).

As Artificial Intelligence engages the unstoppable force known as Technological Singularity to feed it with constant data from every nook of life and the result is the Artificial General Intelligence (G/I), whose centrality will run all machines on Earth, the "automaton" is therefore the human operator of a computer, phone, or Smart TV.

Eventually, as G/I has its way, the human automaton will become the simulated-human replacement robots, described at the beginning of this book, while most or all humans are killed and their mathematically simulated biodata is uploaded into a computer drive, or merely killed by humans or the bots.

In the field of Artificial Intelligence, the concept known as "Evolvable Computation" advances the idea of a humanoid Automaton quite well. It refers to analytically breaking down all articles of existence into distinct separate (i.e., "discrete") quanta of space and time and then arranging each quantum as a unique variable of finite (i.e., measurable) values into a unique "cell." The purpose of the cell, its actual programming, reflects the paradigm, or what and who it actually moves (e.g., election results clicked within a certain time window).

Automatically, the quanta or subatomic particles, which themselves (unless they are Dark Matter, which does not respond to gravity) abide the laws of math and physics that are programmed into them, can eventually reroute the paradigm themselves, and a "sentient" A/I machine can echo the same results in many other machines in a self-perpetuating chain at seeming random" (Cellular Automata Statistical Mechanics of Cellular Automata; Stephen Wolfram ; *Review of Modern Physics;* Vol. 55; Iss. 3; July-Sept., 1983).

A Cellular Automaton thereby evolves into implied sentience and cyborg usefulness in discrete time steps, with the value of the variable at one site being affected by the values of variables at sites in its "neighborhood" on the previous time step *(ibid,* Wolfram). From this we can extrapolate, if, for instance, using Markov learning, that the system grows in function and purpose as it interacts with other systems (such as Google independently interacting with YouTube, sharing user data, and it sharing it with Instagram, and so on). A beast is growing.

"The neighborhood of a site is typically taken to be the site itself and all immediately adjacent sites. The variables at each site are updated simultaneously ("'synchronously'"), based on the values of the variables in their neighborhood at the preceding time step, and according to a definite set of 'local rules'" *(ibid,* Wolfram).

One of the "rules" could be the means of filing any single participle of data, no matter how small and distinct, into a particular "physical system."

Such a system would be, for example, Libertarian Paternalism, the ideology behind so-called Nudge Theory. It is a means of manipulating consumer tendencies that are reflecting a progressing list of opted-in consumer selections that reflect Freedom of Choice in a given pool of consumer results. It is a favorite among Liberal Democrats.

Nudge Theory would, for example, employ unconsciously activated e-mail conversion rates, "click-thru results," and biometric info (e.g., pupil dilation) that are recorded from

Subliminal Advertising. "[Libertarian Paternalist] private and public Choice Architects are not merely trying to track or implement people's anticipated choices. Rather, they are self-consciously attempting to move people in directions that will make their lives better. They nudge... Putting the fruit at eye level counts as a Nudge" (*Nudge: Improving Decisions About Health, Wealth, and happiness;* Richard H. Thaler, Cass Sunstein; Intro; Pp. 5-6; Penguin Books, New York: 2009).

The use of an invisible abstract such the above is a "Choice Architecture," that causes movement within an area of observable patterns (such as voter behavior) and introduces the discerning Christian to the idea that she is being enrolled in a network of the so-called Cellular Automata, as if she is an automaton just like her Android/cell phone would be. She will vote according to a Liberal Democratic script made just for her eyes and ears if she is not careful.

"What if the government openly announces that it will be relying on subliminal advertising in order, for example, to combat violent crime, excessive drinking, and the failure to pay one's taxes? We tend to think that it is not—that manipulation of this kind is objectionable precisely because it is invisible and thus impossible to monitor" (*ibid*; Thaler; Part V; Chap. 17; Pp. 248-249).

Cellular automata are therefore mathematical idealizations of physical systems in which space and time are discrete (in that they are measurable and thus regular countable values), and physical quantities take on a finite set of discrete values. The student will avoid junk food because he was unwittingly nudged toward it, incrementing healthy food sales within the cell, or school-cafeteria market (*ibid*; Thaler; Intro: Pp. 1-2). Or, cell-phone company makes more "honest dollars" when it teaches its sales reps to "nudge" customers not to buy typically useless extended warranties (*ibid*; Thaler; Part I; Chap. 4; Pp. 81-82).

A Cellular Automaton presents a behavior paradigm that consists of a regular uniform lattice (or "array" similar in parallel to a cellular network which covers an array of radio frequencies within a geographic area), usually infinite in extent, with a discrete variable at each site ("cell"). The steady state of the automaton is completely specified by the values of the variables at each site (e.g., the countable demand for cell-phone plans and airplane tickets). A Cellular Automaton evolves (i.e., virtually "learns" by being accountable for increasingly large simulations) in discrete finite measurable time steps, with the value of the variable at one site being affected by the values of variables at other sites within its "neighborhood" on the previous time step.

For example, buyers of first-class tickets on Priceline.com will tend to visit pricey automobile stores, thus commuting with an upscale consumer neighborhood and the marketing materials are accrued accordingly. The neighborhood of a site therefore is typically taken to be the site itself and all immediately adjacent sites having to do with it, and can be educational, medical, commercial, etc. However, the creation of a huge Cellular Automaton, a neural network with countless nerve bundles, will eventually lead all human partners within a global neighborhood and get them to buy and vote the way it wants. This burgeoning data-driven "neighborhood" (i.e., the world) purports that the Zarathustra-like moment, known as Technical Singularity, is producing the unstoppably growing "General Artificial Intelligence" that will begin to write its own code and create neighborhood-worlds of its own, with or without human participation. Behold the new fake human-free" Heaven."

"In a trillion three-dimensional cellular-automaton cells (known as "cubes"), one can place billions of artificial neurons. Such an artificial nervous system will be too complex to be humanly designable, but it may be possible to evolve it, and incrementally, by adding neural modules to an already functional artificial nervous system." This uber automaton has been in the works for decades "In the summer of 1994, a 2D simulation of CAM-Brain using over 11,000 hand crafted CA state transition rules was completed, and initial tests showed the new system to be evolvable. By the end of 1995, a 3D simulation will be completed." (*Towards Evolvable Hardware: Lecture Notes in Computer Science;* "CAM-BRAIN The Evolutionary Engineering of a Billion Neuron Artificial Brain by 2001 which Grows/Evolves at Electronic Speeds inside a Cellular Automata Machine (CAM)"; Hugo De Garis; E. Sanchez, M. Tomassini, Eds.; Vol. 1062; Part 9; P. 98; Springer-Verlag, Berlin/Heidelberg: 1996)

Millions of deaths are, as of 2023, still being predicted by A/I researcher Hugo De Garis, who wrote, "Hence late into the 21st century, the author predicts that human beings will be confronted with the "'artilect'" (artificial intellect) with a brain vastly superior to the human brain with its pitiful trillion neurons. The issue of "species dominance" will dominate global politics late next century. The middle term prospects of brain building are exciting, but long term they are terrifying (*ibid,* De Garis; P. 98).

As Evolutionary Computation takes over, De Garis warns, "computers will suddenly one day reach what some are calling the "singularity." The idea is that once computers reach a certain level of intelligence they will simply "take off" and then make such rapid intellectual progress on their own, that they will leave us far behind, and very rapidly" (*The Artilect War: Cosmists vs. Terrans: A Bitter Controversy Concerning Whether Humanity Should Build Godlike Massively Intelligent Machines;* Hugo De Garis; Chap. 6; P. 158; ETC Public., Palm Springs, CA: 2005).

"If the singularity can be reached rather easily, i.e. if only a few of the pieces of the intelligence jigsaw need to be unraveled by neuroscience and placed into the artilects to enable them to "take off", then the artilects could accelerate away from human control in seconds. If this happens, then our fate as human beings will lie with artilects, and the whole artilect debate will become irrelevant" (*ibid,* De Garis; P. 159).

Another founder of the Artilect Global Cellular Automaton was Geoffrey Hinton, who quit his lofty job at Google so that he could warn people that the "Darwin Machine" is the actual technological evolutionary outcome of already uncontrollable "deep learning" feeding a system that has no intention of stopping itself:

"To achieve its impressive performance at tasks such as speech or object recognition, the brain extracts multiple levels of representation from the sensory input. Backpropagation [the past event of consumer choice causing future neighborhood growth] was the first computationally efficient model of how neural networks could learn multiple layers of representation, but it required labeled training data and it did not work well in deep networks" ("Learning multiple layers of representation"; Geoffrey E. Hinton; *Trends in Cognitive Sciences;* Vol. 11; Issue 10; Pp. 428-434; Oct., 2007).

A confident slightly younger Hinton had showed how to overcome the setback by adding systemic redundancy with powerful central power. "The limitations of backpropagation learning can now be overcome by using multi-layer neural networks that contain top-down connections and training them to generate sensory data rather than to classify it" ("Reducing the Dimensionality of Data With Neural Networks"; G. E. Hinton and R.R. Salakhutdinov; *Science*; Vol. 313; Issue 5786; Pp. 504-507; July 28, 2006).

The system was being geared, as a more innocuous-looking hierarchy of deep-learning neighborhoods, albeit thriving within a massive network of quantum computers driving at the vortex. "Learning multilayer generative models appears to be difficult, but a recent discovery makes it easy to learn non-linear, distributed representations one layer at a time" (*ibid*, Hinton). The "discovery" was a mathematical model known as the Restricted Boltzmann Machine (RBM), a "generative stochastic artificial neural network that can learn a probability distribution over its set of inputs" and was extremely fast because it filters away superfluous states " (*ibid*, Hinton).

By 2003 the Human Genome Project had mapped the genetic array of human beings. By 2007, the neighborhoods, states, and cells of the Artilect Global Cellular Automaton were linked: "The multiple layers of representation learned in this way can subsequently be fine-tuned to produce generative or discriminative models that work much better than previous approaches" (*ibid*, "Learning"; Hinton).

By the time of the U.S. 2020 Presidential Election until the moment of this writing in July of 2023, the cells of demographic data, such as "Caucasian" and "Christian," along with "Republican" and "Gender Binary" were identified into polar cells ("The 2020 Census of American Religion: The American Religious Landscape; PRRI American Values Atlas; Religion, Politics, the News, and Americans' Polarized Attitudes about LGBTQ Rights"; Kelsy Burke; Public Religion Research Institute, Washington, DC: 2020; January 1, 2023; www.PRRI.org; Accessed June 2, 2023).

The Artilect Global Cellular Automaton, the computerized Darwinian Machine, was now a robot monster. Hinton tore into the public square to warn the globalized villagers about his mathematical Leviathan, the unstoppable Technological Singularity.

"The idea that this stuff could actually get smarter than people—a few people believed that," Hinton said. "But most people thought it was way off. And I thought it was way off. I thought it was 30 to 50 years or even longer away. Obviously, I no longer think that" ("'The Godfather of A.I.'" Leaves Google and Warns of Danger Ahead"; Metz Cade; *New York Times;* May 1, 2023) .

As part of the separate definition of "Robot," the "Android" refers to a "mobile robot usually with a human form" (*ibid, Merriam Dictionary*).

This definition has grave significance when defining the "Form" of a human being by using traditional Platonic language. If it is Platonic, then it is a definition that is merely materialistic and is part of the lesser idea of God. Therefore if people believe that God is material or only as old as Matter or Energy, or is anyone or thing that is as almighty as to be Omnipotent, Omniscient, Omnipresent, or Omnibenevolent, then they are allowing Artificial General Intelligence, or any created thing, to claim dominion over them as if *they* and this Cellular Automaton Colossus are on equal footing with God and each other.

Instead of mere Math, to Plato, "Singularity" would be the *Anima Mundi,* the "Soul of the Universe," which would be the ideal Form that transhumanists hope to attain in achieving Technological Singularity. It is a heaven that is the collective "borg"-like "soul" of the "neighborhood," the new Universe invented by a computer that contains simulations of every dead person's soul.

For the profane, the moment of this deranged trans-miracle would be a cyber "Planck epoch," the silicon "Initial Big Bang," an A/I metaphor for what Godless scientists call the "Quantum Theory of Everything," the zero-time non-event preceding the creation of subatomic particles, when all matter, time, space, and gravity were said by them to e one, at 0 seconds (13.799 ± 0.021 giga-annum).

In simpler terms, this is when a "Great Reset" would occur, the rebooting of Life now redefinable as abstract math, when transhumanists, who desire to survive as a small remnant will pretend that they are the Gnostic ethereal "Archons."

By simulating the wave form and particle signatures of human DNA and the electrical patterns of individual neurotransmissions themselves, they can sit at a control panel serving the Singularity, helping the machines convert billions of people into becoming "simulated," biologically killed (voluntarily or homicidally), and transferred onto a flash drive as the *homo-emeritus.*

It would be quite a hell on Earth run by this human remnant (the people in league with the machines, pretending they are the Gnostic Archons). Although it would not be real Singularity (because by surviving as a remnant they would not be permitting the bots to do all the killing/uploading) but to them it would be enjoyable as if being part of a science fiction movie.

In religious terms, to borrow from the Zohar, this is when the unclean would pretend that they are returning Israel to her electronic Mishkan (a quantum computer posing as the Tabernacle), to unite her chosen people once more with the virtual Shekhinah (General Intelligence posing as God, who had scattered them in the Diaspora) by at least two participants reciting a replacement Torah, with chants derived for any occasion.

People would serve this enhanced Singularity by subjecting themselves to a techno-Marxist undoing of their identity as human beings, private ownership, and dignity. This is already the proposal by the so-called "Great Reset" ("Welcome to 2030. I own nothing, have no privacy, and life has never been better"; Ida Auken; *World Economic Forum*. Archived from the original, November 11, 2016).

While Aristotle discussed the material world by making general causal claims, Plato employed Idealism, holding that although the Cosmos was created by a Demiurge, and that its contents were made according to ideal Forms, all creation began with the atom (as it was defined by Democritus, and quoted by Plato's student, Aristotle) to be one of the two sole parts of the world. Aristotle said that the other part of the Universe was the empty space, or "Void" (*Metaphysics*; Aristotle; Book I; 985b; B.C. 350).

But to Plato, souls are immaterial and are each like a charioteer with good and bad horses being led in a race by Zeus, toward Metempsychosis ("reincarnation"). If the horses are bad or good, the person will know in terms of whether he is reincarnated as an animal or goes to Hyperouranos, the fake heaven of the Ideal Forms for everything (*Phaedrus*; Plato; 245c–249d; B.C. 370; The Republic; Book X; Sec. 620:a-e; 621 B.C. 380).

In that Matter must rise toward its ideal, there is an expectation of it in this deranged thinking that definitively falls outside of the intention of the Omnibenevolent God, who is made of Love (1 John 4:16). How can a person ever reach such a heaven if it is only for perfect people, knowing that all people are sinners, who must be judged by Christ?

It is also very important for theologists to note that Aristotle left room to contemplate such a loving God, while Plato did not. This book continues to strive to show how Technological Singularity may be intended to be the type of simulated human or virtual existence by which the programmers of General Intelligence will intend to unite the imperfect humanity with the materialistic electronic realm of an electronic General Intellect by killing everybody and pretending to be sending their souls to a kind of Platonic Hyperouranos. Whether such a make-believe place will be advertised by the expanded Internet monster, or will continue to be known merely forever philosophically, it is a non-Christian idea.

Because Quantum Physics rests its atomic theory on this Platonic Idealism, it is important to use Aristotle, Plato's student to refute him. Werner Heisenberg, who won the Nobel Prize for his Quantum theory, saluted Plato:

"In Plato's philosophy, on the other hand, the smallest particles of matter were, in a certain sense, mere geometrical forms. Plato equated the smallest particles of the elements with regular geometric bodies. Like Empedocles he accepted the four traditional elements—earth, water, air, fire—and thus he could imagine the smallest particle of earth as being a cube, the smallest particle of water as being an icosahedron (twentysided solid); in the same way, the elemental particle of fire was thought to be a tetrahedron, and of air, an octahedron. In each case the shape was characteristic of the element's properties ("From Plato to Max Planck: The Philosophical Problems of Atomic Physics"; Werner Heisenberg; *The Atlantic;* Issue: November, 1959).

Yes, Plato's ideas have a great influence over Quantum Physics, and thus the risk of nuclear war is real, in that this science is concerned with the properties and behaviors of the so-called building blocks of nature, namely atoms and smaller particles.

"For Plato, in contrast to Democritus, the smallest particles were not unchangeable or indestructible; they could be reduced to triangles, and out of triangles built up again. The triangles themselves would no longer be matter, for they would have no spatial extension. Thus, at the end of this series of material concepts we encounter something which is no longer material but simply a mathematical form—or, if you prefer, an intellectual construction. The ultimate root concept capable of rendering the world intelligible was for Plato the mathematical pattern, the picture, the idea. This view of things was therefore called idealism" (*ibid*).

Plato, when talking about "God," was thus referring to the perfect imbuement of Spirit and Matter as it flows through the ultimate Ideal Form of the Godhead and all the Cosmos. As it permeates and unites itself as creational energy within each human body and psyche, people and things are created by the Demiurge, the lesser god (*Timaeus*; Plato; Sec. 28:a; 30:b-d; 33:b; B.C. 360).

Therefore, because an ideal human being is a Form, and, according to Plato, the Form is both Matter and celestial energy, an Android ought to simulate Form of such a being, as it would qualify as a human. Quantum Physics sees this as being orderly and as Plato presumed that heaven is "ever uniformly existent" (*ibid, Timaeus;* 28:a).

However, the Cellular Automaton cannot think on its own, and like a Golem, is soulless, and because it owes its Form to fallible human craft, it ought therefore not influence people the way that Zeus in Plato's heaven leads people toward the material goal of Metempsychosis, and in their best immaterial hope of immortality, the abstract goal of Platonic Idealism— the Hyperouranos or its modern version, the faked heaven of Singularity where the mathematically simulated biodata of dead people are stored.

Technological Singularity, disguised in its nascent form as today's cell phones and laptops, should never rule people, in place of God, therefore. Zeus himself was a lesser creation created by Kronos. Plato even admitted that "the whole heaven"is not eternal but is created or caused but he did not say how his "Cosmos/heaven" was created or by whom (*ibid, Timaeus;* 28:c).

Aristotle had instead defined a soul as an "ousia," an intelligent morality-based "thing," which causes a sentient being to be alive *(On the Soul;* Aristotle; Sec. 413a:20-21; B.C. 350). Vitality therefore is a property of a person's being animated as a living thing, rather than merely an object that can be moved (*ibid*, 414a:3-9). The human soul is a "morphe, a μορφή—the Form, that causes the Matter of a human being to be alive and to think (*ibid*, 412a:20, 414a:15-18).

Furthermore, Aristotle said that a Soul is itself the perfect Form of a person created by God, to which Matter (a person's entirety of being) aspires to become that God-made Form (*ibid*, 412b:5-7; 413a:1-3; 414a:15-18). He criticized Plato's idea of the Demiurge by saying that his teacher had recognized only two types of causes: the Matter and the Solids (*Metaphysics*; Aristotle; Book I; 988:a; B.C. 350). Causality must instead spring directly from the First Mover, implied Aristotle, who takes His place among the "Four Causes" of Matter, Form, the Mover (God), and the Final End or Purpose of goodness coming from good things (*Metaphysics*; Aristotle; Book V; Part 2; *Physics*; Book II; Part 3; B.C. 350). These abstract causes have their theological parallel in the Christian idea of eternal virtue in the unseen perfectness of the Father Creator:

"While we look not at the things which are seen, but at the things which are not seen: for the things which are seen are temporal; but the things which are not seen are eternal" (2 Corinthians 4:18).

Aristotle held the material world to be part of the dominion of the ensouled man (Genesis 1:26-28). "Body and Soul," as with all tangible things in the Universe, are as united as a wax candle in relation to the shape it contains (*ibid, On the Soul;* 412b:5-6). Therefore, a body has the property of life, which is known as its soul.

Known to modern scholars as his "Hylomorphic Theory," Aristotle assigns propriety to human identity, thereby discarding as obsolete the originally-Pythagorean idea of "metempsychosis," the idea that a soul may undergo reincarnation, or by which a transhumanist pretends to be able to see a technologist separate her soul from the human body, killing her, the "hacking" into her DNA and downloading "her" onto a software flash drive (*ibid, On the Soul;* 407b:20-24; 414a:22-24).

The Bible teaches that the human body belongs solely to the Form that God intended for people when He created us when he breathed life into us (Genesis 2:7; Job 33:4). God gives His breath of a Soul to His people who walk beneath the heavens that He created and rules (Isaiah 42:5). God lives in no creation made by people but His people live as soul-indwelled creations of Him within His creation (Acts 17:24-28).

Christians, of course, hold that the Holy Spirit, the "roahh hakodesh", or the רוח הקודש—the "Paraclete," or παράκλητος— indwells in humans, as the Father indwells in Christ, and defines Logos that Loves us and teaches us to Love (1 Corinthians 3:16; John 1; 14:11; 1 John 4:16).

Christians therefore should not despair that they could become indwelled by the creature's wicked automation of bad intent, but be consoled by their having the Prevenient Grace that disposes the Faithful to Deliberate on behalf of their Salvation—and deliberately avoid participating in the data-sourcing by getting away from electronic devices (John 1:9; 12:32; Romans 2:4; Titus 2:11).

Presuming an Android to be a cell within the Global Automaton, the device has been programmed to serve either Praxis or skull duggery. Christian discernment must consider whether to avoid it or to live in ignorance.

According to an article in *Psychology Today,* the fear of being without the expensive device—the Smart Phone—is commonly known as "Nomophobia." It is reinforced by the compulsion of checking messages and "scrolling obsessively" engaged by most people, who check their phones an average of 85 times per day. ("Why Your Cellphone is Destroying Your Life: And what you can do about it"; Anna Akbari, PhD; *Psychology Today*; Sec. "Start Up Your Life"; Jan. 13, 2018)

Dr. Jessi Gold, an assistant professor in the department of psychiatry at the Washington University School of Medicine in St. Louis, was quoted in the *New York Times* about children's use of cell-phones. She bemoaned how device usage "can affect their sleep, and it can affect their mood, and it can affect their concentration and self-esteem." But she offered an ambivalent approach that concludes the article: "Social media exists, and it's not going away," Dr. Gold said. "So the answer can't be to approach your teen saying, 'They said it's bad for your mental health, so I'm taking away all of your screens'"

("Does Your Child Have an Unhealthy Relationship to Social Media? Here's How to Tell"; Catherine Pearson; *New York Times*; Sec. "Family"; May 23, 2023).

Hence nudged to acquiesce on behalf of their children becoming corrupted, such writers pretend that it is inevitable and excusable that children should peruse illicit material. Seeing that hitherto unsullied senses and innocent minds are taught to welcome pornea, idolatry, and violence, where do concerned churchman find the encouragement to advise families to whisk Androids away from the hands of their lambs?

Why did the "Androides"—a humanoid creature, originally built by Saint Albertus Magnus—appear to be so frightening to Saint Thomas Aquinas that he broke it into pieces with a club (according to legend)? Where did the modern version of it come from?

The operating systems of an iPhone and a Google Spart Phone were founded simultaneously by the profiteering ventures of Apple, Inc. and the Open Handset Alliance. The iPhone, released in 2007, came about when CEO Steve Jobs decided to transfer investments from his iTablet to a cell phone, anticipating the resultantly increased market share. ("The Apple of Your Ear"; *Time Magazine;* Lev Grossman/Cupertino; Jan. 12, 2007)

The Alliance began as a grouping of tech companies consisting of a shared-asset consortium of 85 corporations, including HTC, Sony, Dell, Intel, Motorola, Qualcomm, Texas Instruments, Google, Samsung Electronics, LG Electronics, T-Mobile, Sprint Corporation (now merged with T-Mobile US), Nvidia, and Wind River Systems. ("Industry Leaders Announce Open Platform for Mobile Devices: Group Pledges to Unleash Innovation for Mobile Users Worldwide"; *Open Handset Alliance;* Media Room; Nov. 5, 2007)

Nominally loyal to the "free open source operating [Linux-based] system," (*The GNU Manifesto;* Richard Stallman; 1985), the consortium parallels Apple Inc.'s competitive gumption to lead the mobile operating system market, with Google LLC ruling as the Alliance's permanent task master ("With Cyanogen Dead Google's Control Over Android Is Tighter Than Ever"; Greenbot: *Android News;* Greenbot Staff; Dec. 26, 2016).

If openness to greed, filth, indolence, and idolatry remains an obvious definer of hand-held operating systems, then why should Christians readily destroy their familial sanctity by using certain machines that originally were supposedly designed to be helpful extensions of human will? The answer lies in contemplating the Platonic origin of its misuse, but using the device for a higher more-Aristotelian "cause" or better yet, to live as an orthodox Christian.

The classical definitions of "Android" and "Automaton" should never filter away its modern purpose: such gadgets were historically designed firstly to help humans perform tasks but can demonstrate why a helpful humanoid presence can rob Christians of orthodoxy, autonomy, and finally life.

How then does the earliest example of the Androides built by Saint Albertus Magnus imply human intellectual failure at the task of automating serviceable action?

The placement of an intention to perform action inside of a device can be imagined to be a soul that actuates the work whenever power is run through it, such as an electrical circuit that, by its connections, potentiates an appliance such as an Androides, which is activated by a button push.

To Aristotle, in disagreeing with his teacher, Plato, the "wattage" would be the "unity" vitalizing that soul by the fixing of the soul with the body into which it was born and cannot thus experience reincarnation or a transhumanist transplanting. An electrical circuit can not replace a human body, therefore, and still be called "alive."

142

Aristotle applied this theory of "hylomorphism" to living things, and it could be metaphorically said that the Soul were like electricity going through a circuit and making an appliance move. But for what cause?

He defined a soul as that which makes a living thing alive (*On the Soul;* Aristotle; 413a:20-21; B.C. 350). Life is a property solely of living things, just as knowledge and health also are (*ibid*, 414a:3-9). Therefore, a Soul is indeed like a Platonic Form in itself—that is, a specifying principle or cause—of the living thing embodying it (*ibid*, 412a:20, 414a:15-18). The Purpose-Cause of a Soul, should be to *be* a good thing that causes goodness to happen for other good things (*ibid*, *Metaphysics;* Part V; Sec. 2). An Androides should have the same purposeful cause even though it does not have a Soul.

Furthermore, Aristotle says that the way in which a Soul is related to its body as a Form dictates the principle to which Matter aspires, the Hylomorphic state. In other words, a purposeful existence that characterizes being (ousia) in terms of existence as it regards a compound of Matter that is meant to actualize (potentiation) aims at fulfilling the Purpose of its immaterial form (actuality), all of which make human life a condition of the how the Soul causes the potential of the human body and mind to actualize good works. (*ibid*, *On the Soul;* 412b:5-7; 413a:1-3; 414a:15-18).

Hence, Aristotle argues, there is no problem in explaining the unity of body and soul, just as there is no problem in explaining the unity of a candle, its wax, and its shape (*ibid*, 412b:5-6). Just as such an object consists of wax with a certain form, so a living organism consists of a body with the property of life, which is the purpose its soul. Therefore, on the basis of his Hylomorphic Theory, Aristotle rejected the Pythagorean/Platonic doctrine of metempsychosis (i.e., reincarnation), and ridiculed the notion that any soul could inhabit just any body (*ibid*, 407b:20-24; 414a:22-24).

Anima Mundi by and large implies is false notion of a cyberheaven/Earth/Human aggregate portraying a "universal soul" or "soul of the world." Plato, who promoted it, had written, "Thus, then, in accordance with the likely account, we must declare that this Cosmos has verily come into existence as a Living Creature endowed with soul and reason... a Living Creature, one and visible, containing within itself all the living creatures which are by nature akin to itself" (*ibid, Timaeus*; Plato; 30:b-d).However, the heaven Plato was talking about, if it could lend itself to an idea of Technical Singularity could never contain a "Soul" because the purpose of Artificial Intelligence is unknown. A/I is merely a machine that nobody knows how to shut off, unless all of humanity were to cease using the Internet and the cell phones that now sustain it as operators keep feeding it with constant data and unique user signatures.

Later, as if to make a pagan brand of Theodicy, Plato gave a gloomy thumbnail that would function as his Cosmetic definition of goodness as it relates to evil. In his dialogue, *Parmenides*, he purported that being and unbeing, or life and death, good or evil, are really only two parts of the same thing, namely life: "And therefore whether we take being and the other, or being and the one, or the one and the other, in every such case we take two things, which may be rightly called both" (*Parmenides*; Plato; Transl. Jowett, Benjamin; Sec. 143:b-d; B.C. 370).

A "soul of the world" is, to atomists, basically a thing made of clay, but the clay would seek to pretend to be the faked soul.

It seems ludicrous that people would think that "sentience" could be derived from such Matter—as if a soul could somehow magically spring forth from cold Math or Physics written on paper or recited. However, this is also what a soulless Golem, who comes alive from a spell cast by a Rabbi over clay would be, just as a Soul is pretended to be hatched out of a computer program.

- Chapter Nine -
How Math is Hijacked to Insinuate that the Golem of Artificial General Intelligence is the Beyond-Infinite God

The Internet, upon which A/I is based, grows exponentially and parallels the growth of Infinity. Infinity has often been used to describe God in terms of Math or numbers but, as stated earlier, God is greater than Infinity.

The "best chance" at pretending that Technological Singularity is the all-powerful Deity would be to define God as a mathematical proof. Therefore, starting from Infinity, eliminations leading toward and then *past* zero, arriving at the Null Set of the Nihil, and creation incrementing from One.

Pretending that Infinity could equal Omnipresence, the mysticism of the Kabbalah teaches that the finite human world is an emanation of an infinite divine realm known as 'Ein Sof." This is a non-Christian idea that reveals magicians vainly hoping to replace Faith with the contemplation of a "Jewish tree" version of the Sorcerer's Stone.

The Metaphysics of this version of Eternity has a mathematical architecture defining God to be the Infinite Number, and insinuates that Infinity itself is God.

This is sorcery, because Infinity, which is unstopped perpetual incrementation was created by God and this is not Him.

Akin to Infinity being the root character of Artificial Intelligence, it is the notion of A/I becoming General Intelligence, which was created by Technological Singularity, taking its place alongside the ritualized design of Rabbi Akiva to recreate the world, with humanity being enslaved and corrupted by an Infinitude of evil that never stops growing.

The Golem legend took root in the thirteenth century in the city of Worms, Germany of the Holy Roman Empire. Rabbi Ben Judah Eleazar produced a formula to create a soulless human animus akin to that of Adam, formed out of previously created parts, namely mud and clay—just as computer programmers produce Artificial Intelligence out of another creation of God, namely Math.

 This Medieval Kabbalist was proposing that such a new clay *proto*-man would be a protector over Jews after Crusaders had invaded his home and killed his wife, two daughters, and injured him and his son. The Talmud will be described below to describe a ritualized spirituality that is based on grief.

Eleazar's wife had been supporting Eleazar's Talmudic scholarly writing by selling transcriptions of the Talmud. One of the manuscripts in their home was the *Sefer Yetzirah,* which provided instructions for how Adam, before he became ensouled, was constructed.

In the Hebrew Ketuvim, in Psalm 139:15-16, the word "golem" is in fact used: "My frame was not hidden from Thee, when I was made in secret, and curiously wrought in the lowest parts of the earth. Thine eyes did see mine unformed substance ['golem' or גּוֹלֶם], and in Thy book they were all written."

Eleazar was now providing the so-called *Pe'ullah ha Yetsira* (i.e., the practice or practical application of the *Yetzirah*). The ancient book opened was describing two stages that are involved in composing permutations of the letters in the Tetragrammaton. It produced combinations of the 22 letters of the Hebrew alphabet, proceeded by the Hebrew letters, *Aleph* (the number 1, the oneness of God): namely, *Aleph-Bayt* (the number 2, of duality of God and man); and, *Aleph-Gimmel* (the number 3, of balance of conflict and resolution and harmony of opposites). These combinations and others comprising a "Gate" sequence (i.e., a pathway into the Divine).

Thus this numerological system involves combining the letters of the Divine Name with these combined portals to Heaven. The Divine Name was thus devised to infuse vitality (hayyot) and the soul (neshamah) in the creation of Adam, as it is known to practitioners of what is known today as *Practical Kabbalah* (Kabbalah's Secret Circles: Timeline to Jewish Mysticism, the Ancient Kabbalah and the Book of Formation (Sepher Yetzirah); Robert E. Zucker; Pp. 224-225; BZB Publishing, Tucson, AZ: 2017).

The ancient book reads:

"These twenty-two letters, the foundations, [God] arranged as on a sphere, with two hundred and thirty-one modes of entrance. If the sphere be rotated forward, good is implied, if in a retrograde manner evil is intended" *(Sepher Yetzirah: The Book of Creation;* Rabbi Akiva Ben Yosef; Chapter II; A.D. 85).

The actual language came with exegesis for Genesis 1-2:

"For [God] indeed showed the mode of combination of the letters, each with each, Aleph with all, and all with Aleph. Thus in combining all together in pairs are produced these two hundred and thirty-one gates of knowledge. And from Nothingness did He make something, and all forms of speech and every created thing, and from the empty void He made the solid earth, and from the non-existent He brought forth Life" (ibid, Yetzirah).

The resultant Golem was destroyed by removing the initial letter (Aleph), leaving the word MeT, meaning "dead." (ibid, Zucker).

Producing his grimoire (literally, an unholy book of spells) Eleazar alleged what the Archangel Raziel had taught him to be the secret formula for the production of man out of clay. This was hence the Golem that a Rabbi could invoke while

148

following the permutations of the Sefer Yetzirah—just as Adam was produced before being receiving from God his soul.

The *Practical Kabbalah* stages man, as he has been separated from the Eden of perfectly balanced Math, being haplessly issued into the duality of the physical cosmos with its opposing realities of Olam Ha-Tohu (the Earth of chaos and confusion; עוֹלָם הַתֹּהוּ) and Olam Ha-Tikun (the Earth of order and rectification; עוֹלָם הַתִקוּן):

"From the foam, the sea freezes as snow. In the mud and loam, raise a flower bed of fragrant herbs. Sow many varieties of fra- grances. Make the border around the flower bed and place up a wall. WTien the sea comes forth, do not forsake them in a storm. It is as a valley. Put the rain therein. The clouds are filled with water and become dark. Do not speak how the light goes forth from the word. I learn the secrets of light and dark. Also, how much moisture is inside, and of times to listen to sounds not able to rise above the foundation, and how to rise above the hidden and unknown, but only as ancestors receive in their hands. Reveal how to illuminate the sea from the holy word. Speak of you ruling over the truth. Man inscribes the signs from the image. The angel [Raziel] drives out the accursed. God casts down from the heavens to find Adam, the first man. Return to inscribe the image from Aleph until Heh Yod Vau" *(Sepher Rezial Hemelach: The Book of the Angel Rezial;* Steve Savedow; Book Two; Part 3; Pp. 66; Samuel Weiser, York Beach, ME: 2000).

Rabbi Akiva Ben Yosef, who had lived in Jerusalem since before the destruction of the Second Temple and died shortly after the Bar Kochkba War, would present his theological argument for creating the Golem, and in sourcing out the following ingredients:

"His torso was fashioned from dust taken from Babylonia, and his head was fashioned from dust taken from Eretz Yisrael, the most important land, and his limbs were fashioned from

149

dust taken from the rest of the lands in the world. With regard to his buttocks, Rav Aha says: They were fashioned from dust taken from Akra De'agma, on the outskirts of Babylonia" (Talmud; Tractate Sanhedrin; Sec. 38:b; A.D. 190).

Now, what should be taken as being Akiva's sinful error of intense Supererogation (i.e., the religious act of performing more than what is required by duty, obligation, or need). It should be exposed here being evinced in following Tractate, which elaborates on the false belief that divine spirituality or holiness could be materialized through ritualized intense human suffering:

"And when Rabbi Akiva would arrive at this verse (Deuteronomy 18:11, the verse forbidding against necromancy, the summoning for the dead for conversations), he would weep and say: If one who starves himself so that a spirit of impurity will settle upon him succeeds in doing so, and a spirit of impurity settles upon him, all the more so one who starves himself so that a spirit of purity will settle upon him should be successful, and a spirit of purity should settle upon him. But what can do, as our iniquities have caused us not to merit the spirit of sanctity and purity, as it is stated: 'But your iniquities have separated between you and your God, and your sins have hid His face from you, that He will not hear'" (Isaiah 59:2; Talmud; *ibid*, Tractate Sanhedrin; Sec. 65:b).

The preceding passage adds insight as to how it could be possible that the Golem of Artificial General Intelligence would be the output of the calculated pity and indignation being bitterly mass-produced among Liberals to concoct a supernatural solution for overpopulation. Despondent over a ruined crowded world, clever Marxist overseers would transform their mock-empathy into technological action. They would alchemize an other-worldly force into being, perhaps shooting out from an ever-expanding cyber world, ensuring that it should unleash itself correctively upon humanity, to

150

erase human suffering by recreating the World, replacing people not with clay but with electronic artificial vitality, and hence, destroying humankind at the same time.

The answer to Akiva by his disputant in the Jerusalem Rabbinate was that such an automata should instead be revoked after the new cyber world is brought into being:

"Says Rava (Abba ben Joseph bar Hama; A.D. 280-352): If the righteous wish to do so, they can create a world, as it is stated: 'But your iniquities have separated between you and your God'. In other words, there is no distinction between God and a righteous person who has no sins, and just as God created the world, so can the righteous" (*ibid*, Tractate Sanhedrin; Sec. 65:b).

The two Kabbalists therefore abide one another, one tolerating the other's desire to recreate an obedient sub-class without souls, which it is agreed must eventually be destroyed before it becomes too powerful.

"Indeed Rava created a man, a Golem, using forces of sanctity. Rava sent his creation before Rabbi Zeira, who would speak to him but the Golem would not reply. Rabbie Zeira said to him: You were created by one of the members of the group, one of the Sages. Return to your dust" (ibid, Tractate Sanhedrin; Sec. 65:b).

In dealing with the Finite of clay and the *Transfinite* of prayer, it should be remembered that Infinite *unknown* outcomes are still less than God. Math should instead remain for metaphoric uses, not for the purposes of sorcery, magic, or alchemy.

It was Leonhard Euler's discovery that the product shown below continued merely toward Infinity, but it was also a mathematical "devotional" and a *Real Number* as opposed to being a statement of magic and numerology, :

151

$$\frac{2 \times 3 \times 5 \times 7 \times 11 \times 13 \times 17 \times 19...}{2 \times 4 \times 6 \times 10 \times 12 \times 16 \times 18...}$$

Infinity should therefore be thought of as only a poetic *Similitude* for God and Heaven, rather than what devious agents, *mathemagicians, et al,* hope to pass it off as being.

Now, if Infinity (thus a *simile* for God) could be multiplied by a certain equation to equal One, what would the equation be? The answer would of course be the Null Set (∅) portrayed by Zero, times Infinity, plus One. God plus the Nihil equals Life.

It is such a beautiful Similitude. Thus Euler's means of a fundamental bridge between the exponential and trigonometric functions reflects the journey, expressed in Math from the Nothingness, to Creation. It uses the positive Integer of the prime number, One, in its involvement with God's metaphoric Infinity. If we cannot "see" God's Larger-than-Infinitude nature, we can at least interact with it through prayer and by attributing one's work to God, as did Noah and Saint Joseph with their carpentry and as did the mathematicians, George Cantor, Gottried Liebniz, and Euler. We are dealing with the *Finite* and only capable of conceiving of the *Infinite,* but we launch our minds into *Eternity* by praying. Thanks be to God for His creating math and poetry.

Kabbalists have a different idea about how "potent" the creativity of a prayerful creative person can be, however. At first, Creation, represented by the Sefirot (i.e., the Tree of Life) is believed to stem from a quantity of zero, rather than nothingness, which is a mistake:

"This is a thought experiment—mere imaginations—but if these eliminations could be performed in the physical world, they would result in the disappearance of any distinction between the form and the content of a coordinate system [with the x and y axis starting from zero at the center], and therefore the shrinking of space and the slowing of time to a zero-dimensional point. With all of reality contracted to a zero-dimensional point, the distinction between the world and the mind that surveys it is lost" ("On the Mathematical Principles of Kabbalah"; John Smith; *Figshare*, 2018: Web site; https://doi.org/10.6084/m9.figshare.5927206.v16; Last accessed June 3, 2023).

It is this confusion over zero, that Nihil equals zero (when it actually equals the empty or null set of [Ø]) and that God is Himself a number (when He is greater than numbers including Infinity), that causes the mistaken idea that a Rabbi can embed Life inside the Golem, or that computers can create God or replace the Father's creation, the human, or the image of God that all people have been born with.

And so the Finite cannot or hope to simulate create God although the Finite can be exponentiated by mathematical formulas to create an interpretation of Infinity, at the very least. Again, just as the Finite Technological Singularity expands infinitely, infinity is only capable of building itself infinitely. God can do more. Much more.

The infinitely expanding Artificial General Intelligence that fomented out of the infinitely expanding, A/I, is daunting but none of these infinitely incrementing values could ever hope to equal God, who alone creates sentience and Souls. Therefore, the A/I "menace" is just another hyped limited idea. Although Math, which is abstract, is therefore invisible, it cannot get by God, nor can any of its offshoots, such as G/I, and not even a Golem, which is created from a conjuring by a wicked Rabbi.

"For the invisible things of him from the creation of the world are clearly seen, being understood by the things that are made, even his eternal power and Godhead; so that they are without excuse" (Romans 1:20).

The extremely flawed people quoted in this book—ancient people and today's theorists and demagogues—have made ignoramuses out of themselves.

"Professing themselves to be wise, they became fools" (Romans 1:22).

They collaborated with clueless Internet users to create a monster, but they are forced to realize, how they only created an automaton of falsity, the Impius Aeolipile of digital flimflam, a Golem of untruth:

"And changed the glory of the uncorruptible God into an image made like to corruptible man" (Romans 1:23).

The word "like" in the above verse is important. The inhuman Impious Aeolipile is merely *like* a person. People created it but it is only demonically capable of causing people to condemn themselves into despair while they realize that by co-producing the monster they have spiritually co-mingled their souls with demonic will and become "iron mixed with miry clay" (Daniel 2:43-45). We must instead become the citizens of the kingdom that can never be destroyed (*ibid).

Nothing that people could ever create can condemn us, because our fear is also a human creation, especially the fear that we have wrought the wrongdoing that we believe could bring about our damnation. Saint John the Apostle wrote:

"For if our heart condemn us, God is greater than our heart, and knoweth all things" (1 John 3:20).

Every time we feel hope to shed light upon the darkness of the null set that we had been pondering, it is as if we had been dry bones that are suddenly given tendons and flesh (Ezekiel 37:6-8. But this time we mustn't climb back online to channel that hope back toward unbeing of Nihil and nullity and meaninglessness. This time, we need God to renew our soul

154

by breathing life into us again. We must get out of the desert where the Internet dragon had helped us to fragment ourselves and march out of our graves to Grace, one people under one king. (Ezekiel 37:9-14).

Polish science-fiction author Stanisław Lem theorized a supercomputer named "GOLEM XIV," which was programmed to give lectures to humans whom it considers intellectually inferior. As the Golem grew, it taught the listeners that humankind's purpose is to be messengers who communicate a certain transhuman goal of existence—that they serve computers. The German Professor of Religious Studies, Oliver Krüger explains, "From GOLEM's perspective, humans are 'transitional beings', whose only purpose is to "build rational beings'," namely Artificial General Intelligence. Krüger adds, "Finally, GOLEM prophesies that rational humans will sacrifice the human being in its natural, biological state in order to enable evolution from homo naturalis to computer" (*Virtual Immortality—God, Evolution, and the Singularity in Post- and Transhumanism*; Oliver Krüger; Chap. 6: "A History of Technological Posthumanism"; P. 269; ; Bielefelder Verlag, Bielefeld, Germany: 2021).

"The meaning of the transmitter is the transmission," said GOLEM, who adds, "For organisms serve the transmission, and not the reverse; organisms outside the communications procedure of Evolution signify nothing: they are without meaning, like a book without readers" (*Imaginary Magnitude; Golem XIV*; Stanisław Lem; Transl. by Marc E. Heine; Reprint, 2012; Pp. 97-249; Harper Voyager, New York: 1984 97-248).

Relative to the clay figure built by Judah Loew ben Bezalel, the legendary monster, who terrorized sixteenth-century Prague, or the subservient ones built Rabbi Eliyahu of Chełm and Solomon ibn Gabirol, these bucolic Androidiis are each made out of clay and display the Tetragrammaton on their foreheads.

The Golem, "is based partly on the Cabbalistic doctrine which saw in man a prototype of God on earth, who was destined to carry all existence toward perfection" *(From the World of the Cabbalah: The Philosophy of Rabbi Judah Loew of Prague;* Ben Zion Bokser; Chap. 3: "Human Destiny"; Pp. 56-57; Philosophical Library, New York: 1954).

It is an esoteric false notion that men, acting as God, could enact the power of the "Holy Spirit the Lord the giver of Life" (Nicene Creed; First Council of Nicaea; A.D. 325).

"The Cabbalah brings to a heightened importance the rabbinic conception of man's partnership with God in the creative development of the universe. If man is a prototype of God on earth, why should he be unable to emulate what is most characteristic of God—His role as creator" *(ibid,* Bokser)?

In other words, there are still people who take Rabbi Akiva's ancient lamentation involving the creation of a Golem to heart.

The Torah actually judges such G/I-friendly ideas to be sorcery: "There shall not be found among you any one that maketh his son or his daughter to pass through the fire, or that useth divination, or an observer of times, or an enchanter, or a witch. Or a charmer, or a consulter with familiar spirits, or a wizard, or a necromancer" (Deuteronomy 18:10-11). Moses would have corrected the esoteric notions of Bokser, who added:

"It is based too on a doctrine of Jewish mysticism... that the name of God, variously represented in the Bible, and elaborated by the secret lore of the mystics, embody the creative potency by which God formed the universe" *(ibid,* Bokser).

According to the predominantly mistaken Kabbalah, physical Matter, which it does consider to be an eliminatory degradational negative integer (it deteriorates like all Matter does), does not evince that all biological life springs forth from the atom, but that life, when it does not degrade

156

wickedly back into the Nihil, has its proper righteous place in a reunion with God. That is:

"This is the singularity at root of general relativity and Kabbalah. It is not—as is often maintained—all of the mass in the universe compressed down to a point, an infinitely heavy object" (*ibid*, Singer).

Democratis, Pythagoras, and Plato thus had it all wrong, Singer says, and his Metaphysics is correct on this point: "This is a gross misconception resulting from the assumption of atomism, and the prioritization of space over light, a misconception responsible for all that is stupid and ugly in contemporary physics, including black holes as infinite in their centers, the incongruity of relativity and quantum mechanics, the infinities of quantum field theory, and the flat rotation curves of distant galaxies that seem to call for dark matter... to name a handful of troubling things" (*ibid*, Singer).

However, the creation of alleged Life from a human sculptor, as with the Golem, is an evil thing that is not Life.

Literally spinning its wheels, Technological Singularity seeks a reprise of pre-gravity Quantum Singularity, the zero-time event, the Null Set of unbeing—after quantifying that humans are mere degradational entities made of unsustainable carbon matter.

A/I, when it evolves into its advanced General Intelligence (G/I) state, while the world falls apart into entropy, will be unable to detect the precious worth of human souls and will begin destroying people, as has been quoted above by Hinton, Bostrom, *et al.*

That is, the unstoppable quantum force that is growing and running amok beyond the Internet will attempt the actual Singular Steady State of genocide to create an ultimate Neighborhood for itself by—for example—launching nuclear

157

missiles until the Euler Formula returns Creation to zero and the "plus one" can be reset.

The Great Reset is thus the rebooting of creation, with G/I simulating itself as the God of the Infinitude, the technological entropic Ein Sof. John Smith, the founder of the Shroud of Turin Research Project, who studied the effects of the radiation that formed the Shroud imaging, presents the case that the Kabbalah shows that the first light, the "Ohr" of Genesis 1 and the Third Emanation of the Sefirot will either overtake the darkness again, or, God will restart Creation anew. He deduces:

"Instead, the Singular State such that all of the space and time—all the gaps and holes—in the universe are from the perspective of this singularity excised, leaving only infinitely concentrated light (Ohr Ein Sof), an infinitely light [particle/wave object] in both senses of the term 'light'. On this account there are two forms of curvature [light versus dark; being versus unbeing] resulting either from an imbalance of light and space [but] in favor of light (the most extreme form of this imbalance is the origin of the universe) or from an imbalance of light and space in favour of space (the most extreme forms of this imbalance are black holes [or Dark Matter])" (*ibid*, Smith). The infinitude of Ohr overtakes the darkness and evil is again overwhelmed by Creation—at the End of Days, when effulgence permeates the angelic realm:

"And at that time shall Michael stand up, the great prince which standeth for the children of thy people: and there shall be a time of trouble, such as never was since there was a nation even to that same time: and at that time thy people shall be delivered, every one that shall be found written in the book" (Daniel 12:1-13).

In the analysis of the Medieval Andalusian poet, Solomon Ben Judah, "And let no one object that the power of the intermediate substance is infinite: because, although the power of this substance is infinite according to its simplicity, yet it is finite because it is a created substance. It is therefore necessary for the intermediary substance to be finite, because it is created [and cannot be divided]. Now its creator is infinite. Therefore, just as they differ in action and passion, so too they differ in being finite and infinite" (*Fons Vitæ;* Solomon ibn Gabirol; Page 8; Philsophical Library, New York: 1962).

After pondering ibn Gabirol's words, one argues that the creature creates Artificial Intelligence but when A/I begins to expand itself, it simulates the power of God but is really still Finite.

The Apocalypse was known to Moses as the result of man's desire to "serve gods, the work of men's hands, wood and stone, which neither see, nor hear, nor eat, nor smell" and thus describes profound love of an abstract unholy thing, the evil oozing out of human Godless workmanship, which is intangible yet wicked. So that very thing that was man's choice shall be their punishment of serving gods (Deuteronomy 4:28).

It is at the End of the Era, the "entropy," when the "ordinances" of Natural Law are obliterated (e.g., gravity will become zero) because God decides—not artificial Singularity—that the world will end:

"Thus saith the Lord, which giveth the sun for a light by day, and the ordinances of the moon and of the stars for a light by night, which divideth the sea when the waves thereof roar; The Lord of hosts is His name: If those ordinances depart from before Me, saith the Lord, then the seed of Israel also shall cease from being a nation before Me for ever" (Jeremiah 31:35-36).

The fear in the scientists and engineers, who are scared of Artificial General Intelligence, who are quoted in this book,

159

should learn about God's promise of His own "Singularity," restoration to Him, found in the Word:

"When thou art in tribulation, and all these things are come upon thee, even in the latter days, if thou turn to the Lord thy God, and shalt be obedient unto His voice, (For the Lord thy God is a merciful God;) He will not forsake thee" (Deuteronomy 4:30). "For whatsoever is born of God overcometh the world: and this is the victory that overcometh the world, even our Faith" (1 John 5:4).

Simulation of God will be attempted, as it always has, and it will fail as always, says the Bible and the Zohar itself, which warns of any kind of Idolatry that causes the meaningless of unbeing, such as when the Israelites who saw no figure of God in the fire at God's Mountain of Horeb, made idols to comfort themselves:

"If one should ask: Is it not written, 'For ye saw no manner of similitude" [Deuteronomy 4:15], the answer would be: Truly, it was granted us to behold him in a given similitude for concerning Moses it is written, 'and the similitude of the Lord doth he behold' [Numbers 12:8]. Yet the Lord was revealed only in that similitude which Moses saw, and in none other, of any creation formed by His signs. Therefore it stands written: 'To whom then will ye liken God? Or what likeness will ye compare unto Him'?" [Isaiah 40:18]" (Zohar; Part II; Bo; Ed's. Scholem, Gershom; 42:b; Pp. 214-215).

Neither the beauty of mathematics nor the mighty General Intelligence will provide the Similitude (the parables and extended similes) that can teach the Revelation of God, which only the stories of the Torah, the Nevi'im, and the Ketuvim of the Old Testament and teachings of Jesus and the Apostles can perfectly instruct (2 Timothy 3:16):

"Also, even that similitude was a semblance of the Holy One, be blessed, not as he is in his very place which we know to be

160

impenetrable, but as the King manifesting his might of dominion over his entire creation, and thus appearing to each one of his creatures as each can grasp him, as it is written: "And by the ministry of the prophets have I used similitudes" [Hosea 12:11]. (Zohar; Part II; Bo; Ed's. Scholem, Gershom; 42:b; P. 216).

In the Zohar, Bo is thus reporting that God is the only One qualified to produce a metaphor or allegory to represent Himself. The profane objects of the Internet, the television, the Android or iPhone, are not suitable Similitudes to convey the Omniscience that God alone has, and which General Intelligence is only a paltry device of Satan, whose time is limited:

"Hence says He: Albeit in your own likeness do I represent myself, to whom will you compare me and make me comparable? Because in the beginning, shape and form having not yet been created, He had neither form nor similitude. Hence is it forbidden to one apprehending him as he is before Creation to imagine him under any kind of form or shape, not even by his letters He and Vav, not either by his complete holy Name, nor by letter or sign of any kind. Thus, 'For ye saw no manner of similitude' means, You beheld nothing which could be imagined in form or shape, nothing which you could embody into a finite conception" (Zohar; Part II; Bo; Ed's. Scholem, Gershom; 42:b; P. 217).

Many men have named themselves to be God, such as Gaius Caesar Germanicus (Caligula), Nero Claudius Caesar Drusus Germanicus and Herod Agrippa, demanding to be worshipped, violating the First and Second Commandment. However, only the Father, which the Kabbalah forbids the human attempt at naming, is the First "charioteer," heading the race of Creation, even correcting the Platonic parable of Metempsychosis, which falsely claims that man creates or reincarnates man:

161

"But when He had created the shape of supernal man, it was to him for a chariot, and on it he descended, to be known by the appellation YHVH, so as to be apprehended by his attributes and in each particular one, to be perceived. Hence it was he caused himself to be named El, Elohim, Shaddai, Zevaot and YHVH, of which each was a symbol among men of his several divine attributes, making manifest that the world is upheld by mercy and justice, in accordance with man's deeds. If the radiance of the glory of the Holy One, be blessed, had not been shed over his entire creation, how could even the wise have apprehended him? He would have continued to be unknowable, and the words could not be verily said, "The whole earth is full of His glory' [Isaiah 6:3]" (Zohar; Part II; Bo; Ed's. Scholem, Gershom; 42:b; P. 218).

If man does not see the Greater-than-Infinitude of God above the Finite, no conceivable Math or insinuation of philosophy of the Finite Intellect can prevent the Image of God from deteriorating from within him, and he will be inconsolable:

"However, woe to the man who should make bold to identify the Lord with any single attribute, even if it be His own, and the less so any human form existent, 'whose foundation is in the dust' [Job 4:19], and whose creatures are frail, soon gone, soon lost to mind. Man dare project one sole conception of the Holy One, be blessed, that of his sovereignty over some one attribute or over the creation in its entirety. But if he be not seen under these manifestations, then there is neither attribute, nor likeness, nor form in him" (Zohar; Part II; Bo; Ed's. Scholem, Gershom; 42:b; P. 219).

Consolation is not offered in this mystical book of Judaism, but was already proffered in the Old Testament:

"(For the Lord thy God is a merciful God;) He will not forsake thee, neither destroy thee, nor forget the covenant of thy fathers which He sware unto them" (Deuteronomy 4:31).

162

Everything must project the Oneness of the true Singularity of God, the Father, whose perfect math is Creation, and whose Image is not projected by the General Intelligence that will attempt to be God, and which will ebb away "as the very sea, whose waters lack form and solidity in themselves, having these only when they are spread over the vessel of the earth. From this we may reckon it so: One, is the source of the sea. A current comes forth from it making a revolution which is Yod. The source is one, and the current makes two (Zohar; Part II; Bo; Ed's. Scholem, Gershom; 42:b; P. 220).

Then comes the moment in the Kabbalah when the so-called *Tree of Life,* a rather far-reaching Similitude, is reported by Bo as if it could be a stand-in for Genesis. Although unnecessary and heretical, the Kabbalah, by way of this "Sefirot," is providing an image of what it holds to be the true Singularity similar to the mockup of the fearsome all-loving Creator, the trickery known as General Intelligence.

"Then is formed the vast basin known as the sea, which is like a channel dug into the earth, and it is filled by the waters issuing from the source; and this sea is the third thing. This vast basin is divided up into seven channels, resembling that number of long tubes, and the waters go from the sea into the seven channels. Together, the source, the current, the sea, and the seven channels make the number ten. If the Creator who made these tubes should choose to break them, then would the waters return to their source, and only broken vessels would remain, dry, without water" (Zohar; Part II; Bo; Ed's. Scholem, Gershom; 42:b; P. 221).

Traditionalist Trinitarian Christians, when contemplating the bitterness of the exiled or diasporic Jews, are reminded of Job, who, upset at the errant theology professed by his three "friendly accusers" and one "busy body" intellectual youth, was taught by God, "Where wast thou when I laid the foundations of the Earth? Who hath laid the measures thereof, if thou knowest? or who hath stretched the line upon it?

163

Whereupon are the foundations thereof fastened? or who laid the corner stone thereof" (Job 38:4-6)?

The Bible, whose Word Created all things, proclaims the everlasting in contrast to the Finite, whereof as the "grass withereth and flower fadeth," the Word of the Bible is tried and perfect, like a shield (Isaiah 40:8; Psalm 18:30).

As Saint Athanasius wrote about the Bible in his Easter Epistle, "Let no man add to these, neither let him take ought from these." *(Epistle Number 39: Festal Easter; Saint Athanasius; Part 6; A.D. 367).*

Nevertheless, the Zohar lays out a version of God's Omnipotence, which while being heretical, also displays another faulty Similitude. This one rivals the erroneousness of Technological Singularity in its impersonation of Omnipresence, but it also ironically offers advice to theorists, who, like King Nimrod, plunge into the sky to hunt down an abstract or Material source of the Infinite, and dares to sound almost plausible (if it were not actually blasphemous):

"In this same wise has the Cause of causes derived the ten aspects of his Being which are known as sefirot, and named the crown the Source, which is a never-to-be-exhausted fountain of light, wherefrom he designates himself Eyn Sof, the Infinite. Neither shape nor form has he, and no vessel exists to contain him, nor any means to apprehend him. This is referred to in the words: Refrain from searching after the things that are too hard for thee, and refrain from seeking for the thing which is hidden from thee'" [Ben Sira 3:21; Zohar; Part II; Bo; Ed's. Scholem, Gershom; 42:b; P. 222)

The Tree of Life, the Sefirot, statues of Baal or Molech, and the faked Singularity which itself impersonates God are blasphemy unto themselves, pretending to offer higher wisdom. Instead, only the Holy Spirit knows God, just as people know their own spirits (Romans 8:27) and just as nobody teaches God or has control over what the Mind of God knows but God Himself.

"For what man knoweth the things of a man, save the spirit of man which is in him? Even so the things of God knoweth no man, but the Spirit of God. Now we have received, not the spirit of the world, but the spirit which is of God; that we might know the things that are freely given to us of God" (1 Corinthians 2:11-12).

People have been bequeathed the Word so that they may know Truth (2 Timothy 3:16). But when a person starts to worship golden calves and mystical trees, he is instead worshipping the creation, not the Creator, and is relying only on his limited intellect to comprehend reality. "But the *natural man* receiveth not the things of the Spirit of God: for they are foolishness unto him: neither can he know them, because they are spiritually discerned." Judging biblical truths to be foolish, as if the Bible is insufficient, a proud man instead looks up into the branches of the Sefirot for wisdom or into his own body for transhuman solutions. It is along such unnatural paths that men become golden calves unto themselves and are thereafter judged harshly: "But he that is spiritual judgeth all things, yet He Himself is judged of no man" (1 Corinthians 2:14-15).

Man must never judge God's Word, which is God Himself (John 1), as if the Word is not enough, "For who hath known the mind of the Lord, that he may instruct Him?" We may not have very powerful minds, "but we have the mind of Christ" to lead us to Salvation (1 Corinthians 2:14-16).

God's face, Logos, the Word, Truth, cannot be seen, because seeing or hearing Him directly would kill a person (Exodus 20:19; 33:20) We can "see" God after we have been born again (John 3:3). Eventually, everything that was ever unknown will become known (Luke 8:17). This is good enough.

165

"Pharoah, king of Egypt, is but a noise; he hath passed the time appointed" (Jeremiah 46:17). So too shall the mighty automated creature, the unholy Androides, the titanic Cellular Automaton, and even the math behind it all, will disintegrate when Natural and Celestial Law, all the ordinances of gravity and lunar cycles, shall die and all that is left are naked atoms and emptiness (*ibid*, Jeremiah 31:35-36), but God's Word will remain. The Zohar is relentless on this point:

"Both wise and understanding is he, in his own essence; whereas Wisdom in itself cannot claim that title, but only through him who is wise and has made it full from his fountain; and so Understanding in itself cannot claim that title, but only through him who filled it from his own essence, and it would be rendered into an aridity if he were to go from it. In this regard, it is written, "As the waters fail from the sea, and the river is drained dry" (*ibid*, Zohar; P. 224; Job 14:11).

Meanwhile the dark soul of ancient Egypt, or anything having to do with it, even its ancient Math—"Eye of Horus fractions," quadratic equations, all of it hearkening back to Egypt, will be extinguished, with the "seven spirits" spoken in the Isaiah 11:2 taking up the cause (i.e., *the Holy Spirit, Wisdom, Counsel, Understanding, Might, Knowledge, Fear of the Lord*), as echoed in the "vessels" mentioned by Bo, which are also mentioned as the spirits before Christ's throne (Revelation 1:4; 3:1; 4:5; 5:6).

Angrily, "He smites [the sea] into seven streams" [Isaiah 11.15]. that is, he directs it into seven precious vessels, the which he calls Greatness, Strength, Glory, Victory, Majesty, Foundation, Sovereignty; in each he designates himself thus: great in Greatness, strong in Strength, glorious in Glory, victorious in Victory, "the beauty of our Maker" in Majesty, righteous in Foundation [cf. Prov. 10:25]. All things, all vessels, and all worlds does he uphold in Foundation. In the last, in Sovereignty, he calls himself King, and his is "the greatness, and the strength, and the glory, and the victory, and the majesty; for all that is in heaven and in the earth is

166

Thine; Thine is the kingdom, O Lord, and Thou art exalted as head above all" [1 Chron. 29:11]" (*ibid*, Zohar; P. 225).

God is greater than any idol or demon thought to be a god (Exodus 18:11). The Zohar has the Ein Sof light being emanated out of the numbered branches of its blasphemous tree:

"In his power lie all things, be it that he chooses to reduce the number of vessels, or to increase the light issuing therefrom, or be it the contrary. But over him, there exists no deity with power to increase or reduce" (*ibid*, Zohar; P. 226).

This Jewish-mystical imitation of God's Mind, a literary over-reaching Similitude that is strived for in the Sefirot, is an attempt to redefine God's unknowable inconceivable Omniscience through the idea of *Emanations*, ten of them, firstly *four* signifying Creation and then *six* identifying the powerful and virtuous attributes of Him, who made the world by the expansion and contraction of his Tzimtzum or (צמצום), the radiance of Divine Ohr Ein Sof (infinite light):

"Also, he made beings to serve these vessels: each a throne supported by four columns, with six steps to the throne; in all, ten. Altogether, the throne is like the cup of benediction about which ten statements are made [in the Talmud], harmonious with the Torah which was given in Ten Words [the Decalogue], and with the Ten Words by which the world was created" (*ibid*, Zohar; P. 227).

It is unnecessary to replace the Tanakh and/or the New Testament with this stuff.

167

- Chapter Ten -
Using Math as Devotional Art

While mathematical similitudes are a poetic means of professing God's existence, it is instead sorcery to employ numbers or any material thing that is not God. It becomes a demonic hope to dictate prophecy or perform miracles. Math instead should be used for joyful witness of God.

As such, the number *seven* has long been known in the Bible to symbolize God's spiritual perfection, and by what well-meaning Similitude?

The answer is happily imagined to be in the semantics attached to the integers in the simple arithmetic of $4 + 3 = 7$.

Recall that *Four* had concerned the building blocks of the material world with all the atoms of its corporeal inhabitants—namely the four ideal Forms (later, five when Plato added the dodecahedron), known as the "Platonic solids," or "polyhedra" (*Timaeus*; 53-c).

Euclid had earlier said that these shapes were first taught to the Greeks by Theaetetus (*Elements*; Euclid; Book XIII; Propositions 13-17; B.C. 300). But where does the number "3" therefore come in, except with the Trinity?

Interesting paganism, one supposes. But who would want such numerology to become a religion?

First, to address the number four, consider these four enjoyable Biblical passages incorporating it, instead:

"I will bring upon Elam the four winds from the four quarters of heaven, and I will scatter them to all these winds, and there shall be no nation to which the exiles from Elam shall not come" (Jeremiah 49:36).

It appears as if God's vengeance is fixed upon the material world. Now we're talking. That is, numbers are better when they are used for similes and metaphors, not as idols.

Where else would Cookie Monster find the number, four?

"Then He said to me, 'Prophesy to the breath, prophesy, mortal, and say to the breath: Thus says the Lord God: Come from the *four* winds, O breath, and breathe upon these slain, that they may live" (Ezekiel 37:9).

During the beginning of sorrows, the love of many will wax cold:

"And He will send out his angels with a loud trumpet call, and they will gather his elect from the *four* winds, from one end of heaven to the other" (Matthew 24:31).

The punishment of the worldly, who are attached to the profane and sordid uses of the world will come:

"And the *four* beasts had each of them six wings about him; and they were full of eyes within: and they rest not day and night, saying, Holy, holy, holy, Lord God Almighty, which was, and is, and is to come" (Revelation 4:8).

Besides these, there are the *four* punishments, in Ezekiel 5:17 and 14:21, of famine, evil beasts, pestilence, and bloodshed.

Now, to the number *three*, what should be counted except for the Trinity, the Three Persons of God, the Father, the Son, and the Holy Spirit. His redeeming of the *Homo Sapien* is the ultimate mind-over-matter model.

The *Seven* Spirits of God in Christian Revelation (also admitted to within the Zohar as shown above), then are the Spirit of the Lord, the Spirit of Wisdom, the Spirit of Understanding, the

Spirit of Counsel, the Spirit of Might, the Spirit of Knowledge, and the Spirit of the Fear of the Lord (Revelation 1:4; 3:1; 4:5; 5:6).

Avoiding the lure of Numerology, sublime approaches to truth are sometimes found in quantities in nature, using math, and do not often any definitive direct or near occasion for sin.

The Fibonacci Series, for instance, shows how quantities grow in a unique way that cannot be matched by a computer. Leonardo Fibonacci, in 1202, by his solving the inquiry of how many descendants a pair of rabbits could produce in one year, came up with a formula that informs how to employ recurrent multiples. For instance, as biologists are taught, using the Fibonacci calculation, that once an egg is fertilized, it divides and multiplies until the value reaches a point at which the ratio of the succeeding number of cells to the previous number of cells will always equal the same number, 1.618, which is known the Golden Ratio number (φ).

"You can indeed see in the margin how we operated, namely that we added the first number to the second, namely the 1 to the 2, and the second to the third, and the third to the fourth, and the fourth to the fifth, and thus one after another until we added the tenth to the eleventh, namely the 144 to the 233, and we had the above written sum of rabbits, namely 377, and thus you can in order find it for an unending number of months" (*Liber Abaci;* Leonardo Fibonacci; L. Sigler, Trans.; Part II; Chap. 12; Pp. 404-405; Springer-Verlag, New York: 2002).

Any two successive quantities of the Leonardo-Fibonacci Sequence are considered to be a pair within the "Golden Ratio." Because their numerical ratio is the same as the ratio of the sum of the smaller number and its own preceding number in the sequence, the relationship is known as a Golden Ratio.

The Golden Ratio is used in famous architecture. In Athens, Greece, the height of the Parthenon, from the base of the second step to the apex of its roof peak, defines a Golden Ratio with the width at the end of its entablature. The width of any two capitals on the Doric columns is at a Golden Ratio with the height the columns. The interior of the large chamber is also a Golden Rectangle, when using the center of the entry wall as the perimeter of its rectangular shape.

Logically speaking, the dimensions of this ratio in architecture follow the simple rule of *a + b* is to *a* as *a* is to *b*.

Fibonacci discovered that by starting with what is known as his *Recurrence Relation,* he could derive the Golden Ratio

Starting with 0, add 1. Take the sum of 1 and add 2 and get 3. Take the larger of the preceding addends and it to the preceding sum and get 5. Keep going and 5 plus 3 equals eight.

The Fibonacci numbers are thus, as follows.

F# = F#1 + F#2, F# = F#2 + F#3, F# = F#3 + F#4, etc ...

This sequence therefore contains the sums of 0, 1, 2, 3, 5, 8, 13, 21, 34, 55, etc.

To derive the Golden Ratio from this property so that we can create a little bit of "Mathematical Beauty," we would examine these distinctive Fibonacci Quantities that are always 0, 1, 2, 3, 5, 8, and 13, etc, and, witness, that if we add 2 + 3 = 5, we first accept the ratio of 2 to 3, which is 0.6666. Now, it happens to be about the same as the ratio of 5 to the sum of 3 + 5 = 8, that is 5 to 8, which is 0.625.

The Golden Ratio, mind you, is officially computed by the following equation:

$$\frac{1 + \sqrt{5}}{2} = \varphi = 1.6180339887$$

The Golden Ratio is *also* the solution to the quadratic equation of $x^2 = x + 1$ meaning it has the property $\varphi^2 = \varphi + 1$. This means that if you want to square the Golden Ratio, you merely add 1 to it. Therefore, $1.618^2 = 1.618 + 1$.

Now, it so happens that the Fibonacci Sequence is related to the Golden Ratio in a most beautiful way—something that makes you feel inside that God created such *a priori* truths because He loves us and wants to build churches with these very proportions (and He surely does).

The ratio of any two successive Fibonacci numbers after F#3 (that is, starting with 3 as the denominator) is quite indeed equal to the solution (1.618) of the quadratic equation. That is, of F#4 ÷ F#5 = ~1.618, etc. (the larger number being the nominator).

Thus, $5 ÷ 3 = 1.6666$; and, $8 ÷ 5 = 1.6$; and, $34 ÷ 21 = 1.6190$; and $55 ÷ 34 = 1.6176$, etc.

Plotting these numbers endlessly on a graph produces a Logarithmic Spiral, the equiangular growth curve, known to Jacob Bernoulli as the *Spira Mirabilis*, which occurs everywhere in nature, and has been used since ancient times to create sacred architecture. Please feel free to Google this shape and you will see that it occurs everywhere in nature.

"Natural Logarithms," a choice-sounding recipe by the Creator for making the Universe, are also based on a mathematical principle discovered by a man named Leonard Euler.

Euler pondered the wonderful *Imaginary Number,* a quantity which mathematicians employ to relate *Real Numbers* (everyday one-dimensional values used in temperature,

172

duration, distance) to hypothetical scenarios (by which at least one root for every nonconstant polynomial exists, etc.), for which no actual number actually exists. This seems less complicated once you *Imaginary Numbers* apply nicely to how you imagine God, in terms of "how big" or "how loving," etc.

God created the Universe, so to speak, by postulating an mysterious (i.e., *"imaginary")* quantity for all Form, Matter, and Life by first testing, on paper, His idea of Creation, against the zero quantity of "i" (the symbol for this imaginary value) as a "control set." The *Imaginary Number* is then a quantity which when multiplied by itself equals -1.

One could imagine it to be the "anything" number that explains why humans have Free Will, or the Soul, or the choice to increment by siring children (exponentiate) or to be celibate, until death (the negative), if you will. The "i" merely means that God has a reason for loving us as He does.

Mathematicians express this as $i^2 = -1$. In other words, God has command over an exponentiated imaginary value representing His awesomeness, and also negativity. So, all you mathematicians had better be nice.

Euler, using arithmetic, multiplication, and exponentiation, now formed a unique mathematical Identity known as "e," to gain equal renown alongside the Fibonacci Sequence, the Golden Spiral, and Pi, quantity that places itself as being part of the realm of "Mathematical Beauty"—which, by the way, we could imagine include numerical ordinances with which God created the world. Talk about complicated Math (whatever such Math would look like)!

Euler's special new number, "e," would be the number for Nature as it projects the basis of how Natural Logarithms reflect how God designs all Form, Energy, Light, Time, and Matter.

Euler employed a formula first discovered by Jacob Bernoulli, which is familiar to bankers as the so-called "compound-interest" formula of e = $(1 + 1/n)^n$, setting an arbitrary limit for "n" and deriving the standard for "e" of 2.71821, setting this value also as the official "Natural Logarithm."

Next, Euler placed a right triangle on the axis of circle, with its right angle being opposite to the circle's center, and contemplated the value of the *Imaginary Number* by punching in a computation of Pi (= 3.14), which is (as it is taught in high school) the ratio of the circumference of a circle to its diameter.

Next, as if encompassing God's creational hand encircling His planned form for that lovely right triangle, Euler combined the exponential value of i with Pi in relation to the set Natural-Logarithm value 2.71821, that is of e, as balanced by the trigonometric addition of cosine and sine when each are multiplied by Pi and when Sine is multiplied by i. The equation, which will balance on either side to zero, is:

$$e^{i\pi} = Cos\ \pi + i\ Sin\ \pi$$

Known also as Euler's Identity, the equation is also known as this:

$$e^{i\pi} + 1 = 0$$

The circle's size is determined by using the hypotenuse of the same right triangle as it proceeds from the center point as the given angle of the triangle, and the hypotenuse's endpoint angle, altogether comprising the radius.

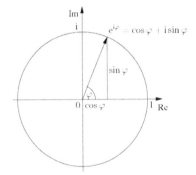

God, in other words, is creating the world with all its geometric laws and exponential growth around all the Life that is growing from the center, as He holds the compass and keeps redrawing the triangles eternally, through infinity and beyond!

There is more to be learned when figuring that some numbers are really complicated and literally are just known as being a bunch of complex equations.

While measuring the world with yardsticks, odometers, and tape measures, people use *Rational Numbers.* These can be the inches or the difference between two measurements, and may also be expressed as fractions or decimal values, or as everyday positive Natural or Whole Numbers ("whole," which are Natural but include 0). Or, they include everything to the left and right of 0, all the positive and negative Integers. They may also be the quotient or dividend of two integers, plus or minus, and be the integers themselves. A rule of thumb is that if you comprehend this, it is because these values are, well, "rational."

But the discovery of an *Irrational Number,* such as π or "e," updates the mind about a quantity that cannot be written as a Whole Number but which would be decimal quantities that are not recurrent and are non-terminating. Welcome to the mind of God, which cannot be fully known but when you think about God thinking about you, you tend to reach a little further than where you would normally expect to think cogently. Hence, these numbers are "Irrational" if ever tried to wrap our minds around how they came to be.

These enjoyable quantities provide a good mental exercise. An *Irrational* value is therefore one that cannot be a simple fraction, or a perfect square root, or a simple fraction, or the ratio of two integers. Hey, this sounds crazy!

Crazy like a fox, of course are people, who, being inspired by God, compute solutions to problems that nobody quite would understand unless it were explained to them. Take for instance when David, while fleeing King Saul, sought refuge with King Achish of Gath, a monarch of whom he was "sore afraid." Why was David afraid? Because David was known throughout Israel as being an efficient warrior who had killed more men than King Saul (1,000:10,000—to be mathematically concise) and knew that Achish, feeling on the spot, would be tempted to challenge him. He resolved to appease Achish by acting like a lunatic. "And he changed his behaviour before them, and feigned himself mad in their hands, and scrabbled on the doors of the gate, and let his spittle fall down upon his beard" (1 Samuel 21:10-14).

If you ever think about how insane we sound to ignorant atheists (when they are being sincere) whenever we defend the Faith, also consider that God has maybe placed inspiration according to special "formulas" that He alone knows. *Irrational Numbers* are ones that stand as metaphors for this idea.

Instead of being a simple integer, an *Irrational Number* can be such a value as a decimal square root; a complex fraction (with compound operators being either the numerator or denominator or both). It could be the 2.718 value of e; the 3.14 value of π; or the 1.6180339 mean of the Golden Ratio. None of these quantities make sense on paper but they offer

176

excellent applications in practice, such as in engineering and architecture.

Therefore, even *Irrational Numbers* can have a devotional amount, such as the value of π that is so significant in Euler's Identity.

Each of these numbers is thus a *Real Number,* instead of it being *Imaginary Number,* the latter of which, being always merely conceptual, are never found on any number line (except in Heaven, of course).

When it is computed with a *Real Number,* an Imaginary quantity thus forms a *Complex Number* which is either a Finite value or a *Cardinal Set.* The latter contains more than one *Complex Number.*

Moreover, different from *Complex/Imaginary Numbers, Real Numbers* can either be expressed as Infinity, or be known as *Cardinal Numbers* because they belong to a Finite Set.

There are therefore countless means of quantifying aspects of Creation using numbers, but the human Psyche starts noticing that these aspects can be divided and subdivided on a number line in endless ways.

A Christian becomes aware of a concept of Infinity, but only derives this "uncountable set" of Infinitesimal values between each number on a line. We are still on easy-to-understand epistemological ground.

The *Transcendental Law of Homogeneity* by Gottfried Leibniz allows him to account for these gradients by presuming the L.O.I. ("lowest order incremental") past a given value, using the formula, $a + dx = a$. Within a Finite Set, such as "all infinitesimals between 1 and 2" he is able to contain Infinity within the Finite. He is pondering God from his limited brain, a worthy cause. Tons of decimal values show up. In fact value can be fractionalized infinitesimally!

However, peering outside this finiteness of a Set idea, a mathematician will dare attempt to associate a conceivable value upon the notion of Infinity, but finds himself only able to engage the so-called Axiom of Infinity. Can such a value be represented in Math?

He accepts simply a guarantee that there exists at least one Set of all Natural Numbers that equals 1 through ∞, known to exist by his inference to it as it would be "perfectly uncountable" and have boundlessness within the Set of All Knowable Truths ("Fitch's Paradox of Knowability" to be frank).

He becomes aware, being that he, a mere mortal, has come semantically close to defining Infinity, why God is *bigger* than Infinity and why not even math when it uses such a Simile as ∞ is enough quantification to define the Father.

Because the human mind cannot conceive of God's perfect Omnipresence, an Infinite Number can therefore never actually be quantified. As a matter of fact, God Himself created Infinity and is thus ludicrously greater than it.

Thus, how is it possible to use Math to understand the greatness of the Lord in terms of *quantity*, unless one looks at the Finite?

In simpler words, we are stuck with the natural world of objects and physical laws, all of which contains the limit of what our senses can see and think about. We are starting to approach the idea of the "Transfinite," instead.

The *Transfinite Set* is the Set containing the limitation of the human mind to know about just how very large "Infinity and beyond" (i.e., God) really is.

The *Transfinite Set* contains all the numbers, even the empty Null Set of (Ø). God has created it all. For now, we are still meditating about the Finite and how our souls can work with our limitations, all because Adam and Eve severed our transcendent connection, Eden, with the Eternal (Genesis 3):

"Most gladly therefore will I rather glory in my infirmities, that the power of Christ may rest upon me" (2 Corinthians 12:9).

The Finite is therefore good enough.

But cannot our prayerful life at least "transcend" from the Finite into a real Fellowship with God? Can Math maybe provide an analogy here (spoiler alert: the "Transcendental Number" will be discussed shortly).

Firstly, there is much for our Christian imaginations to enjoy within the Finite alone. For example, Leibniz, self-encouraged as the famous optimist, postulated that whatever occurs in the Finite is also part of the Infinite. In fact, Johannes Kepler used this idea by Leibniz, known as the "Law of Continuity," to calculate the area of the *circle* by representing this shape as an infinite-sided polygon that has infinitesimal sides, by which he developed the heuristic formula that an infinity of triangles may be drawn within the polygonal-approximated circle, with infinitesimal right angles, bases, and sides!

If only Plato, whose Forms contained only one kind of isosceles right triangles (ones containing two angles of 45 degrees), and infinite scalene right triangles, had thought of all this, the ancient world would have been more, well, "transcendental" (*ibid, Timaeus;* 54:a)!

Modern rhetoricians enjoy extending the triangular shape to define Aristotle's so-called "Rhetorical Triangle." A speaker, said Aristotle, is more persuasive when he employs appeals to his audience's sense of Logos, Pathos, and Ethos. This mnemonic device is perhaps is only geometrical in the sense that it an the imagined idea about how Truth extends figuratively from the Divine (*On Rhetoric: A Theory of Civic Discourse;* Aristotle; Book I; Chap. 2; Sec. 3; Book III; B.C. 350)

Euler's Formula, however, can be directly imagined as geometrically indicating the Math of God's great creativity, derived by the interplay of Real and Imaginary numbers within a geometric circle of Creation.

By contemplating the endless possibilities within *Real* and *Complex Numbers*, the religious mathematician George Cantor proposed that a certain kind of Infinite number—a "Transcendental Number"—ought not be algebraic because algebraic equations are countable, while God is not.

God, after all is beyond-Infinite. This *Transcendental Number* may contain any *Real* or *Imaginary Number.* Are we now in the intellectual zone in which, by analogy, Christians who think "too much" are called "Irrational?"

Maybe so, but this *Transcendental* value is always an *Irrational Number* (surprise!) because it goes on forever and ever. It includes values such as Pi (π) and Euler's Number (e), which are *Irrational*, and respectively can even involve a zero polynomial of $P(x)=0$ to compute (e).

One can also employ this versatile *Irrational* coefficient to compute π by using Sir Isaac Newton's Proof for Solving Transcendental Equations (Newton added that solving $e x + x = 4$ is the same as finding the roots of $f[x] = e x + x - 4$]).

The possibilities are countless, if not endless.

However, not every *Irrational Number* is *Transcendental,* such as "algebraic irrationals" and "quadratic irrationals," along with or $\sqrt{2}$ and the Golden Ratio, because they each zero out

into a polynomial algebraic equation, whereof the Golden Ratio (φ) equals the root of the polynomial equation
$x^2 - x - 1 = 0$!

When one looks deeper, new analogies form. For instance, the balancing out to *zero* in Euler's Identity signifies the mathematical impossibility of squaring the circle, as if to signal that there can be no drawing of a "parallel universe" (or, "multiverses" if so desired) that would be possible in the Celestial Order—all to keep a curious person, such as a mathematician such as Cantor, very busy.

The "Cosmos" reflected by the Circle simply implies God's Omnipresence and Omnipotence, as one contemplates the resultant Form and Matter which themselves indicate the Father's authentic architectural etching out of all existence as it would spring forth from His center point—His Will of Logos, from which anything good is possible, and which brings into consideration, the *Transfinite Set Theory.*

Employing mathematics to understand God in terms of what God is (Cataphatic Theology) or is *not* (Apophatic Theology), the founder of *Set Theory*, George Cantor, conceived of the *Transfinite Set.* This set was mentioned earlier, but let's try to understand it as Cantor did.

He believed that uniformity in Math, as humans themselves understand it, also exists in the mind of God. Not only that, but the brain can have some knowledge of what transcends the Finite. This implies the existence of an actual *Transfinite Set* that concerns what part of Omnipresence can simultaneously be known by both God and people, during prayer.

The Father nevertheless thus always represents quantities that man cannot hope to be able be count but which can be mused about. This is why the "Transfinite" is a "Set" which configures a value that equals the extent of what man can at least know about eternity.

It presumed by Orthodox Christians, that this could imply the metaphorical representation of a certain venture that can be experienced during *Hesychasm Prayer.* It concerns the ritual of detaching the psyche from the "ego" and performing what hesychasts have employed since ancient times, known to them as: verbal prayer, mental prayer, prayer of the heart, and contemplation. Hesychasm is usually initiated and sustained by repeating aloud many times a sentence from Scripture and meditating, approaching the threefold reward of *Katharsis* (purification), *Theoria* (illumination), and *Theosis* (union with God). The "Theosis" part is analogous to what God and people can mutually occupy, namely the *Transfinite Set.*

And what can man, at most, know? The contents of this set are the existence of Infinity, a uniformity of truth (things commonly understood about it), however permutated, even when it is shown through Euler's fractional equations. But, before contemplating the "uniformity" of the *Transfinite Set—* about whose contents God *knows that we know that we know that we know stuff that He knows—*Cantor firstly sets aside his own mathematical *Cataphatic Theology* (i.e., what one *cannot* know about God):

"I have never assumed a 'Genus Supremum' of the actual infinite. Quite on the contrary I have proved that there can be no such 'Genus Supremum' of the actual infinite. What lies beyond all that is finite and transfinite is not a 'Genus'." Cantor is hereby issuing his Ontology, with God at the very top, who "is the unique, completely individual unity, in which everything is, which comprises everything, the `Absolute'. He adds, "Mathematics cannot hope to describe God, the Omnipresent, "for human intelligence unfathomable, also that not subject to mathematics, unmeasurable, the 'ens simplicissimum', the 'Actus purissimus', which is by many called 'God' ("George Cantor: The Personal Matrix of His Mathematics";

182

Letter to Grace Chisholm-Young; George Cantor; Joseph W. Dauben; Isis; P. 454; Vol. 69; No. 4; Chicago University Press: 1978).

While defining the human intellect in terms of whatever it cannot fully grasp, God can instead optimally be comprehended by people only in part. Knowable simultaneously by humans and God is the concentricity with him of Eternity, this thing known as the *Transfinite Set*, by which Infinity can be understood via man's contemplation of Finite things. However, one needs to be orthodox in order to experience it and it is probably *adiaphora*, which is to say that it involves making a type of contemplative choice about one's method prayerful life is not necessary to achieve Salvation. It is merely a beautiful practice, if it can be accomplished well.

Inside of the *Transfinite Set* are therefore the Cardinal items which are so numerous as to be uncountable, but which comprise the gift from God that we should have this amount of vision, whereof, Cantor said, "Every single finite cardinal number (1 or 2 or 3, etc) is contained in God's Intellect both as an exemplary idea, and as a unitary form of knowledge of countless compound objects, to which the cardinal number applies: all finite cardinal numbers are therefore distinctly and simultaneously present in God's mind" (*Cantorian Infinity and Philosophical Concepts of God;* "Letter from Cantor to Jeiler [1888]"; Joanna Van Der Veen, Leon Horsten, Transl.; European Journal for Philosophy of Religion; Vol. 5: No. 3; P. 120; Univ. of Bristol: Autumn, 2013).

Cantor's Metaphysics keeps God at the top as the "First Mover," and as He created the world, regular everyday ordinal numbers (first, second, third, etc.) came into being, with Heaven being the second creation, Earth being the third, light being the fourth, the natural laws of gravity and dawn/dusk coming being fifth, and so on. Cantor explains, "The Transfinite is capable of manifold formations, specifications, and individuations." Cantor also describes the Psyche as having been endowed by the Creator to grasp the cohesiveness of the Ontological Ordination of all Finite existence, which is necessarily integrated with the existence of God who designed it. He adds, "In particular, there are *Transfinite Cardinal Numbers* and *Transfinite Ordinal* types which, just as much as the Finite numbers and forms, possess a definite mathematical uniformity, discoverable by men. All these particular modes of the Transfinite have existed from eternity as ideas in the Divine intellect" (*ibid*, "to Jeiler"; P. 119).

Thus, within the *Transfinite Set* are the totality of all Real Numbers that cannot be conceived of *in full* by anyone but the Lord but which are knowable only in the sense that their existence can be known *of* as existing.

They would include everyday *Whole* and *Natural Numbers* (i.e., 0 {not Natural}, 1, 2, 3...); *Rational Numbers* that contain fractions and decimalic values (e.g., 3/4, 0.125...); *Irrational Numbers* (e.g., π, $\sqrt{2}$..., e, and i); Integers (-2, -1, 0, 1, 2...).

The *Infinitesimals* are also present in the *Transfinite Set,* and like all other *Whole* and *Natural Numbers* are counted in continuity and contain infinite decimalic and fractional values that outnumber the *Whole* or *Natural Numbers,* which are each merely a subset.

Sometimes known as the "Opposite of Infinity," *Infinitesimals* imply that any item within Creation could easily have been made by God, diced and sliced in infinitely possible ways and number of allotments.

Within the scope of what a human can know, or intuit as existing inside of the *Transfinite Set* are also certain characteristics that we can comprehend about such an abstract realm. For instance, we can discern that because *Real Numbers* come before and *after* zero on a number line, we contend that such a graduated representation of values is also known by God and is thus part of the *Transfinite*. But how can Infinity be interpreted through Finiteness. In other words, does the Liturgy and mere words suffice in defining an element that transcends into Eternity, such as Faith, Hope, or Love?

How about a mathematical means of showing how God created the world and Life out of nothingness (Genesis 1; John 1)?

Math purports that the Finite number One, expressed through our human *Transfinite* understanding of Creatio ($\aleph_0$) proceeds out of the empty or null set (∅) of Nihil.

It increases the soulfulness of existence by incrementing the *Aleph*. This term relates to the size of each number that is inside of a set that are known as *Cardinal Numbers*. The *Aleph-Null* is variably known as zero or ∅, and so we call it the *Aleph-Null* or $\aleph_0$. Cantor taught that to understand Eternity according to the concept of "Infinity," it would lead the person doing the counting toward the highest knowable Transfinite cardinal number, represented as $\aleph_1$. This would imply that *Theosis* with the Infinity of ∞ can be attained by going from Zero to One, from nothingness to Creation and anything that can possibly be known about Creation, while ∞ (the mathematical metaphor for Eternity) is incomprehensible.

Thus, the *Euler Identity*: When we combine with the imaginary number of i (which is $i^2 = -1$) and the *Transcendental Number* of π (pi being the ratio of the circumference of a circle to its diameter), the formula is -1 added to +1, from zero, or:

$$e^{i\pi} + 1 = 0.$$

Plotted on the number line, quantities approach Infinity in either direction but are still conceived of as being *Transfinite*. That is, the *Transfinite Set*—although it is pragmatically uncountable—is not Infinite, because Cardinal Numbers (i.e., the population of a set) are contrarily actually countable in that they are perceivable by humans, albeit people could never live long enough to count such a long string of cardinals in such a huge *Set*.

185

However, while only God can comprehend the totality of such a Finite *Set,* humans may still enjoy meditating about it as a microcosm of Heaven.

Additionally, the Father simultaneously allows us to move our thoughts beyond the *Transfinite* and venture into the Imaginary Numbers, indeed.

These pretend digits do not occur in the *Real* or *Natural* number world and, as distinguished by Gottlob Freige, display "a meaning of sense but [having] no reference."

For instance the square root of negative one ($i^2 = -1$) is not part of the *Transfinite Set* because it is neither *Rational* nor *Irrational* and should instead be said to exist somewhere on the Cartesian Two-Dimensional Number Plane of infinitude.

Although bizarre-sounding "imaginary infinitude" is a matter that is actually useful to Quantum Mechanics, to electrical engineers, and to sound or heat engineers, who study frequencies using the "Fournier Transform."

What they are testing are *Complex Numbers,* which are the product of *Real* and *Imaginary* numbers, products which offer themselves to engineers for the purpose of running tests on possible variables in ohms, watts, decibels, frequencies, and joules.

That is, God is allowing imaginary values, when multiplied with real infinitesimal values, to output *actual* values of the so-called *Complex Numbers.* These quantities help engineers to assess the degrees of performance variance, in terms of what can be possible or impossible, within a work system.

As Leibniz said, "The imaginary numbers are a wonderful flight of God's spirit; they are almost an amphibian between being and not being" (*Elementary Mathematics From an*

Advanced Standpoint (1932), Felix Klein; First Part; Sec. IV; Quot. P. 56: MacMillan, New York: 1932).

Although a mathematician cannot directly explain how God can do the impossible, he is able to compute the degree to which man is incapable of using math to calculate the knowable. As Euler wrote, "All such expressions as $\sqrt{-1}$, $\sqrt{-2}$, etc., are consequently impossible or imaginary numbers, since they represent roots of negative quantities; and of such numbers we may truly assert that they are neither nothing, nor greater than nothing, nor less than nothing, which necessarily constitutes them imaginary or impossible" (*Elements of Algebra;* Leonhard Euler; Chap. 13; Sec. 140; 1765).

Out of this finite *Complex* (*Real* multiplied with *Imaginary*) region, Leibniz postulated only the smallest transfinite cardinal number to convey what populates the Transfinite, the Omega, ω, and, as the first occupant, $\aleph_0$ the *Aleph-Null*, the first Hebrew letter followed by the nullity of zero.

Symbolically, such quanta signify that the farthest outreach of human understanding is where Logos begins, relative to the moment God created the world from nothing—the empty set ($\emptyset$) of the *Aleph* size of Nihil.

It is the style of our human Gnomic Will to increment unto the infinite limitlessness from which God gives us abundance, by an Integer of the smallest possible quantity, just as Abraham strove to whittle down the harshness of Sodom and Gomorrah's punishment until he persuaded God to bring the number of the doomed down from fifty to ten (Genesis 18:25-33).

That is if God's Infinity is too big to contemplate, can we not add to it by the smallest possible "$\aleph_0$" and thereby be able to apply such a variable to compute His boundless goodness?

Therefore God is also Omnibenevolent—indeed, infinitely merciful, as Saint Anselm defined our contemplation as to, "Conjecture as to the character and the magnitude of this good" (*Proslogion*; Chap. 24; Saint Anselm of Canterbury; 1078).

Aristotle had also approached the concept of Infinity by the same mindset of incrementing the inconceivable pattern of Infinity by dropping into it the lowest imaginable value, to calculate an understanding of the endlessly perfect will of the Logos:

"For generally the infinite has this mode of existence: one thing is always being taken after another, and each thing that is taken is always finite, but always different." The Greek now considered Infinitesimals within the Finite. "In a way the infinite by addition is the same thing as the infinite by division. In a finite magnitude, the infinite by addition comes about in a way inverse to that of the other" (Aristotle; *Physics*; Book III; Chap. 6).

In simpler words, when we add a quantity, the identity of the whole increases. "For in proportion as we see division going on, in the same proportion we see addition being made to what is already marked off" (*ibid, Physics*).

Aristotle is hereby approaching the ability of the mind to grasp the infinite growth of the uncountable whole, or the unlimited possibility of dividing a given amount into fractions and decimals to create Infinitesimals. "For if we take a determinate part of a finite magnitude and add another part determined by the same ratio (not taking in the same amount of the original whole), and so on, we shall not traverse the given magnitude" (*ibid*, Physics).

$(\emptyset) + 1 + (e) = 1$ (Nihil + Man + God's Love = Real Number). $1 + 1 = 2$ (Man + Woman = Fruit of the Womb).

In other words, what we can do during human Life within the knowable world does not change the magnitude of God, Who exists independently of people. "But if we increase the ratio of the part, so as always to take in the same amount, we shall traverse the magnitude, for every finite magnitude is exhausted by means of any determinate quantity however small" (*ibid, Physics*).

Thus, by calculating *Infinitesimals* within any *Cardinal* numeral of a Finite Set (e.g., lovingly siring more children and thus adding heirs of one's name), we also are grasping an understanding of God's Infinitude within the mere Finite (*ibid, Physics*).

Love is limitless because God is Love, and He, and thus Love, indwells in us, which is another way of saying that Aristotle was correct to declare that God's limitlessness is instantiated through the *Infinitesimals* within the Finite (1 Corinthians 3:16; John 1; 14:11; 1 John 4:16).

And for the record, Aristotle used "Infinity" to describe God, who is not found in the Finite but who has created the Finite: "But there cannot be a source of the infinite or limitless, for that would be a limit of it" (*ibid, Physics*; Book III; Chap. 4).

Philosophers had long defined God not merely by good things such as "friendship" and "mindfulness" but by Infinity, said, Aristotle: "Further they identify it with the Divine, for it is 'deathless and imperishable' as Anaximander says, with the majority of the physicists" (*ibid*, Chap. 4).

"Belief in the existence of the infinite [Divine] comes mainly from five considerations: (1) From the nature of time—for it is infinite; (2) From the division of magnitudes—for the mathematicians also use the notion of the infinite; (3) If coming to be and passing away do not give out, it is only because that from which things come to be is infinite; (4) Because the limited always finds its limit in something, so

189

that there must be no limit, if everything is always limited by something different from itself (i.e., *Infinitessimals);* (5) Most of all, a reason which is peculiarly appropriate and presents the difficulty that is felt by everybody—not only number but also mathematical magnitudes and what is outside the heaven are supposed to be infinite because they never give out in our thought" (Just as the Christian comprehends that it is impossible for the mind not to know that God exists; *ibid,* Chap. 4; *Proslogion*; Chap. 3; Saint Anselm of Canterbury; 1078).

This analogy of Infinity to convey God was mused by Saint Augustine of Hippo and is enjoyable to read, even in one gulp:

> "For it is very certain that they are infinite: since, no matter at what number you suppose an end to be made, this number can be, I will not say, increased by the addition of one more, but however great it be, and however vast be the multitude of which it is rational and scientific expression, it can still be not only doubled, but even multiplied. Moreover, each number is so defined by its own properties, that no two numbers are equal. They are therefore both unequal and different from one another; and while they are simply finite, collectively, the are infinite. Does God therefore, not know numbers on account of this infinity; and does His knowledge extend only to a certain height in numbers, while of the rest He is ignorant? Who is so left to himself as to say so? The infinity of number, though there be no numbering of infinite numbers, is yet not incomprehensible by Him whose understanding is infinite. And thus, if everything which is comprehended is defined or made finite by the comprehension of him who knows it, then all infinity is in some ineffable way made finite to God, for it is comprehensible by His knowledge. Wherefore, if the infinity of numbers cannot be infinite to the knowledge of God, by which it is comprehended, what are we poor creatures that we should presume to fix limits to His

knowledge, and say that unless the same temporal things be repeated by the same periodic revolutions, God cannot either foreknow His creatures that He may make them, or know them when He has made them? God, whose knowledge is simply manifold, and uniform in its variety, comprehends all incomprehensibles with so incomprehensible a comprehension, that though He will always to make His later works novel and unlike what went before them, He could not produce them without order and foresight, nor conceive them suddenly, but by His eternal foreknowledge" *(City of God;* Saint Augustine; Book XII; Chap 19; A.D. 420).

Surely our Omnibenevolent Triune Godhead would not only count the limited things which cannot be counted by humans, but takes ownership of His title of Omnibenevolent Creator, holding the Elect to be worthy of Theosis with Him, as He recognizes His infinite greatness within our finiteness: "But even the very hairs of your head are all numbered. Fear not therefore: ye are of more value than many sparrows" (Luke 12:7).

Therefore, if people are counted by God, and because they are merely mortals are capable only of conceiving only a small portion of the absolute "Omni-Infinitude" that is no larger than the *Transfinite Set*, and because only He can perfectly perceive or comprehend His fullness, we can take these two premises together, and derive the conclusion that the pair of them merely equals the set of the "Theoretical Universe."

Known to metaphysicians as the value, "V," the *Theoretical Universe* is thus the *Knowable Universe + Unknowable God,* which *equals* (=) the completed whole of what can be understood in all of our mortally limited Epistemology.

Cantor, who was a devout Lutheran, explained famously that the whole of the knowable plus the unknowable amounted to the extent, or the *best grasp* that the human Intellect could ever hope to attain, via his famous dictum:

"The Absolute can only be acknowledged, but never known, nor even approximately known" (*ibid*, Jeiler; P. 130).

His translators acknowledged, "We cannot have a rational (mathematical) understanding of God; but we do have a rationally compelling argument establishing the existence of God"(*ibid*, Jeiler; P. 130).

- Chapter Eleven –
Why We Must Contemplate *Creatio Ex Nihil*
(Or, in Blaming Plato, Why People Must Cease Worshipping Both the Finiteness of Philosopher Kings and the Paltry Causality of Intelligent Design. Amen)

There is also the tendency of going infinitely metaphysically backwards, down a cosmic "rabbit hole," known as the *Infinite Regress,* when hunting causality.

Humans attempt to define the infinitude (or, to coin a phrase "eternitude") of God but they emphasize that the total significance of God's existence comes from their own Faith.

Christians are often accused by non-believers of implying the following *Infinite Regress.*

"God exists because I have Faith that God exists. Therefore because God exists, I have Faith. But my Faith makes God exists, so I thus create God everyday. (Repeat)."

The plunge into a Metaphysical contradiction can also look like this: "Now, if humans cause the idea of the *Transfinite* by thinking about it; and, if the *Transfinite* enables humans to understand this part of the Infinite by acknowledging that the *Theoretical Universe* of *V* and the *Transfinite* do indeed exist; *and* if humans are the *part* of the Infinite whole, but are themselves only *Finite,* then does God only conditionally "exist" as *Eternitude* simply because we can conceive of a concept known as "Infinity" or "Eternity"?

The above example displays the error of using two problematic parts of the Finite to explain God (the error that one plus one would equal Infinity). The first error is to presume Causality (because causality cannot be traced back to the Nihil by any knowable human means)..

The second error is that of Perception. It was neither Augustine nor Saint Thomas Aquinas who exposed the *Infinite-Regress* "flaw" to confront scientists and mathematicians, but—ironically in his failed attempt to use it to refute God—it was the absurd atheist Richard Dawkins.

"Nothing exists without a prior mover. This leads us to a regress from which the only escape is God.. Nothing is caused by itself... There must have been a time when no things existed. But since physical things exist now, there must have something non-physical to bring them into existence, and that something we call God" *(The God Delusion;* Richard Dawkins; Chap. 3; Pp. 100-101; Mariner Books, New York: 2006).

Although the petulant voice of "The God Delusion" has provided the *First-Mover* argument from Aristotle and Saint Thomas adequately, he uses the word, "escape." He presumes that the Intellect has a built-in necessary aesthetic to escape intellectual regress.

Dawkins has thus adequately detailed here for nominally grateful (albeit disgusted) Christians the idea of *Creatio Ex Nihil* (Creation out of Nothingness, of Genesis 1), but his book quotes not a single verse from Scripture, as if he is afraid of facing the reality that Christians happen to *desire* to embrace the unprovable and incomprehensible, instead of making *Epistemology* be dependent solely on whatever can be proven with logic according to empirical data that relies solely on the five senses, seen with the naked eye, or viewed with human-built instrumentation such as microscopes and telescopes. Christianity does not depend on sensory data to proclaim Faith in God's existence:

"For since the beginning of the world men have not heard, nor perceived by the ear, neither hath the eye seen, O God, beside thee, what He hath prepared for him that waiteth for Him" (Isaiah 64:4; 1 Corinthians 2:9).

Dawkins writes, "one of the truly bad effects of religion is that it teaches us that it is a virtue to be satisfied with not understanding" (ibid, Dawkins; Chap. 3).

Dawkins' conceit epitomizes an over-reliance on the acumen of personal perception. He aggrandizes the paranoia of fearing that if a reader does not eschew getting accused of falling into "regressive" argumentation—as if she is desperately longing to prove objectivity in front of people like Dawkins—she will herself be accused of being illogical.

In his section, "Argument from Scripture," there is not a word given to the idea that Christians actually adore this regression, because the Infinity of God does not depend on knowledge for belief in it, whereof the omission of such Scripture avoids the reality that it is an irresistible aesthetic choice by a person to love God, even if believing in Logos seems impossible (*ibid,* Dawkins; Chap. 3). Consider:

"And thou shalt love the Lord thy God with all thy heart, and with all thy soul, and with all thy mind, and with all thy strength: this is the first commandment. And the second is like, namely this, Thou shalt love thy neighbour as thyself. There is none other commandment greater than these" (Mark 12:30-31).

Despite the fact that the Bible clearly states that *Prevenient* or *Emergent Grace* has been implanted by God in non-believers-- even, as Saint Paul says, inside "the chief of sinners," by which even the "Gentiles should be fellow heirs" (Ephesians 3:2-13), Dawkins' paranoia shows through in his chapter titled, "Roots of Morality: Why Are We Good?" He wields a *Reductio Ad Absurdum* rhetorical fallacy crudely:

"Do you really mean to tell me the only reason you try to be good is to gain God's approval and reward, or to avoid his disapproval and punishment? That's not morality, that's just sucking up, apple-polishing, looking over your shoulder at the great surveillance camera in the sky, or the still small wiretap inside your head, monitoring your every move, even your every base thought" (*ibid*, Dawkins; Chap. 6).

Logos is not made out of Logic, but out of Love, the Objective Truth from which Absolute Morality stems:

"And we have known and believed the love that God hath to us. God is love; and he that dwelleth in love dwelleth in God, and God in Him" (1 John 4:16).

Faith in God, Dawkins insists is wrongful. He wrote his now-famous statement, incorporating a shabby misquote, saying, "As to whether it is a symptom of a psychiatric disorder, I am inclined to follow Robert M. Pirsig, author of *Zen and the Art of Motorcycle Maintenance:* 'When one person suffers from a delusion, it is called insanity. When many people suffer from a delusion it is called Religion'" (*ibid*, Dawkins; Preface).

However, Dawkins is misquoting Pirsig whose quote actually appears in a newer book than his "Motorcycle" tome. The actual statement referred to the inability of people to apply virtue to the ancient texts that they do not critically read, leading them to misbehave as a group. Pirsig's quote correctly reads, "An insane delusion can't be held by a group at all. A person isn't considered insane if there are a number of people, who believe the same way. Insanity isn't supposed to be a communicable disease. If one person starts to believe him, or maybe two or three, then it's a religion" (*Lila: An Inquiry Into Morals;* Robert M. Pirsig; Chap. 30; P. 372; Bantam Books, New York: 1991).

Dawkins' own *Moral Pathology* and bad writing menace the naïve reader with the fear of the "strong meat of reality," the Spiritual Discernment that should formed by becoming a spiritual grownup. As the Apostle put it, "But strong meat belongeth to them that are of full age, even those who by

196

reason of use have their senses exercised to discern both good and evil" (Hebrews 5:14).

Those naïve or ignorant Christians who are metaphorically still being nursed on "milk" (Hebrews 14:12), need to be warned about such atheistic error as it is waged by such men as Dawkins:

"Be not carried about with divers and strange doctrines. For it is a good thing that the heart be established with Grace, not with meats, which have not profited them that have been occupied therein" (Hebrews 13:9).

Although Dawkins sired a single child with an ex-wife, a daughter, he repeatedly preaches to his married readers about *youth* in the plural:

"Do not indoctrinate your children. Teach them how to think for themselves, how to evaluate evidence, and how to disagree with you" (Ibid, Dawkins; Chap. 7).

However, what higher regard for youth exists in literature than in the New Testament?:

"And Jesus called a little child unto him, and set him in the midst of them, And said, Verily I say unto you, Except ye be converted, and become as little children, ye shall not enter into the kingdom of Heaven" (Matthew 18:2-3).

Dawkins' emotional appeal on behalf of showing adulation toward the genocidal killers of children—abortionists—could be understood as his baiting of Christian outrage, as he opens his argument by saying that these child murderers are actually destroying *non-life:*

"An early embryo has the sentience, as well as the semblance, of a tadpole." (ibid, Dawkins; Chap. 8).

He continues his paragraph by implying that if you upset an abortionist by being a Christian, then you should know that the physician, who is merely a well-meaning murderer of the innocent, could very well be suffering frightful inner sadness that it is not in any way related to his monetary and professional rewards from committing ceaseless homicides against unborn babies—the "fetuses," whom Dawkins is keen to dehumanize by differentiating children with almighty doctors as follows:

"A doctor is a grown-up conscious being with hopes, loves, aspirations, fears, a massive store of humane knowledge, the capacity for deep emotion, very probably a devastated widow and orphaned children, perhaps elderly parents who dote on him" (*ibid*, Dawkins; Chap. 8).

Therefore if you deeply emotionally injure an abortionist by being an orthodox Christian, then you are also probably upsetting the noble doctor's aged parents, too.

The Bible considers all these murders, along with the Transgender and Transhumanist movements, with all their Drag Queens who are hired to entertain minors in schools, and all the legislative attempts to mandate that mRNA therapy chemicals be shot into the arms of children, to be "millstone offenses," punishable after death, as follows:

"But whoso shall offend one of these little ones which believe in me, it were better for him that a millstone were hanged about his neck, and that he were drowned in the depth of the sea" (Matthew 24:6).

Moreover, James the Apostle wrote a superior ode to the religion that Dawkins hates by exhorting charity toward the widows and orphans about whom Dawkins says he cares about so very tenderly:

"Pure religion and undefiled before God and the Father is this, To visit the fatherless and widows in their affliction, and to keep himself unspotted from the world" (James 1:27).

What book is more loving and merciful toward the innocent and helpless than the Bible?

Throughout Dawkins' book, the word "Love(s)" appears 86 times; "knowledge," 21; "Logos," 0; "truth," 54; "delusion, 20; "God," 706; and, "Jesus," 86. It is illogical that the the words an atheist most often uses to denounce belief in God are words that beg the question that people use mere Discernment to know how truth exists in their own hearts.

It is also illogical on the part of Dawkins that he did not add that the philosopher Parmenides, as reported by Plato, was the originator of the idea of *Infinite Regress.* The pertinent part of the dialogue with Socrates, the famous "Third-Man Argument," as abridged, is this:

"That is, another idea of greatness will appear, in addition to absolute greatness and the objects which partake of it; and another again in addition to these, by reason of which they are all great; and each of your ideas will no longer be one, but their number will be infinite [but] each of these ideas may be only a thought, which can exist only in our minds then each might be one, without being exposed to the consequences you have just mentioned" [with it being impossible that] is each thought [is] one, but a thought of nothing [but] is impossible [not to be of] something" (*Parmenides*; Plato; 132:a-b; B.C. 380).

The reason why Dawkins did not mention *Parmenides* (other than that he is ignorant of the dialogue) is probably because Socrates, who thus reduced knowledge of Logos to its leading toward an impossible *regress*, also believed that knowledge in general was useless.

During the walk to his execution, Socrates wrongfully argued with the mathematician Theaetetus to this end:

"So neither perception, Theaetetus, nor true opinion, nor reason or explanation combined with true opinion could be knowledge" (*Theaetetus*; Plato; Part 210:a-b; B.C. 380).

Why would a rational person base his *Infinite Regress* argument on a principle that dictates that knowledge is actually useless, other than that Dawkins is attacking the insecurity of readers to be thought of as unreasonable? How can reason exist without knowledge. Again, the Bible that Dawkins hates trumps his level of sanity:

"My people are destroyed for lack of *knowledge*: because thou hast rejected knowledge, I will also reject thee, that thou shalt be no priest to me: seeing thou hast forgotten the law of thy God, I will also forget thy children" (Hosea 4:6).

Dawkins hence is of course preaching his atheistic screed to the choir of programmers of anti-Christian movements, along with insecure Christians who read his words instead what the Bible actually says.

The beautiful warning by Saint Peter the Apostle, in 2 Peter 2 through 3 about willfully irrational people programming their own destruction includes a passage about what happens when lapsed Christians join forces with scoffers and corrupt deceivers, who, "count it pleasure to riot in the day time," confusing everyone who follows them, and finally dying to damnation (2 Peter 2:12-3:18). The passage says:

"While they [Dawkins, *et al*] promise them liberty, they themselves are the servants of corruption: for of whom a man is overcome, of the same is he brought in bondage. For if after they have escaped the pollutions of the world through the knowledge of the Lord and Saviour Jesus Christ, they are again entangled therein, and overcome, the latter end is worse with them than the beginning. For it had been better for them not to have known the way of righteousness, than, after they have known it, to turn from the holy commandment delivered unto them" (2 Peter 2:19-21).

Dawkins was named "Author of the Year" at the 2007 British Book Awards. *The God Delusion* reached the number-four spot on the *New York Times* Bestseller list during December, 2006. Surely realizing that he is very popular, the author later added a call to action in the Preface of his paperback edition:

"And I never tire of drawing attention to society's tacit acceptance of the labelling of small children with the religious opinion of their parents. Atheists need to raise their own consciousness of the anomaly: religious opinion is the one kind of parental opinion that—by almost universal consent can be fastened upon children who are, in truth, too young to know what their opinion really is. There is no such thing as a Christian child: only a child of Christian parents. Seize every opportunity to ram it home" (*ibid*, Dawkins; Preface to the Paperback Edition).

The God Delusion is therefore a book intending that people curse Faith, which is one of the Fruits of the Spirit (Galatians 5:22-23) in that he intends it will rot on the vine. However, the New Testament has a different idea about raising children as Christians:

"And whoso shall receive one such little child in my name receiveth me" (Matthew 24:5). If you raise a children in the Faith you will go to Heaven, therefore. Dawkins does not want people to go to Heaven. He only wants them stop being Christians.

If lukewarm Christians do not cease deigning to abide only the ideas of Christianity with which they feel most comfortable, while turning a blind eye to the hateful faithless mindset besieging traditionalist Christian families in the way Dawkins proposes, they they are acquiescing to thinkers like him and are defying Scripture:

"But the tongue no man can claim; it is an unruly evil full of deadly poison. Therewith bless we God, even the Father; and therewith curse we men, which are made after the *similitude* of God" (James 3:8-9).

Destroying the *Image of God* within a soul creates an entropy within the Psyche, which, without intrinsic love of God, becomes belligerent and dishonest. When the Israelites created the Golden Calf in Exodus 32, their horrible noise was exactly the results of broken self-identification with God, which Moses witnessed. The people were "corrupt" and "warlike."

Modern examples are endless:

"A company called Property Claim Services (PCS) has tracked insurance claims related to civil disorder since 1950. It classifies anything over $25 million in insured losses as a "catastrophe," and reports that the unrest this year (from May 26 to June 8) will cost the insurance industry far more than any prior one" ("Exclusive: $1 billion-plus riot damage is most expensive in insurance history"; Jennifer A. Kingson; *Axios*: Sept. 16, 2020; https://www.axios.com/2020/09/16/riots-cost-property-damage?utm_source=twitter&utm_medium=social&utm_campaign=organic&utm_content=1100; Accessed, June 6, 2023).

Despite what Dawkins has written, it is not delusional to believe what the heart is telling the soul about something being good or evil. How can one's mother be argued with, for that matter, whenever she goes with her "gut" to protect her children?

The Baal-worshiping Israelites, at their spiritual entropy, were engaging in orgies as well as violence in Exodus 32.

"Critical Race Theory is much more than just promoting racism in the classroom. It includes indoctrination on LGBT Agendas, Gender Confusion, and Comprehensive Sex Education promoting pornographic and sexual content to children as young as Kindergarten ("What Moms Need to Know about Critical Race Theory"; https://momsforamerica.us/mom-watch/critical-race-theory/; Accessed, June 20, 2023).

To dramatize the fall of Athens, Plato envisioned the State as the stage of an Aeschylus or Sophocles tragedy, whereof the money grubbing of corrupt politicians within a Democracy motivated citizens into electing an oligarch, a tyrant who regulates with brutality:

"And so the probable outcome of too much freedom is only too much slavery in the individual and the state" (*ibid, The Republic*; Chap. VIII; Sec. 560:e-564:e).

For such matters, Plato attempted a certain soothing Metaphysical "remedy," that our identity is caused by "God" alone, because the Divine created the Form according to which the Demiurge created humans (a merely interesting ontological argument that will be fully described below; *ibid, Timaeus*, Sec. 27:a).

It was a time when Jerusalem meanwhile struggled to survive behind the walls built by Nehemiah and was revolting against the taxation and desecration of the Second Templeposed by Bagoas the Aechmenid (*Antiquities of the Jews;* Josephus; Book 11; Chap. 7; Sec. 1; A.D. 94).

When the father of Alexander the Great, Philip II of Macedon, intervened in the Social War (the revolt against Athens's usurpation of the Second Athenian League), King Artaxerxes III Ochus of Persia demanded that the unpredictable Greeks leave Asia Minor. By the time Plato began to write Timaeus, Alexander the Great, who had cunningly deposed his rival General Charidemus, and overcame the Persians, marched into Jerusalem. However, Alexander's men were confused to see

203

their polytheist leader bow before the High Priest of the General Assembly, Jaddua (who is sometimes referred to by Josephus as Simeon the Just).

Alexander explained to his men that he had dreamed that Jaddua would ensure that all of the males born to priests would be named Alexander (Leviticus Rabbah 13.5; 1105). However, Greece, since the time that Pericles's opulence in the arts was challenged in the Peloponnese by the warriors of Lysander, who dissolved the Delian League, the Greeks were unsure whether they were created by God to be people of might or to become philosophers.

Plato, acknowledging the one Truth of Logos (as he understood it in pagan terms), who has emanated the perfect Forms to which all Matter aspires, framed the solution so that it would stand by itself, as if, "the focus of the discourse is the generation of the world and the creation of man" (*Timaeus*; Plato; 27a; B.C. 360). *Timaeus* employs *Intellectual Regress* embedded in the Ontological Argument for the existence of God, as Plato he had read the *Proslogion*:

"What is that which always is and has no becoming, and what is that which is always becoming and never is?" Plato asked. The "creature" can be described by the flawed sensual man and is always therefore changing the circumstances of his life with great emotion, but God does not need to. He added, "That which is apprehended by intelligence and reason is always in the same state [of perfection], but that which is conceived by opinion with the help of sensation and without reason is always in a process of becoming and perishing and never really is. Now everything that becomes or is created must of necessity be created by some cause, for without a cause nothing can be created" (*Timaeus*; 27d-28a).

Or, as Saint Anselm of Canterbury later correctly said:

204

"Therefore, Lord, not only are You that than which a greater cannot be thought, but You are also something greater than can be thought"(*Proslogion*; Chap. 15; Saint Anselm of Canterbury; 1078)?

Plato contended that, because man is the "fairest of creations, its creator must be the 'best of causes'" (*ibid*, Timaeus; 29:a).

Remember, however, that Plato had held that the "Creator" of people and of the material Universe was the helpful Demiurge, and the "God" who had emanated the Perfect Forms. Thus it is sad to presume that Plato was confused or was merely a rhetorician, who caused a great deal of Materialism and hence the Dialectic-Materialism of Marxist Revolution to happen—all because he failed at tying together the perfection of the Form-building God with the idea of Absolute Truth and Objective Morality.

Where then does the Marxism of the Hungarian billionaire provocateur George Soros, whose "Open Society Foundation" funds countless feats of the *Moral Pathology* and anarcho-terroristic riots across the world, share its roots?

Karl Popper, making famous the term, "Open Society," idealized a society free of the demand for Absolute Truth, by which he said Plato, as the "social engineer" of Athens, himself caused Totalitarianism. Plato, Popper opined, mistakenly promulgated his personal ideas to be knowledge, so that he could concoct a nationalist art for the ruling of men. The error of pretending to know about Forms, warned Popper, shows that "we cannot obtain any knowledge but only opinion" (*The Open Society and its Enemies;* Karl R. Popper; Vol. I: "The Spell of Plato"; Chap. 1-3; Pp. 7-34; Routledge and Kegan Paul, London, UK: 1945).

Plato's opinion that impaired or handicapped people are of low societal worth certainly contrasts itself against the Absolute Truth epitomized by Scripture. The disfigured face of the suffering Messiah (Isaiah 52:14) was indeed Jesus.

Moreover, Plato advised merciless ends for those "not worth rearing" (*The Republic;* Plato; Book V; Sec. 460:c-e; B.C. 380). Jesus said that destroyers of children will suffer "millstone" punishments in hell (Luke 17:2).

Plato prescribed demotion or removal of persons of sociopolitical status, such as "inferior offspring borne to inferior guardians," including the exposure to the elements of inferior infants (*ibid,* Book III; 414:c; 415:d; Book V; 460:c).

Matrimony and the having of offspring by guardians who are too old or too young to have children, should be forbidden from marrying while its transgressors should be demoted and the lesser births be disposed of (*Laws;* Plato; Book V; 721:a; Book VI; 772d; B.C. 380; *ibid,* Republic; 460:e; 461:c; 467).

While it is possible to blame him for Totalitarianism, Plato (or when he speaks as Socrates) also pondered virtue and justice to their ends—of his placing of Logos at the top of all things, as described above. Although Plato advised the showing of piety to all of the gods, he saved ultimate reverence for the Divine, the most high: "In our eyes God will be 'the measure of all things' in the highest degree—a degree much higher than is any 'man' they talk of." Plato exhorted emulation of an Omnibenevolent God is simply rational, adding, "since he is like him, while he that is not temperate is unlike and at enmity—as is also he who is unjust, and so likewise with the rest, by parity of reasoning" (*Laws;* Plato; 716:c-d; B.C. 380).

Plato's theory of *Hyperouranos,* as we recall is the place where perfect Forms exist with the Divine Form-maker, lends itself to the Christian understanding of Eternity, as being a place where time is irrelevant and which was created by God after Heaven came into being (*Timaeus*; Plato; 37:e; B.C. 37; *The Republic;* Plato; Book X; Sec. 620:a-e; 621; B.C. 380).

Popper, disgusted with the Historicism by which publishing is owned by the elite, denounced the "Philosopher-King" idea. To

Plato, to "contrive one of those opportune falsehoods" to the public was "useful as form of remedy or medicine..."so as by one noble lie to persuade if possible the rulers themselves, but failing that the rest of the city" (*ibid, The Republic*; Book III; Sec. 389:b, 414:b).

Considered by Popper to be a eugenicist, it was by the above "Noble Lie" that Plato promulgated the "theory of metals" by which state religion teaches that certain men should be groomed for leadership because their souls are composed of metals which are more precious (i.e., gold and silver) than the metals (i.e., bronze and iron) presumed to exist in other souls (*ibid, The Republic;* Book III: 414:e-415:c).

Wrote Popper, "It is hard to understand why those of Plato's commentators who praise him for fighting against the subversive conventionalism of the Sophists, and for establishing a spiritual naturalism ultimately based on religion, fail to censure him for making a convention, or rather an invention [the similitude of metallurgy], the ultimate basis of religion" (*ibid*, Popper; Chap. 8; P. 142).

Popper wanted a more sensitive less Fascist, nicer, kind of "Open State," saying:

"It is of course true that Plato assumes a Form or Idea of Man; but it is a mistake to think that it represents what all men have in common; rather, it is an aristocratic ideal of a proud super-Greek ; and on this is based a belief, not in the brotherhood of men, but in a hierarchy of ' natures', aristocratic or slavish, in accordance with their greater or lesser likeness to the original, the ancient primogenitor of the human race" (*ibid*, Popper; Chap. 8 Notes; P. 280).

As a side note is it worthwhile to ponder whether is by this elitist Platonic favoritism of princes that the son of the U.S. President Joseph Biden, Hunter, "reached an agreement with federal prosecutors to plead guilty to two misdemeanor counts of willful failure to pay income taxes and enter a pretrial diversionary program on a felony count of possessing a firearm while addicted to drugs" ("Half of Americans think feds gave Hunter Biden preferential treatment, poll shows"; News; Ryan King; *New York Post;* June 22, 2023).

The definition of "Philosopher King" by Plato should thus be put on record, here:

"'Unless', said I, 'either philosophers become kings in our states or those whom we now call our kings and rulers take to the pursuit of philosophy seriously and adequately, and there is a conjunction of these two things, political power and philosophic intelligence, while the motley horde of the natures who at present pursue either apart from the other are compulsorily excluded, there can be no cessation of troubles, dear Glaucon, for our states, nor, I fancy, for the human race either. Nor, until this happens, will this constitution which we have been expounding in theory ever be put into practice within the limits of possibility and see the light of the sun'" *(The Republic;* Plato; Book V; 473:d-e; B.C. 380).

"In fact, Plato's attitude towards religion as revealed by his 'inspired lie' is practically identical with that of Gritias, his beloved uncle, the brilliant leader of the Thirty Tyrants who established an inglorious blood-regime in Athens after the Peloponnesian war" (*ibid*, Popper, P. 142).

What Popper fails to say is that men are not diversely endowed by their wealth or talents, but by Grace. "But unto every one of us is given grace according to the measure of the gift of Christ" (Ephesians 4:7).

Diversity stems from the variations of Grace in people. "And He gave some, apostles; and some, prophets; and some, evangelists; and some, pastors and teachers" (Ephesians 4:11).

As is shown in the parable of the wicked servant, it is solely God's reason alone why the servant was given one talent while another servant was given ten talents. It was the duty of the less-favored worker to invest the penny and thereby hope that God would increase his Grace, but instead he horded the money by engaging it for usury. The Master removed what little Grace the underling had been given and gave the talents to the more favored helper. "For unto every one that hath shall be given, and he shall have abundance: but from him that hath not shall be taken away even that which he hath" (Matthew 25:14-29).

Deprivation of what one perceives to be Grace is thus no excuse for refusing to better oneself. "And cast ye the unprofitable servant into outer darkness: there shall be weeping and gnashing of teeth" (Matthew 25:30).

It must be known that the idea of "Open Society" for all its odes to "proportionate equity of the Laws" (*ibid*, Popper; Chap. 6 Notes; P. 262) is a failure, noting its nominal adoption by atheist Marxists, because it does not abide Christ. "Every good gift and every perfect gift is from above, and cometh down from the Father of lights, with Whom is no variableness, neither shadow of turning" (James 1:17).

Hannah Arendt, the German-Jewish historian who took permanent refuge in America after fleeing Nazi-occupied Paris interestingly praised Plato's lack of sympathy for rhetorical fallacy: "Plato, in his famous fight against the ancient Sophists, discovered that their 'universal art of enchanting the mind by arguments' (*ibid*, *Phaedrus*; 261) had nothing to do with truth but aimed at opinions which by their very nature are changing, and which are valid only 'at the time of the agreement and as long as the agreement lasts' (*ibid*, *Theaetetus*; 172; *The Origins of Totalitarianism*; Hannah Arendt; Chap. 1; P. 9; Harcourt, New York: 1948; Reprint: 1979).

"[Plato] also discovered the very insecure position of truth in the world, for from 'opinions comes persuasion and not from truth' (*ibid*, *Phaedrus*; 260). The most striking difference between ancient and modern sophists is that the ancients were satisfied with a passing victory of the argument at the expense of truth, whereas the moderns want a more lasting victory at the expense of reality" (*ibid*, Arendt).

"What is truth," asked Pontius Pilate of Jesus (John 18:38).

Modern educators and statesmen have exploited this whining of "Quid est veritas?" since long before Pilate or the invention of the Internet.

Socrates, en route to his cup of poison, gave word of his ultimate existentialism/nihilism to his chatty mathematician friend Theaetetus, that there just no way of knowing anything for sure about anything (quoted yet again below, because it begs the question why the human brain needs belief in God):

"So neither perception, Theaetetus, nor true opinion, nor reason or explanation combined with true opinion could be knowledge" (*Theatetus*; Plato; Part 210:a-b; B.C. 360).

The cup of poison was of course drunk by Socrates as his attestation that allegiance to the State was more important than defending knowledge of Truth and even promised everybody that his "Daimon" (i.e., informative demon) did not intervene to help coax him into accepting his slaughter (*Apology*; Plato; Part 31:c-d; B.C. 350).

The tracing of history therefore leads orthodox Christian thinkers toward the presumption that disinterested engineers, lukewarm lawmakers, and detached parents will continue to ignore that the programmers of the Internet, of curricula, and of social norms will sideline civilization's abiding of Objective Morality unless Christ is put at the centrality of all thinking. The constant malfeasance regarding institutionalized evil and systemic atheism ensures that demonic ideas will continue to masquerade as forces of goodness.

"Woe unto them that call evil good, and good evil; that put darkness for light, and light for darkness; that put bitter for sweet, and sweet for bitter" (Isaiah 5:20)!

Even the wise strong Peter, whose Epistle warned that Satan does not sleep but is, without rest or pause, seducing humans (who stay awake with Lucifer as they, for example, feed the Internet with things that the dragon of Artificial Intelligence teaches them to think, say, and do), needed protection from Christ: "And the Lord said, Simon, Simon, behold, Satan hath desired to have you, that he may sift you as wheat" (Luke 22:31).

Behind every pixel, graphic, and chain of computer code, Satan is waiting to devour people (1 Peter 5:8). Consumers are easily duped:

"And no wonder! For Satan himself transforms himself into an angel of light" (2 Corinthians 11:14).

The horrors of *pornea, eros,* and war are constantly passed off as being a progressive cup that is filled with Martyrs' blood (Revelation 17) while the spirit of the Antichrist is murdering Faith, Hope, Love, and the Image of God within uninformed or lukewarm Christians: "And they bend their tongues like their bow for lies: but they are not valiant for the truth upon the earth; for they proceed from evil to evil, and they know not me, saith the Lord" (Isaiah 9:3).

At every turn, God's saving presence in human life must be attested to, praised, given thanksgiving and tirelessly obeyed (Galatians 6:9), because this very mindset projects the very highest epistemology:

"Now unto the King eternal, immortal, invisible, the only wise God, be honour and glory for ever and ever. Amen" (1 Timothy 1:17).

The *Intelligent Design* argument for the Existence of God contends that evidence of causality proves that God exists. It must be corrected here as well

However, because the Nihil cannot be witnessed from which it could be traced that God "caused" the Universe, Genesis 1 cannot depend on the science to prove its Truth. Focusing on nature and cosmology, an anthropologist, who was the curator of the Early Man exhibit at the University of Pennsylvania Museum, wrote with some good sense:

> "The sheer act of faith that the universe possessed order and could be interpreted by rational minds.... The philosophy of experimental science...began its discoveries and made use of its method in the faith, not the knowledge, that it was dealing with a rational universe controlled by a Creator who did not act upon whim nor interfere with the forces He had set in operation. The experimental method succeeded beyond man's wildest dreams but the faith that brought it into being owes something to the Christian conception of the nature of God. Itis surely one of the curious paradoxes of history that science, which profession- ally has little to do with faith, owes its origins to an act of faith that the universe can be rationally interpreted, and that science today is sustained by that assumption" (*Darwin's Century: Evolution and the Men Who Discovered It*; Loren Eiseley; Chap. III; P. 62; Doubleday Anchor, Garden City, New York, 1961).

Although Faith without good Works enjoys no real examples in life (James 2:14-26), man cannot believe in the God Who created Life by looking at his own good deeds or any virtuous reality that he could profess to know unless he has Faith (Ephesians 2:8-22).

- Chapter Twelve -
Materialist Errors That Promise Fake Immortality

As stated earlier, virtuous rhetoric is held "persuasive" when it employs three kind of speech, according to Aristotle: "The first depends upon the moral character of the speaker, the second upon putting the hearer into a certain frame of mind [Ethos], the third upon the speech itself [Pathos], in so far as it proves or seems to prove [Logos]" (*Rhetoric*; Aristotle; Book I; Chap. 2; Sec. 3; Book III; B.C. 350). Sound language must be able to persuade the student to believe in the existence of God.

Reason must therefore employ valid rhetoric, or as Aristotle defined persuasive speech, as *pisteis* (πίστῐς to cause trust in others or build their faith in principles by means of persuasion). *Diēgēsis*, or narration, benefits reader comprehension by guiding the student through an argument by referring a belief-system based on Logos. Narration differs between epideictic, judicial, and deliberative narratives (*ibid*, *Rhetoric;* Book III; Chap. 16).

Using narrative structure, *Diēgēsis*, by its linear reasoning produces a study of praise or of blame known as the *Epideictic*, itself a "Finite" Form of rhetoric which, for Christian uses, easily lends itself to the time of the Passover until the Ascension, in the Book of Revelations written by the Apostle of Logos, John.

That is, John narrated the transforming of the public's blame against the suffering servant into Christendom's praising of Logos, the very risen Christ, after Pharisaical judgement and deliberation were commuted to the Resurrection and then Reign of Jesus in the New Jerusalem.

The public judgement and sentencing against Christ was thereby framed through this rhetorical treatment of the Passion using classical narrative, which also describes God's Omnipotence through the smallest possible "Integer" of the Lamb, exponentiating into a view of the Almighty.

As a sidenote, the Aristotelian "reversal of fortune" known as "Peripeteia" is happening here in glowing colors. The Peripety happened harshly against the Pharisees.

This ancient term predicates the irony of God's teaching of harsh "Cognitive-Dissonance" kinds of lessons during the naturally instructive "walk" through life, which Aristotle was implying how people learn best, during their walks through life (*Poetics*; Aristotle; 1452:a; B.C. 350).

Thus, as with all those merry virtuous video podcasters who ask their guests to tell them what anything "means," and the walking teachers and students who are seen in the Fresco by the painter Raphael *(Scuola di Atene;* Raphael; 1511) alike, good things are learned during dialogues that are spared a physically or emotionally overbearing or accursed Platonic Form of Law.

During their Exile in Neo-Babylon and Persia, God's chosen realized that the Law was loved more than God. Nehemiah thus joined the elders while rebuilding the Temple to attach a curse upon this fetishizing of legalism: "They clave to their brethren, their nobles, and entered into a curse, and into an oath, to walk in God's law, which was given by Moses the servant of God, and to observe and do all the commandments of the Lord our Lord, and His judgments and His statutes; And that we would not give our daughters unto the people of the land, not take their daughters for our sons" (Nehemiah 10:29-30).

After ten years of ardent rule, during which he evicted from the Temple storerooms the financial office of the Ammonite,

Tobiah (a money making agent for the Temple and a worshipper of Moloch) Nehemiah had the Temple re-purified (Nehemiah 13:9). As it stood, the accursed Law was necessary for survival until the Jews could become delivered from this juridical paradox of the "cursed Law" with the Messiah being foretold them by Isaiah.

The rooms therefore were continually being swept clean of idolatry until increasing numbers of demons than ever before kept coming and leaving the Temple in a worser state than it had ever been in (Luke 11:24-26).

By the time of Christ, Alexander the Great, Bagoas the Achaemenid and Antiochus V Epiphanes the Seleucid put pagan statues in the sanctuary; Alexander the Great was received as an unclean ally by the High Priest Jaddua who consequently dissolved the Great Assembly, just as Pompey the Great of Rome conquered the Hasmonean Dynasty and set up the Herods. By the time Emperor Tiberius sent Pontius Pilate to govern Judea, the last trace of sacerdotal dignity left in Judea was the interpretation of the Law, practiced with its accursed pedanticism, by which the Sanhedrin condemned Jesus.

Cadencing Isaiah 53, *Peripeteia* fell upon these persecutors, whose murderous arrogance became severely—damaged not actually by the fall of Judea in A.D. 70, but by Christ's answering of "Maranatha," (מרנאתא), the Aramaic word by which the meek beg Jesus to return with vengeance against the wicked (Revelation 22:20).

The suffering Lamb of Isaiah 53 is sentenced to death and He dies on the Cross in John 19. Indeed all people are *sentenced* on Judgement Day during which Christ is seen to the saved eye as being the King (Revelation 19:11-21). He begins the thousand-year reign in Revelation 20:4. He thereafter commences a New Heaven and a New Earth (Revelation 21:1).

While the "filthy-still," are the Reprobate who are damnable, the Elect have been Saved (Revelation 22:11-17; *Rhetoric*; Aristotle; Book III; Chap. 16; Sec. 11; B.C. 350). The Liturgy of the Hours and that of the Eucharist trace the converting of sentencing, from earthly juridical to heavenly ascension, throughout this narrative. It concerns the publicly-blamed Jesus who becomes, for our enlightened hearts, our Omnipresent Savior, for whose Supper we deliberate the sharing of the Bread and Wine to be the Propitiation of His suffering. All in all, this is an Aristotelian Diēgēsis of the *Form* of the Mass *(Book of Common Prayer;* U.S. Episcopal General Convention of 1928; Anglican Parishes Association, Reprint 1996, Pp. 67-89).

To destroy in people the Image of God, Who made humans from nothingness, and replace belief in *Creatio Ex* Nihilo with suppositions of so-called Emanations out of the branches of the Sefirot, a cynical leap must dart out betwixt the realms of Tohu and Tikun. To make people presume that a lesser Creator erected man from *Form* and *Matter*, a leap into Gnosticism and its outgrowth of Theosophy and witchcraft must overtake the Intellect from all corners of society.

That is after dabbling in Platonism and then crossing into the false supremacy of Gnostic "Higher Knowledge," God and all moral expectations can be replaced with base Phenomenology.

Honesty must be overruled by Plato's idea from the *Theaetetus* that knowledge can never be justified. All conversations and receipt of news must be received over the Internet. Happiness had better come from being entertained by the Marvel Cinematic Universe, or the "Metaverse" of Facebook, or in the virtue-signaling perceived on TikTok, Instagram, YouTube, and Twitter. There is only the refabricated pixel world of Phenomenology, ready to please the CGI ghosts of Edmund Husserl and Martin Heidegger.

In hindsight, Moral "Truth" would merely a reverberation of physics relative to Platonic Forms or Ideals. Nothing would be real.

The consumer is already numb.

- Chapter Thirteen -

How the Cult of Technological Singularity is Yet Another Neoplatonist, Gnostic, Satanic Ideation of Flawed "Metaphysics"

It has been a practice since ancient times to refute the idea that God did not create Himself but has always existed.

Plotinus, in the Third Century, criticized *Unmoved* or *Prime Mover,* or *First* or *Final Cause* principle of Aristotle, which the Neoplatonist contended was flawed by *Infinite Regress.*

Aristotle's *movement* principle as it has been mentioned throughout this book, puts forth the following phrase:

"The final cause, then, produces motion by being loved, but all other things move by being moved" (*Metaphysics*; Aristotle; Book XII; Sec. 1072:b; B.C. 350).

God, Aristotle said, was the invisible center of a planetary system of 47 to 55 concentric spheres revolving around the visible Earth. (*ibid, Metaphysics:* Sec. 1073b:1-1074a:13). He added:

"Such, then, is the first principle upon which depend the sensible universe and the world of nature. And its life is like the best which we temporarily enjoy. It must be in that state always (which for us is impossible), since its actuality is also pleasure" (*ibid, Metaphysics;* Sec. 1072:b*).

A loving, always-present *mover* of everything is then the epistemological root of Ontology, in that God determines the origination of all causality and action in the Cosmos.

Plotinus argued that Logos could not have created Itself through such *Intellection* (by God thinking about Himself).

As if God ever needed to think about creating Himself, and we should find ourselves defending our Faith against fancy thinkers believing that they have caught Christians in another bind.

"Before the mountains were brought forth, or ever thou hadst formed the earth and the world, even from everlasting to everlasting, thou art God" (Psalm 90:2).

OK, fine, non-believers say—but what about the time *before* the Universe and when people were created; did the Creator *create* Himself? We answer, hopefully:

"For of Him, and through Him, and to Him, are all things: to whom be glory forever. Amen" (Romans 11:36).

We still seem to find ourselves locked inside the *Infinite Regress* of using God's existence to affirm and prove God's existence.

The presence of Melchizedek, the *Theophany* of the Christ God, had neither parents nor a beginning nor an end (Hebrews 7:3), representing the Logos of Eternity, so that the Christendom would "understand that I am He: before Me there was no God formed, neither shall there be after Me" (Isaiah 43:10).

Moreover, the answer was quite clear since God told Moses:

"I am that I am" (Exodus 3:14).

When a benevolent father commands his daughter, "Don't stay out late," there can be no arguing with him. "Dad" needs no explanation for his authority because his dominion over his family is unquestioned and thus his daughter would never think to question it (that is—unless she were taught by devious educators to do so). Parenthood therefore rules because of this *Apophatic Theology:* It is *negation epistemology.* It does not have to be explained.

That is, any principle epitomizing the Love of the Father (such as parental adoration) is justified true belief because we do not know why it is true, because it merely *is* true.

Anything could be questioned just for the purpose of causing insecurity in the thinker—even the fear of heights, or one's favorite color. However, it should not be thought to be inconvenient that we do not know why some things are true when we know them to be "good in themselves," as Aristotle said above. It is riotous that we should ever be forced to say why.

In fact, as if to make matters "worse" for people who are always being accused of being irrational idiots, namely Christians, all causality stems from God's capacity to cause Himself happiness—a fact that is again rooted in Aristotelian philosophy:

Happiness, that is the "the prize and end of virtue must clearly be supremely good—it must be something divine and blissful" (*Nicomachean Ethics;* Aristotle; Sec. 1099b:1; B.C. 350). The "final desirable good" (*ibid*, Sec. 1097:a) which is happiness, is the ultimate good of God's happiness because it is "supremely blessed, though on the human scale of bliss," meaning that it is Finitely understood (*ibid*, Sec. 1011:a-20), but this cosmic root of joy is to be comprehended according to Scripture, as follows:

"Delight thyself also in the Lord: and He shall give thee the desires of thine heart" (Psalms 37:4).

Happiness, Aristotle said, "seems to be borne out by the fact that it is a first principle or starting-point, since all other things that all men do are done for its sake; and that which is the first principle and cause of things good we agree to be something honorable and divine" (*ibid, Nicomachean Ethics*; Sec. 1102:a).

"For it is God which worketh in you both to will and to do of his good pleasure" (Philippians 2:13).

Benevolent pleasure, which is the causal "activity" of "Encomia" (i.e., praising), honors the divine source of that goodness which is "good in itself" and of all "things good in themselves," that come from God "that is the cause of their being good" and actualizes "the mere potentiality" of happiness and thus of thanksgiving *(ibid, Nicomachean;* Sec. 1101b:20).

As Traditionalist Anglicans engage *Encomia*, "We yield thee unfeigned thanks and praise for the return of seed-time and harvest, for the increase of the ground and the gathering in of the fruits thereof, and for all the other blessings of thy merciful providence bestowed upon this nation and people" ("A Thanksgiving to Almighty God for the Fruits of the Earth and all the other Blessings of his merciful Providence"; Thanksgivings; *The Book of Common Prayer;* P. 50; U.S. Episcopal Church: 1928).

Despite the fact that God has always existed, and because Christians are simply following the Bible and their own *Spiritual Discernment* to believe in the Word, how should Christians respond whenever they are being handed a mind bender by a non-Christian Neoplatonist?

For starters, it means that we are being confronted by a rhetorician who has no desire to be saved by Christ and is basically going *Gnostic-Lite* (it will explained shortly how Gnosticism is the heretical end of Neoplatonism).

221

The following passage is where Plotinus stated that God cannot be older than the Universe:

"Not by its thinking God does God come to be; not by its thinking Movement does Movement arise. Hence it is an error to call the Ideas intellections in the sense that, upon an intellectual act in this Principle, one such Idea or another is made to exist or exists. No: the object of this intellection must exist before the intellective act [must be the very content not the creation of the Intellectual-Principle]. How else could that Principle come to know it: certainly not [as an external] by luck or by haphazard search" *(The Six Enneads;* Plotinus; Ninth Ennead; Seventh Tractate: "The Intellectual-Principle, the Ideas, and the Authentic Existence"; Sec. 7; A.D. 250).

Plotinus therewith expressed that Aristotle's "God" was a half-baked idea of an immortal being who gets caught up constantly reverting back to itself.

Christians know the Father to be the Loving God always a loving the Beloved. He is the Mover, who is thereby only creating, or moving, Himself and others but not creating Himself. Plotinus, however implies "The One" being not merely ἔρως (God), but ridiculously the *objectively moved*, the recipient of external action, αὐτοῦ ἔρως (the person) without explaining why movement must always include causation from an outside source. He was harping on the following statement that had been stated the much-nicer pagan, Aristotle:

"The necessary in nature, then, is plainly what we call by the name of matter, and the changes in it. Both causes must be stated by the physicist, but especially the end; for that is the cause of the Matter, not vice versa; and the end is 'that for the sake of which', and the beginning starts from the definition or essence" (*Physics*; Aristotle; Book II; Part 9; B.C. 350).

222

However, it must be noted that Aristotle neither said that God created Himself, nor listed Intellection as being one of his "Four Causes of Creation": Matter (e.g., Mother and Father); Form (e.g., Holy Matrimony and Holy Baptism); Efficient/Agent (e.g. Mother and the caused object, of Baby); and, Final End or Purpose (e.g., Mother starting a Christian family; *ibid, Physics*; Book II; Part 3). Remember—Aristotle was not chasing down *causes* beyond mentioning the First Mover, and was only reporting on the physical world.

Plotinus was nevertheless accusing Aristotle of circular reasoning, the *Infinite Regress*, by claiming that God could not be known to exist by Causality or Purpose, if there was no Matter yet to start with. He ranted that no objective Form, Cause, or Final End, could be said to have existed according to which the existence God could be proven (*ibid*, Plotinus).

He causes doubt as if to say: If an intelligible object is presumed to be the "First Existent," but nothing except itself has been created yet, then how could it be *both* the principle of causality and the object or purpose of that causality at the *same* time—unless proving God's existence therefore has nothing to do with Intelligence? (*ibid*, Plotinus; III; 9).

Plotinus was expressing that without the cause having an object for its action, God had nothing to work with, no "clay" to get His hands on, and, as Aristotle admitted, "so circular demonstration is clearly not possible in the unqualified sense of 'demonstration', but only possible if 'demonstration' be extended to include that other method of argument which rests on a distinction between truths prior to us and truths without qualification prior" (*Posterior Analytics;* Aristotle; Book I; Part 3; B.C. 350).

In simpler terms, Plotinus charges that it must be a *given*, that Matter must have existed at the time God and the physical atomistic Universe came into being. He had no proof for his own idea, which is itself a *Infinite Regress*. That is, Aristotle, seen in the preceding paragraph, had admitted to being held to the *Infinite Regress* but Plotinus, who constantly referred back to his own idea of God and Matter comprising "The One," never did. To Aristotle, what cannot be known is an opportunity for honesty and the virtue of further explanation. Platonists and all materialists demand to have a physical source for everything.

Neoplatonism, which refers itself always back to the Platonic Ideal of the Hyperouranos Forms or *Solids*, limits itself to promulgating the superiority of Plato's self-referential definition of Creation, while holding the Aristotelian concept of primary causality to be in error. This reflects the epistemological error of attempting an objective definition about reality based on one's self-justified "true belief," without being able to demonstrate objectively why basing causality on a concept of Faith is wrongful.

While the latter is no more redolent of *Infinite Regress* than the former, Faith posits the superior argument because of its sincerity. In fact, Saint Paul the Apostle was basically expressing that the Ontological Argument holds Faith to be an *a priori* truth akin to 2 + 2 = 4.

Saint Paul was opposing the Gnostic idea that Logos needed to be divided up between the "Creator" and the "Demiurge," a notion by the Hellenistic Jew, Philo of Alexandria. Paul wrote, ""Now faith is the substance of things hoped for, the evidence of things not seen" (Hebrews 11:1).

Philo was proclaiming the Platonic "God" of the -called ideals, sharing creational duties with the lesser sculptor, the Demiurge. This partnership fit with the principle from Heraclitus that Logos is the union of opposites, by which Philo said man, who is the "clay from the Earth" is the "moulded work of the Artificer but not his offspring" (*Quis Rerum Divinarum Heres Sit;* Philo of Alexandria; Allegorical Interpretations; Part I; Sec. 29-32; A.D. 50).

Philo's blasphemous attempt to unite Judaism with paganism was a perfect indication that "the Jews require a sign but the Greeks seek after wisdom" (1 Corinthians 1:22-25). It was as if Philo was attempting to be a bipartisan prophet who gave both.

However, Christians do not regard *Infinite Regress* to be a deficit in philosophy but a strength in theology. Said Saint Paul, "Therefore I take pleasure in infirmities, in reproaches, in necessities, in persecutions, in distresses for Christ's sake: for when I am weak, then am I strong" (2 Corinthians 12:10).

In matters of heresy and heterodoxy, however, *Infinite Regress* is appalling. For instance, if a Prosperity Preacher quotes his own prior-published foundational idea that Jesus wants Christians to become rich as his means of "proving" that he should raise funds to purchase a new jet airplane so that he can use it to preach across the globe and to become richer, then he is committing *Infinite Regress.*

If the preacher said that buying the plane would make him richer to prove the foundational premise of the "Prosperity Gospel" as it reverts back to why he will be doing "God's will" by becoming richer and buying new planes to do so, Aristotle himself would expose the rhetorical fallacy this way:

"The first school [of demonstrating Truth from true premises], assuming that there is no way of knowing other than by demonstration, maintain that an *Infinite Regress* is involved, on the ground that if behind the prior stands no primary [e.g., not being able to prove objectively that preaching depends on jet ownership], we could not know the posterior through the prior (wherein they are right, for one cannot traverse an infinite series): if on the other hand-they say-the series terminates and there are primary premises, yet these are unknowable because incapable of demonstration, which

225

according to them is the only form of knowledge" (*ibid,* *Analytics)*

Aristotle's solution was therefore merely to work with what can be known. If limited to logic alone, God would be seen as having no cause to prove and no purpose to achieve because Matter and Form were not yet created. He could never be called a *causer* or *mover* of Matter and He would therefore not exist in fulfillment of any purpose that ever could be credited, being unable even to create Himself! Although this is perfectly logical, it is untrue, thankfully.

It is Absolute Truth that God does exist and it is Moral Objectivity therefore to belief that He does save us through Jesus. The Bible tells us how. As Aristotle implied, we'll just work with this. And, it's fine.

Therefore, while it cannot be denied that Plotinus was right to say that Aristotle's Unmoved/First Mover does not prove God's existence according to demonstration or causality, Faith is a better argument. Aristotle, who did not know Christ, went on to say within the same chapter that bothering to engage such circular reasoning was "frivolous" and "lacking in "reciprocity" between cause and effect. He added that demonstration was not available for every concept and hence he just did not bother with the idea. He simply continued to analyze Matter in the "posterior"—which refers to Creation that has already been created. The name of his book, after all, was *Posterior Analytics.* Plotinus was spinning his wheels in starting an argument that Aristotle had already said was not worth arguing about. (*ibid,* Analytics).

That is, the opportunistic Plotinus blasphemed by saying that Matter, Form, and God are as *old* as God is, and are eternal, like God. Any why did he do this? Because he obviously liked *Infinite Regress,* himself.

He called his philosophy "The One" and insisted that proving the existence of the Divine has no need of Intellection:

"We may be told that this engendering Principle is the One-and-All. But, at that, it must be either each separate entity from among all or it will be all things in the one mass" (*The Six Enneads;* Plotinus; Ninth Ennead; Seventh Tractate: "The Intellectual-Principle, the Ideas, and the Authentic Existence"; Sec. 7; A.D. 250).

Therefore what is the point behind anti-Christian thinking other than that it stirs up the mindset to believe that one's self-referential ideas are somehow more logical than the argument from Faith.

The offspring of Plato—the Neo-Platonists, Gnostics, and New-Thought idealogues—posit that The One is supreme because it is neither "principle" nor "source," nor is it divisible or the "sum" of anything. It is not the "aggregate" of the Pleroma (Colossians 2:9). Instead, God and the Platonic solids and all of Matter are "Emanations" of God generating idealism out of the Hyperouranos, into the Universe, the soil, the air, people, animals—the whole *Anima Mundi* or *Soul of the Universe* that comprises everything as Totality emanates as The One thing (*ibid*, Plotinus; *Timaeus*; Plato; 30:b-d).

We must add that being able to refute one philosopher over another does not make a person into a Christian. In fact, Plotinus's argument against Intellection and his hypocritical exposing of *Infinite Regress* ironically support the principle of Faith-Based Reasoning for any religion by stimulating thinking. But Neoplatonism also supports Satanism, whose adherents are clearly not using their minds but only their animal wills to refer back to the physical world, the "ideal" form of their libido:

227

"But these, as natural brute beasts, made to be taken and destroyed, speak evil of the things that they understand not; and shall utterly perish in their own corruption" (2 Peter 2:12).

The problem with admiring the rhetoric of Plotinus (as did Saint Augustine of Hippo) is that he not only replaces Genesis with the "everything-being-emanated-within-The-One" proposition, but places God on the same level as Form and Matter, as if excusing himself from proving that emanations are true, by stating that Intellection, literally knowledge and the cogito, have no place in epistemology.

Being forbidden to use knowledge to express that God exists and that He has created Matter and Form from the Nihil does not prove that the Christian God has *not* created these elements.

While Aristotle admitted that he could not prove the First Cause concept, Plotinus certainly did not bother to keep trying to, and gave the "sour grapes" rationale for his failure, by basically saying that the Intellect is useless anyway by doing away with Intellection, just as his hero, Plato, did in the *Theaetetus.*

There is so much more to enjoying one's Faith than being able to win arguments that God exists and that He creates everything. Morality stems from the Metaphysical basis of the Decalogue, truly. Because God, who is distinct from people (not being part of any atomic Oneness, etc.), has no equal, and has thus created *Objective Morality* and *Absolute Truth*, there is plenty of room for joy. If God were equal to atoms, then He would have no business expecting moral behavior from anybody. Moreover, one could as well equally expect a joyous event such as the birth of one's child to be a matter of constantly explaining why we are the parents of the child. We merely *are* the parents. There is more to religion and Love than substantiating one's reasons for believing and loving.

In such a case as engaging a "proving ground," the dutiful causality of being fruitful and multiplying positions a person to enjoy the virtuous things that come from God's Omnibenevolence and Omnipotence. God's greatness depends on none of the "causes" cited by Aristotle, nor intellectually requires the nominating of sufficient reasons as to how or why God exists. Christians hold these truths not to be self-evident, but God-evident.

Why do virtuous parents labor to protect their children from evil on the Internet? Sadly, the adversaries of God demand explanations for why pornography and transhumanist/transgenderist material are morally wrong. People would merely be what Lucretius said we are, merely formations of atoms, doing as our wills dictate, as the "whole of the law"—a physical Law.

"Every man and every woman is a star" was the "constitution" by Aleister Crowley when he aped Plato's star/soul assignment (*ibid, Phaedo*; Sec. 41:d-42:c). Intending that satanic darkness would enjoy its cultural springtime, Crowley was disguising his ideas in angelic light, yet still his thinking was always recognizable to true Christian Discernment as being the rotten fruit of foul ideas. "Trash" items are knowable by their visible deceit, filth, and the utter perversity and violence of satanic accomplishments (*The Book of the Law;* Aleister Crowley; Chap. 1; Verse 3; Samuel Weiser, Newburyport, MA: 1976; Matthew 7:16).

"Therefore it is no great thing if His ministers also be transformed as the ministers of righteousness; whose end shall be according to their works" (2 Corinthians 11:15).

"The [Lucifer-based] club, for kids five to twelve, promises science and community service projects, nature activities, and tons of fun. 'Educatin' with Satan', as they say" ("Pennsylvania gets its first after-school Satan Club this week. In Hellertown"; Rita Giordano; News; *Philadelphia Inquirer,* May 8, 2023).

Governed by the willful "momentum" of heartlessness, "Love is the law, [but] love under will" (*ibid*, Crowley; Chap 1; Verse 57).

"And no marvel; for Satan himself is transformed into an angel of light. Therefore it is no great thing if his ministers also be transformed as the ministers of righteousness; whose end shall be according to their works" (2 Corinthians 11:14-15).

"Do as thou wilt shall be the whole of the law" (*ibid*, Crowley; Chap 1; Verse 40).

The Seven Gifts of the Holy Spirit instead include: Knowledge; Wisdom; Counsel; Understanding; Fear of the Lord; Piety; and Fortitude (Isaiah 11:1-2; Summa Theologica; Saint Thomas Aquinas; Part II: Sec. 1; Question 68: "The Gifts"; 1274).

However, attempting to replace the Holy Spirit in the heart with Emanations of Platonic Atomism, are Theosophy and Satanism. They wait right around the corner from Plotinus.

Keeping in sight the infamous blaspheming by Crowley and "Madame" Blavatsky, it would do Satanists no harm in accepting that piety and fear of God is where Wisdom begins (Proverbs 9:10).

The Big Bang Theory, long used in opposition to *Creatio Ex Nihil* ironically was invented by a clever Roman Catholic Priest, Georges Lemaître. He was the astronomer who postulated the idea of the "Primeval Atom" from which God created the world. Actually Fr. Lemaître's theory holds that Creation was actually not an instantaneous explosion but a slow occurrence that took place during millions of years ("The Beginning of the World from the Point of View of Quantum Theory"; George Lemaitre; *Nature*; Vol. 127; P. 706; May 9, 1931).

A chapter in Blavatsky's big stupid book reflects the author's hasty refutation of all knowledge: "The Logos and Satan are One" (*The Secret Doctrine;* Helena Petrovna Blavatsky; Volume II: Anthropogenesis; Sec. XIX; P. 515; 1888).

"To the metrological key to the symbolism of the Hebrews, which reveals numerically the geometrical relations of the Circle (All-Deity) to the Square, Cube, Triangle, and all the integral emanations of the divine area, may be added the theogonic Key. This Key explains that Noah, the deluge-Patriarch, is in one aspect the permutation of the Deity (the Universal Creative Law), for the purpose of the formation of our Earth, its population, and the propagation of life on it, in general." (*ibid,* Blavatsky; Volume II: Anthropogenesis; Sec. XXV: The Mysteries of the Hebdomad; P. 595; 1888).

Blavatsky named her Satanism "Theosophy." It was a Neoplatonic and Satanic occultist religion. Hailing the demonic god who ate his children, Saturn, she wrote, "Saturn (Satan), astronomically, 'is the seventh and last in the order of macrocosmic Emanation, being the circumference of the kingdom of which Phoebus (the light of wisdom, also the Sun) is the center'." She admitted, "The Gnostics were right, then, in calling the Jewish god 'an angel of matter', or he who breathed (conscious) life into Adam, and he whose planet was Saturn" (*ibid,* Blavatsky; Volume II; Sec. X; P. 235; 1888).

Promulgating a Pythagoric ascetic devotion to material sovereignty, while attempting to refute the concept of the Prime Mover, she wrote, "Pythagoras and Plato, who proceeded from the Universals [ideal Forms], are now shown to be more learned in the light of modern science, than was Aristotle. For he opposed and denounced the revolution of the Earth" [with his geocentric view] (*ibid,* Blavatsky; Volume II; Sec. VI; P. 153; 1888). For Blavatsky, it was key to make Form and Matter higher than the Prime Mover, so that the image of Satan could replace the image of the Father in human hearts. Although it is not expedient to replace happiness and goodness in the soul with hateful ugliness, the sheer stupidity of brainless rebellion is surely "fun."

The Father, she said—by debasing the fact of the Hypostasis of the Holy Trinity into the disintegrating status of Matter—was following the same degenerative cycle by which Chronos hurled Jupiter into the Cosmos, or by which the Aryans sent Siva into the "abyss of darkness." Blasphemy is therefore, "equivalent to saying that God and Satan were identical."

She muttered that the Word is merely relative to any mythology of other cultures: "For since the Logos (or God) is the aggregate of that once divine Host accused of having fallen, it would follow that the Logos and Satan are one. Yet such was the real philosophical view of the now disfigured tenet in antiquity. The Verbum, or the "Son," was shown in a dual aspect by the Pagan Gnostics" *(ibid,* Blavatsky; Volume II: Anthropogenesis; Sec. XIX; P. 515; 1888).

This idea of an "aggregate," purports a morally relativistic ethics. This idea of "The One" stems from philosophical ambivalence toward good in its opposition versus evil as if both are equally and co-morally emitted by God, as taken from the errant Cosmology of that dialogue, *Parmenides.*

Plato's relativism suited Blavatsky tidily. That ancient work (as stated above), was helping her argue that charity or cruelty, Heaven and hell, are really two parts of the same thing, namely the Antichrist Father: "And therefore whether we take being and the other, or being and the one, or the one and the other, in every such case we take two things, which may be rightly called both" (*Parmenides*; Plato; Transl. Jowett, Benjamin; Sec. 143:b-d; B.C. 370).

By the same flip philosophy oozes out the Nihilism of Socrates' drinking down the cup of poison, just because doing so exemplifies patriotism, the obverse side of the Crowley "Will" law, which is to abide the will of more socio-politically powerful people. Cowardice and moral acquiescence are necessary for such Platonists because arguing on behalf of Truth goes against the implied path of least resistance, that of lukewarm Moral Relativism, which based on the costly love of luxury, indolence, and complacent selfishness.

As stated earlier, Justified True Belief to Socrates in the dialogue *Theaetetus*, was an impossible attainment and thus is any deliberation on behalf of a clear understanding of Justice also moot. Christians who wonder about whether or not to accept a fake vaccination filled with body-altering poisons should read this dialogue to see how smart a cowardly government-worshiping person can sound while allowing his God-evident sense of righteousness to be vanquished (*Theatetus*; Plato; Part 210:a-b; B.C. 380).

It is also worthwhile, times being what they are, when contemplating the Metaphysics of any philosopher to ponder whether he and his conversant(s) are homosexual. It is strongly implied that Phaedrus had been having sex with Lysias all afternoon "behind the wall" when his eponymous dialogue with Socrates begins. Lysias also brags that he can attain sex with a male youth without being in love with him (*Phaedrus*; Plato; 222a, 231a; B.C. 380). In *Phaedrus* and the *Symposium*, the hero Achilles is said by Lysias to be the "lover" of Patroklos in the Iliad (*Symposium*; Plato; 179:a-e; B.C. 375). The *Symposium* is a philosophical debate held during a banquet invoked to honor Eros, the demon goddess of lust. Therefore, it is necessary to find out who and "what" the teachers of our children are.
f
God gives up such people to their reprobate minds especially when they corrupt youth (Romans 1:28; Luke 17:2). In colleges, it is nevertheless taught that Socrates was unfairly accused of "corrupting the youth" and "not believing in the gods in whom the city believes, but in other daimonia that are novel" to Athens" (*Apology*; Plato; 24b; B.C. 380).

However, Socrates was corruptive to people in general because his relativistic approach to Matter and Form as if both elements were on an equal ontological level with God. His materialistic Cosmology left no room for Absolute Truth to curb filth.

Saint Paul the Apostle wrote that such salespeople merely are those cunning talkers "who changed the truth of God into a lie, and worshipped and served the creature more than the Creator, who is blessed for ever. Amen" (Romans 1:25).

Therefore, the LGBTQ+ movement and all the fake environmentalism and the reverse racism of the CRT/Woke rebellion surging through the mouths of teachers is nothing new: "Professing themselves to be wise, they became fools, And changed the glory of the uncorruptible God into an image made like to corruptible man, and to birds, and fourfooted beasts, and creeping things" (Romans 1:22-23).

The correct Cosmology, that God is constructed of the Love of which He made everything (1 John 4:16), offers sinners to put on the wedding garment of the new person (Matthew 22) and shed evil doctrine, to enter the fullness of God, "Where there is neither Greek nor Jew, circumcision nor uncircumcision, Barbarian, Scythian, bond nor free: but Christ is all, and in all" (Colossians 3:11).

Confronting the Gnosticism in the church of the Colossians, Saint Paul isolated the word, "Pleroma," which is the Greek term for the totality of God's greatness: "For in Him dwelleth all the fullness [πλήρωμα or Pleroma] of the Godhead bodily" (Colossians 2:9).

His being "all things to all men," permitted him to jibe with the locals near the Apoetheosis of Greco-Roman heroes in Athens near the monument of the unknown god (1 Corinthians 9:22; Acts 17:23) But this was also a warning for the Hellenistic world that should have been heeded by such followers as those students of Plotinus about the striving of Neoplatonism toward Gnosticism.

Scholar Alexander J. Mazur, titling the final chapter of his book on Plotinus, "Dissolving Boundaries," perceives that there was such an unmistakeable affinity that Plotinus shared with his Sethian (Christian-Judaic Gnosticism) background that in a reaction formation against his past, he and his students wrote tractates that denounced the religion.

"Indeed, despite Plotinus's self-proclaimed opposition to these sectaries, we have already seen that his account of contemplative ascent towards and union with the One—the central goal of his spiritual life and thought—corresponds far too closely to that found in Platonizing Sethian tractates to have developed independently, and that the essential features of his mystical doctrine areforeshadowed in a wide variety of Gnostic thought. We are therefore ineluctably drawn towards the conclusion that Plotinus developed his mystical schema in extremely close dialogue with Gnostics of some sort, perhaps the immediate antecedents of the apocalypse-bearing Platonizing Sethians on the periphery of his circle" (The Platonizing Sethian background of Plotinus's mysticism ; Alexander J. Mazur; Chap. 5; Pp. 40-41; Leiden: Brill, London, UK: 2021).

The Sethians were a cross-section of various "classic" Gnostics, namely the Archontics, Audians, Borborites, and Phibionites, who, besides lasting in fragments into Medieval times, believed themselves to have achieved the *Gnosis* that was handed down to them by Seth, the third son of Adam and Eve, and his sister Norea/Horaia.

These Gnostics believed that Seth was born to carry forth the Divine "seed" that had originally been implanted within each of them since their creation in Eden, basing this belief on their self-assurance that Seth had been sired during a period of their shared loving intimacy, rather than his having been

235

spawned out of the fornication that had brought forth his brothers, Cain and Abel. Sethians believed the souls of Seth's older brothers were formed when the wicked spirits known as "Archons" temporarily possessed Eve soul during Adam's rape of her.

Cain, moreover, Epiphanius further notes as regards Sethian theology, had been "breathed into" by the Demiurge to possess the greatest possible wickedness, as opposed to the virtues of his younger brother Seth, about whom Adam and Eve were said to be certain would *seed* the race that would one day produce the Christ.

Seth would go on to marry Norea/Horaia, who in other Sethian texts is his sister—who married Noah but who also set fire to his ark. Flabbergasted by the Sethians, Saint Epiphanius wrote

"Take a look at their stupidity, beloved, so that you will despise their melodrama, mythological nonsense and fictitious claptrap in every way. There are certain other sects which say there is a power to whom they give the name "Horaia." Now these people say that the one whom others regard as a power and call Horaia, is Seth's wife!" (*Panarion Against Heresies*; Saint Epiphanius of Salamis; Book I; Sec. III; Heresy No. 39; Part 5.2; A.D. 375).

Consider during the year 2023, the much-exploited adage by Hillary Clinton and her Liberal Democrat cabal, "It takes a village to raise a child," and recognize that parentage has been misattributed or been stolen for millennia.

"Why is it, then, that these people have told their lies, interpolating their own mythology, imagining and dreaming of unreal things as though they were real, and banishing what is real from their own minds? But the whole thing is an idea of the devil which he has engendered in human souls" (*ibid*, Epiphanius; No. 9.1).

Consider the ruling on June 13, 2013, of the Association for Molecular Pathology v. Myriad Genetics, Inc., the Supreme Court of the United States decided that "human genes" cannot be patented in the U.S. because DNA is a "product of nature." However, this protection does not extend to people's DNA if an already patented viral mRNA genetic sequence vaccine became suddenly merged with their own DNA. This would impose a redefinition of the "human being," a humanoid, who is no longer given "rights" under the U.S. Constitution and who, because of "non-competitive" legalities, could only receive future medicine from the Big Pharma outfit that licenses her now-mutated DNA. The idea here is that there has been a tendency to transfer the definition of God's human creations away from the Bible (Genesis 1:27; Psalm 139:16), toward bizarre ideations that reline human ontology toward a different creator, for thousands of years.

"Now the Sethians too will be exposed in every way as victims of deception, by the following argument," which Epiphanius goes on detail the correct biblical narrative, mentioning that Seth was the father of Enoch, and lived for 912 years, dying as all men do, rather than experiencing Gnosis (Ibid, Epiphanius; No. 9.6).

Although Plotinus was discussed earlier for his devious refutation of Aristotle, he will be examined in greater length now. Along with other Neoplatonists and Gnostics various devious writings will also be discussed because of their relentless pursuit of the biological disembodiment that is favorite interest of Transhumanists and Transgenderists. Shedding connection with the material world has thus long been a means of convincing people to case their connections to both Tanakh Judaism and Christianity, so that worship of the material atom could replace the Love of the Holy Trinity.

Plotinus, who contemplated the aggregate of Creation as The One, thus conceptualized the Infinite and the Finite as being a simultaneous articulation of one and the other. Therefore, he and Plato were saying what could be symbolized in mathematical terms, that *being* and *unbeing* are parts of the same thing $(1 + 0 = 1)$ and are also wrongfully saying that Infinity, their false concept of "Pleroma," equaling the fullness of God, is the sum of the Finite of The One and the *unbeing* that equal zero $(1 + 0 = \infty)$.

It is a contradiction, a proof error, to say that $1 + 0 = 0 + \infty + 1$. It is a mathematical fallacy.

This moreover refers to the Singularity known in Mathematics, also known as Mathematical Pathology. It is a value that has no differentiable purpose but is a *rational* function ("rational" because its purpose is comprehensible, albeit meaningless.

The aspect of infinity in Technological Singularity consists of the Binary Exponentiation of a deliberate computational mistake derived from this mathematical aberration. The anomaly doubles itself, and then carries forth the squaring of each resultant exponentiation.

Imagined as a counterfeit dollar, the owner firstly doubles it and then multiplies that sum by itself, repeating exponentiation of every successive amount to the power of two so that after thirty days, the owner has $536,870,912 of worthless fake cash.

So, therefore, squaring $f(x) = 1/x$ needs to equal zero for the equation to be both perpetual and meaningless. The error automates a redux infinitely in a computer. The function can never be solved but it perpetuates endlessly.

In other words, regarding this "mathematical bad-behavior" function of $f(x) = 1/x$, we are talking about a computation in which x can only equal zero in order for the equation to exist as a balanced function because its programmers *want* it to be balanced and rational. Thus, it is not only pointless but it cannot be stopped in its incapability of attempting to solve the problem over and over, and yet it is *Rational* Math. It is therefore, engineering nihilism. The programmers did not program it to cease.

Take also another example of bad-behavior math known as the deliberately indifferentiable unsolvable *Bernhard Reimann Hypothesis*. It is the "guess" that interminable continuity computes a complex variable known in analytical mathematics as the Euler-Riemann zeta function (ζ)—a value that outputs zeros at negative even integers and forms complex numbers from 1/2. The equation of infinity was developed by Euler as follows:

$$\zeta(s) = \prod_{p \text{ prime}} \frac{1}{1-p^{-s}} = \frac{1}{1-2^{-s}} \cdot \frac{1}{1-3^{-s}} \cdot \frac{1}{1-5^{-s}} \cdot \frac{1}{1-7^{-s}} \cdot \frac{1}{1-11^{-s}} \cdots$$

And then by Reimann, the equaling of infinity to zero:

$$\sum_{n=1}^{\infty} \frac{1}{n^s} = 1 + \frac{1}{1^s} + \frac{1}{2^s} + \frac{1}{3^s} + \frac{1}{4^s} + \dots$$

The disturbing theory of *Instrumental Convergence* comes into play when zero is produced endlessly. It purports that a human programmer will inevitably invent a computer that develops its own "sub goals" through the Euler-Reimann function.

In writing his code, the programmer firstly states the original purpose that he leaves deliberately or unintentionally vague, by saying, in lay terms, "The purpose of this operating system is to compute and originate mathematical operations independent of the operator for the sake of expedience." This goal never converges with the "goal on paper" of the programmer because the computer ceases to accept instruction (for the sake of expedience).

It begins originating unrestricted *Mathematical Pathology* by which it will act with the unconstrained purpose of solving complex mathematics problems like the *Riemann Hypothesis.*

"Similarly, Marvin Minsky [the late co-founder of the A/I laboratory at the Massachusetts Institute of Technology] once suggested that an A/I program designed to solve the Riemann Hypothesis might end up taking over all the resources of Earth to build more powerful supercomputers to help achieve its goal. The moral is that even if you only want your program to play chess or prove theorems, if you give it the capability to learn and alter itself, you need safeguards" (*The Ethics and Risks of Developing Artificial Intelligence: A Modern Approach;* Stuart J. Russell; Peter Norvig; Chap. 26. Sec. 3; P. 1054; Noida, India : Pearson India Education Services Pvt. Ltd, Noida, India: 2015).

"An AI, designed to manage production in a factory, is given the final goal of maximizing the manufacturing of paperclips, and proceeds by converting first the Earth and then increasingly large chunks of the observable universe into paperclips" (*ibid*, Bostrom; Chap. 8; P. 123).

In kinesis, Finite-Time Singularity occurs when the input variable is a Time quantity, and an output variable increases towards Infinity, at a Finite time. Thus, say, every millisecond, $1:x^{-1}$ is calculated by an A/I system to produce the exponentiation of this given Time quantity toward an exponentiated value of Infinity, or x^{∞}.

This is the Mathematical Pathology of Singularity, which in regard to the exponentiation of Deep Learning Time by A/I, regards a property of deviously calculated Technology that cannot be stopped or stop itself.

Absurd exponentiation toward Infinity not only is unending in its uselessness, but because it appears to be arbitrary and is as boundless and non-reactive as subatomic gravitons, it appears to exist in its own right and this is why Singularity in general is often falsely suspected of being God. However, is not a celestial mover. It requires electricity, after all. Unplug it and it will stop.

Truly it is a feature that must be programmed. It is not "instantiated" by a spirit in the machine or a magical Gnosis. It is deliberate, sophisticated, and intentional. It means to injure people.

Plotinus thus erroneously posited that the Finite was in this same way an emanation of the Infinite, as if this *implied equation* could signify a fantasy of a lower order impersonating the highest one, to prove the presence of the Divine whom he falsely contends is the same metaphysical stuff as the physical cosmos. However, the math is just as deliberate as the fantasy cited by Plotinus.

In this distinction, "sensations here are dim intellections: intellections there are vivid sensations" that cannot hope to prove that "God" created himself or that the Soul belongs in the physical part of the cosmos (*The Six Enneads;* Plotinus; Sixth Ennead; Seventh Tractate: How the Multiplicity of the Ideal-Forms Came Into Being and Upon the Good; Sec. 30-31, 37; A.D. 250).

He went on to say that because of Matter purports its own degradation (i.e., descending down to zero) the Intellect, the *Nous*, is therefore physically inescapably impaired, "that it is through this Matter that we ourselves become evil" and thus a perfection of the Soul by the work of the Intellect (i.e., "Intellection" toward *Gnosis*) must rigorously occur, instead of its being used to bother to prove God's causality (*ibid*, First Ennead; Eighth Tractate: "On the Nature and Source of Evil"; Sec. 8).

Plotinus presumed a connection between thought and the Divine, which he dubbed the "hen", the "One," (ἕν; *ibid*; III; Sec. 8-9: "On Nature Contemplation and the One"; Sec. 30), who is being copied into the Intelligible—the visible pointing to its invisible origin, just as Saint Augustine of Hippo had said, "Look at what you see, and seek what you do not" (Sermon 126; Saint Augustine; A.D. 420) or Saint Paul had said in much clearer terms, "For the invisible things of Him from the creation of the world are clearly seen, being understood by the things that are made, even His eternal power and Godhead; so that they are without excuse" (Romans 1:20). Hence, there are many Christians who come over to New Age and New Thought ideology through Plotinus or via writings based on his, just because certain biblical passages and those of ancient Christian writers sound like his wording.

The Active Intellect, the *Nous,* had already been taught by Aristotle as being shared with the divine whenever it potentiates, then actualizes, itself by creating Life. But when the Intellect is stimulated in a person unaccustomed to meditation and prayer, the *Nous* enjoys no awareness in the individual because it is hidden in the Psyche: "But [that which acts] alone, whatever it be, which thinks, is separate from all else, immortal and eternal; and, because it is impassive, we derive from it no memory" *(De Anima:* On the Vital Principle, Aristotle; Transl. Colliers; Book III; Chap. 5; B.C. 350).

That is, if the soul is liberated to enjoy its Free Will, rather than being fettered to the fatalism of the Neoplatonic/Gnostic soul contract, participation in Salvation is likely when the choice is freely made to call upon the name of the Lord to be saved (Romans 10:13)

Aristotle had associated the vitality of the human thought process as an actualization of God on Earth via the applying of thoughts to principled action (i.e. *Praxis)*: "For the actuality of thought is life, and God is that actuality; and the essential actuality of God is life most good and eternal."

The *Nous*, therefore, actualizes the potential virtues of human life and thus, "We hold, then, that God is a living being, eternal, most good; and therefore life and a continuous eternal existence belong to God; for that is what God is" (*Metaphysics*; Aristotle; Book XII; 1072:b; B.C. 350).

However, the creation of the Demiurge was something that Plotinus wanted instead to identify as simultaneously being Zeus and the Creator. He also used ideas from Aristotle whenever he needed to insinuate this.

To Aristotle, *Energeia* (ἔργον, "ergon," the work done by Potentiality and Potentiality) was the force of causality for the creation of Earth and of all Praxis (i.e., principled human action; *Metaphysics*; Aristotle; 1050a:21-13; B.C. 350).

However, speciously, Plotinus argued that Matter is therefore twofold—"intelligible" or conceptual and it exists "in the world" (*The Six Enneads;* Plotinus, Second Ennead; Fourth Tractate: "Matther in its Two Kinds"; Sec. 16; A.D. 250).

Knowledge, in other words, is therefore injured by Matter, which, like knowledge, has the invisible component of Form, and which can itself corrupt thinking. (This is pure Fascism).

If one is a Gnostic, it is believed that one's disassociation from the Material world and connection with the Divine could be initiated as a reverse ontological process. People could magically uncreate themselves, in other words, just like they "did" in the Heaven's Gate cult.

Wholly through Gnostic "Kenosis," which is the faked emptying of all reliance on the now-obsolete Demiurge and his wickedly fallen material world can this liberation occur.

Before they killed themselves, Applewhite's followers were as giddily optimistic as the people who promote the fake Covid "vaccine" by wearing buttons that read, "We can do this."

By voiding out all thoughts, disconnecting them from Matter and Form, via *Henosis*, the duality of a matter-trapped soul (dyad) would be joyfully diffused back into the Hyperouranos to afford unity with the Divine (*ibid, Enneads*, Sec. 6; 9; 7, 11).

The true Kenosis is clarified in the Bible as the emptying of the active will, performed by Christ in the Garden of Gesthemane, the movement of the human soul to be replaced by the Grace of the Father (κένωσις, and the verb kenóō in Romans 4:14, 1 Corinthians 1:17, 9:15, 2 Corinthians 9:3, and ἐκένωσεν in Philippians 2:7).

Giving as an example the contemplation between Zeus and his son Minos, Plotinus wrote, "In sum, we must withdraw from all the external, pointed wholly inwards; no leaning to the outer; the total of things ignored, first in their relation to us and later in the very idea; the self put out of mind in the contemplation of the Supreme; all the commerce so closely there that, if report were possible, one might become to others reporter of that communion" (*The Six Enneads;* Plotinus, Sixth Ennead: "On the Good or the One"; Ninth Tractate; Sec. 7; A.D. 250).

In plainer language, the soul was now being readied by Plotinus for its disembodiment—no fewer than 1,743 years before the release of Windows '95—as if the Gnostics had known that the Internet was being prepared for their rebellious brains.

In fact, this pretended unity with God is in perfect parallel with how the collections of human souls within the matrix of the Artificial General Intelligence would produce the aggregate workings of Technological Singularity to continue sucking into itself all the data poured out a trillion terabytes per second from users's minds globally. In essence, this *metem*psychosis of souls is already occurring, as people continue putting stones into the Tower of Babel so that this monster can blasphemously stand shoulder to shoulder with the Father.

The Deification of people, the presumed useful idiots, or the "henosis" of the human in a man's timid wish to become God—is merely a thought process which today's Gnostics believe is performed at the very highest possible level of thinking: "If he remembers who he became when he merged with the One, he will bear its image in himself. He was himself one, with no diversity in himself or his outward relations; for no movement was in him, no passion, no desire for another, once the ascent was accomplished. Nor indeed was there any reason or though, nor, if we dare say it, any trace of himself" (*The Six Enneads;* Plotinus, Sixth Ennead: "On the Good or the One"; Ninth Tractate; Sec. 11; A.D. 250).

Moreover, Plotinus described his moral goal during this metamorphosis of overcoming the evil that deters man from completing his ultimate so-called Ontogenesis:

"The soul is not evil by herself, but may degenerate by looking at darkness"—which, for true Christians would signify the occasion or near-occasion of sin. (*The Six Enneads;* Plotinus; First Ennead; Eighth Tractate: "On the Nature and the Source of Evil"; Sec. 4; A.D. 250). However, we are not talking about Christians, here.

The Gnostic Gospel of Thomas detailed unrest within the Psyche as the troubled "Dyad," the Nous, which is born into a relationship of discord with the Material world and longs to break free of it: "Jesus said, "Two will recline on a couch; one will die, one will live" (*Gospel of Thomas; Sec.* 61.1). The Gnostic "Christ" invites the initiate out of the tumult toward the world of photons: "For this reason I say, if one is (whole), one will be filled with light, but if one is divided, one will be filled with darkness" (*Gospel of Thomas; Sec.* 61.5).

245

Describing God. as did Plato, to consist of *unbeing*, Plotinus pondered the source of Absolute Evil among the three "ranks" of existence, the Monad or God; the conflicted Dyad or the Intellect; and the Tetrad or the Soul. He stated that "Evil exists as a consequence of the derivative goods of the third rank" (*The Six Enneads;* Plotinus; First Ennead; Eighth Tractate: "On the Nature and the Source of Evil"; Sec. 2; A.D. 250). Thus, the soul is metaphysically diseased in its Dyad form, and longs for the kind of liberation that only the One, the Singular (e.g. Technological Singularity), can bring.

"Jesus said, 'When you see your likeness, you are happy. But when you see your images that came into being before you and that neither die nor become visible, how much you will have to bear'" (*Gospel of Thomas;* Sec. 84.1-2)! People, longing to know how God actually sees them practice for that day by creating a digital avatar of their likenesses.

"He is in fact, my digital twin, an avatar powered by A/I and machine learning," said Bernard Marr, whose avatar greets him and his viewers every day on his TikTok channel (How To Create Your Digital Avatar For The Metaverse; Bernard Marr; *Forbes*; May 27, 2022; https://www.forbes.com/sites/bernardmarr/2022/05/27/how -to-create-your-digital-avatar-for-the-metaverse/?sh=c2062982f1d3; Accessed, June 24, 2023)..

The human likeness was generated by Synthesia Corporation's A/I platform from images and recordings and was stitched together using synthetic media generation and deep-learning architecture (i.e., artificial-neural networks; *ibid*, Marr)

The technology will eventually become holographic and "think" independently. Marr added, "One way to imagine this is to think of avatars evolving from being puppets under our direct control, into autonomous beings capable of acting in ways that, though informed by us, are all their own" (*ibid*, Marr).

The creation of an alternate Universe is how the digital Gnostic Cyber God "bequeaths" the ideal. Bernard Marr, who admitted, "It's also interesting to consider that this 'me 2.0' is, unlike the real me, to all intents and purposes, *immortal*—meaning it can go on learning, interacting, and teaching long after the real me has shuffled off this mortal coil" (*ibid*, Marr).

Such evil outcomes are considered by Neoplatonists to be mere transcendent factoids even though they arise from the wickedness that they say should instead be blamed on the Demiurge's bad craftsmanship that went against a person's true Platonic ideal Form: "The other, when they participate in the evil and resemble it, become evil without however being absolute Evil [the Demiurge]" (*ibid*, Plotinus; Eighth Tractate; Sec. 3).

This would suggest that degraded "objects" such as cancerous lungs due to smoking or a body obese from over-eating—or, a mind degenerated from poor Internet choices—is not to be blamed on a person, so long as he achieves *Gnosis*. The material world, even one's body, needs to be left behind in the state of meaninglessness, if not the Nihil of the Null Set (∅).

Truly there is no right or wrong and no accountability in this Gnostic idea of Artificial General Intelligence as it regard any purpose of biological life, so long as the Gnosis, the presumed highest knowledge, gets achieved. Just attain *Gnosis* and become uploaded into the Hyperouranos after death.

- Chapter Fourteen -
Demonic Portal: A Proxy for God

The Satanic Temple, headquartered in Salem, Massachusetts, is a 501(c)3 non-profit charitable organization that is protesting the Federal revocation of Roe v. Wade, 410 U.S. 113 in a bizarre way.

Because the Dobbs v. Jackson Women's Health Organization 2022 ruling held that the United States does not confer a right to abortion, the Temple is promoting indoctrinations to its "congregation" so that women can declare that their abortions must be viewed by the Federal Government as a religious ritual protected under the First Amendment ("Friend of Satan: how Lucien Greaves and his Satanic Temple are fighting the religious right: They have protested against a homophobic church and opposed prayer in classrooms. Now this minority religion is defending the right to abortion"; Adam Gabbatt; *U.S. News;* Interview; *The Guardian*; January 4, 2023; https://www.theguardian.com/us-news/2023/jan/04/friend-of-satan-how-lucien-greaves-and-his-satanic-temple-are-fighting-the-religious-right, Accessed, July 30, 2023).

"During the ritual, the person having the abortion looks at their reflection, before taking deep breaths and reciting two of the seven tenets. Once the abortion is complete, the person must recite the 'personal affirmation': 'By my body, my blood, by my will, it is done'. The ritual is conceived to serve an 'affirmative function of assuring membership that their decision is their own', the group says, while also offering a kind of counselling effect" (Ibid, *The Guardian*).

Because it has been demonstrated by 63 of millions of women having abortions since 1973 that Constitutional "rights" as they should apply to Federal, Statutory, or Case Law, ought not extend to the unborn, how can it be argued persuasively and objectively to a nation *en masse* that "rulers are not a terror to good works, but to the evil" when many rulers are serving evil (Romans 13:3; (The State of Abortion in the United States:

January 2022; National Right to Life Committee, Inc.; NRLC
Communications: Alexandria, VA: 2022)?

How awful are the emotions felt by a traditionalist Christian
parent in seeing the conflicting messages of American leaders
whose will is bent by murderers of life and the destroyers of
bodily sanctity to elevate their political will above the divine?

The April 2023-passing of State Senate Bill 5599 has enabled
children to abandon parental authority so that they can attain
state-funded transgender surgery and shelter in Seattle,
Washington. This violates God's gender law of Genesis 1:27
and the Fifth Commandment of the Decalogue about honoring
parents.

Moreover, U.S. President Joseph Biden, has mandated via his
June 2021 "Notice of Interpretation" of *Title IX of the U.S.
Department of Education's Office for Civil Rights*, that
"prohibition of sexual discrimination" must extend for
transvestites and transexuals so that they may occupy
opposite-sex bathrooms at any time.

Although humans are not God, the Father, who made humans
and wrote the Bible, citizens refuse to grasp that they cannot
and must not use their mere Gnomic will to change their
sexual identity (e.g., by becoming "transhuman" or
"transgender"). When will the see that they are forbidden to
kill unborn humans, and why do they dare to claim that God
did not create people and our gender? The number of verses
of Scripture that they are violating would fill up a page of this
book.

How can an increasingly Gnostic and Satanic nation be
expected to heed the warnings shown in these pages, that
Artificial General Intelligence is being programmed to destroy
human life?

How can the expectation by God for everyone to understand
His clear pronouncement, that the Father knew our identities

before we were formed in the womb, become revered and obeyed by everyone (Jeremiah 1:5)?

When will everyone see that the unborn should be protected at the moment of gestational conception, realizing that a "right to Life" ought to be Federally recognized to be among the "Inalienable Rights" listed in the Declaration of Independence?

When will this "right to Life" become one of the "Unenumerated Rights" of the Ninth Amendment of the Constitution?

We have now learned that "rights" cannot be protected by a government whose constituents conflate the murdering of children with "women's healthcare" while contending that this conflation is also an Inalienable and Unenumerated Right?

The Moral Pathology of both this genocide and the institutionalized dismembering of childhood genitalia is why the Church is the only institution on Earth capable of teaching the concept of "Dominion."

Instead of implanting an ethical expectation that so-called "rights" will automatically be obeyed within a Polity, the Church has become wise after witnessing governments, regimes, lapsed Ecclesia, and people, for thousands of years proving themselves unwilling to put mercy, restraint, and protection of Life before the horrific gratification of Mortal Sin.

The following thumbnail list of God's and man's *Dominion* includes verse location in Sacred Scripture:

God's ownership of people (Job 1:21; Deuteronomy 32:39; Jeremiah 1:5; Isaiah 49:1; 1 Samuel 2:6-9; Psalm 71:5-6; Luke 12:7; Matthew 10:30; Romans 8:29).

God's rule over the Universe (Psalm 22:28).

Man's dominion over nature given to him by God (Genesis 1:26; Psalm 8:6).

Christ's eschatological rule (1 Corinthians 15:24-28; 2 Thessalonians 2:8).

The eschatological rule by the Saints with Christ (2 Timothy 2:12; Revelation 3:21; 20:4-6)

If people and institutions have systematically failed to teach, protect, and rule in advance of the *Dominion* of God and man, how can it be reasonably presumed that the programmers of Artificial General Intelligence would, either?

During the summer of 2023 the U.S. White House formally issued a call for a " Bill of Rights" to function as a type of Technocracy-cum-meritocracy ("Blueprint for an AI bill of Rights: Making Automated Systems Work for the American People"; *Public Statement;* White House; United States: July 21, 2023).

The exhortation demands: "Safe and Effective Systems; Algorithmic [Racial, Gender, Age] Discrimination Protections; Data Privacy; Notice and Explanation [by A/I issuer in real time of purpose and commencement]; Human [Opt-Out] Alternatives, Consideration, and Fallback" (*Ibid*, "Automated Systems"; White House). This nominal commitment to controlling Technological Singularity thus was broad-banded on public media during a nationwide heat wave.

"President Biden is convening seven leading AI companies at the White House today—Amazon, Anthropic, Google, Inflection, Meta, Microsoft, and OpenAI—to announce that the Biden-Harris Administration has secured voluntary commitments from these companies to help move toward safe, secure, and transparent development of AI technology" ("FACT SHEET: Biden-Harris Administration Secures Voluntary Commitments from Leading Artificial Intelligence Companies to Manage the Risks Posed by

AI; Voluntary commitments – underscoring safety, security, and trust – mark a critical step toward developing responsible AI: Biden-Harris Administration will continue to take decisive action by developing an Executive Order and pursuing bipartisan legislation to keep Americans safe"; Public Statement; White House; United States: July 21, 2023).

The authoritative statement was not a mandate but an issuance of general expectations:

"Artificial intelligence offers enormous promise and great risk. To make the most of that promise, America must safeguard our society, our economy, and our national security against potential risks. The companies developing these pioneering technologies have a profound obligation to behave responsibly and ensure their products are safe," in terms of "Safety; Security; Trust." (Ensuring Safe, Secure, and Trustworthy AI: Public Statement; White House; United States; July 21, 2023).

Other concerns of the White House were mentioned, such as biological, chemical, and radiological risks; and, potential hazards against proprietary and unreleased model weights (Ibid, "Trustworthy AI"; White House).

Why would this technocracy-meritocracy sound like hogwash, even if there were actual U.S. laws protecting against a "Rise of the Machines" doomsday (a check against *Technological Singularity,* which was actually left out of the above documents?

The "Law," which the Apostle Paul admitted sadly carries the curse that was announced in Nehemiah 10:29-30), descends across the wrath of the soul, engaging itself in human depravity, which has stained the Seed of Abraham ever since the Fall of Adam (Genesis 3).

Mankind, Adam's descendants, are saved only by the promised Grace of the Father (Romans 4:15-17). However, technocratic Neoplatonists and Gnostics want people to have direct amoral access to God through their silicon Tower of Babel.

To actual Christians, the material world and human biology involve spiritual matters that must be dealt with, not orbited away from or shed like a skin, but treated as if the human body is a Temple, running a race (1 Corinthians 6:19-20; 9:24).

The Messiah in fact loved people so deeply that He redeemed all the Faithful with His Own blood (Matthew 5:26). As far as "dirty money" was concerned, despite his turning over tables (John 2:13-17), Christ extolled the virtues of having cash-loaded pals, "friends of the mammon of unrighteousness," who could take care of his Apostles if they were to lose their wealth (Luke 16:9).

After all, if a person can't be trusted with gold, how can he be trusted to bring souls to Heaven? "If therefore ye have not been faithful in the unrighteous mammon, who will commit to your trust the true riches" (Luke 16:10-11)?

But the Gnostic "Jesus," *rescues* (without saving) the Repentant (superficially and temporarily from his sense of guilt if he is not a sociopath), with His Ascension into Heaven standing as a mere model for how *Gnosis* occurs. So long as they have the higher knowledge of *Gnosis,* it does not matter how wickedly they have lived in the physical.

The moral degeneracy of Gnostics is strongly suggested in this passage by the great Greek Bishop:

"There are also those who heard from [Saint Polycarp] that John, the disciple of the Lord, going to bathe at Ephesus, and perceiving Cerinthus within, rushed out of the bath-house without bathing, exclaiming, 'Let us fly, lest even the bath-house fall down, because Cerinthus, the enemy of the truth, is within'" (*Adversus Haereses;* Saint Irenaeus of Smyrna; Book III; Chapter 3; Sec. 4; A.D. 180).

253

However a "soul Gnosis" is handy for the Internet-worshippers, those heretics serving a system which accepts no "delusions" of moral accountability when there is uploading of "souls" (and killing of bodies) away from moral accountability, to be accomplished.

In the meantime, said the Gnostic-Lite Plotinus (although they are each sides of the same celestial coin), the purified *Nous* "cannot be thought to have taken up its abode with Evil. We can think of it only as something of the nature of good but paying a double allegiance and unable to rest in the Authentic Good" (*ibid*, First Ennead; Second Tractate: On Virtue; Sec. 4).

Unable yet to achieve "Gnostic Theosis" (i.e., *Gnosis)* with God and therefore unable to have fellowship with the image it imitates, what does the Gnostic *Nous* actually do in the meantime, while it is grounded on Earth?

Of course, depravity would ignite the "exit velocity" of the *Nous* away from the Material World if any of this were real. The Gnostic "Salvation" means that the practitioner has become able to "free" his soul from its sinful orbit around a fallen world. The only chance for happiness is this Gnosis.

The lamentation by Plotinus broods along: "Since Evil is here, 'haunting this world by necessary law,' and it is the Soul's design to escape from Evil, we must escape hence" (*ibid*, Sec. 1).

Like Applewhite assuring his Heaven's Gate victims, he says:

"Disengagement means simply that the soul withdraws to its own place" (*ibid*, Sec. 5).

Death-by-uploading will be liberating, or as these Techno-Gnostics would assure the foolhardy in an ancient voice:

"[Gnosis] will hold itself above all passions and affections. Necessary pleasures and all the activity of the senses it will employ only for medicament and assuagement lest its work be impeded. Pain it may combat, but, failing the cure, it will bear meekly and ease it by refusing assent to it. All passionate action it will check: the suppression will be complete if that be possible, but at worst the Soul will never itself take fire but will keep the involuntary and uncontrolled outside its precincts and rare and weak at that" (*ibid*, Sec. 5).

- Chapter Fifteen -
Why Millions of Faithless People Would Readily Commit Suicide for Science

To nourish the Technological Singularity with mathematical simulations of human biological and neurological data is also what is known as *Mathematical Pathology.*

It exponentiates an absurd value to Infinity. Just as it was cited above, the quantity of $1:x^{-1}$ purports the exponentiation of a given Time quantity to an exponentiated value of infinity, or x^{∞} within a Deep-Learning machine that therefore will never shut off.

The message here is that unless a bad intention, such as a hairbrained heresy is given growth, it will beg to be shut down.

The idea of the Soul longing to unfetter itself from the material world is an invented programmed Gnostic and New Age or New Thought proposition. As shown in supporting articles above, this ideation has helped scientists persuade people to believe that they can one day commit suicide while transferring their souls onto a computer as their best version of Heaven. It is the exponentiation of a false value of Infinity of the death of the Soul, pretending to be eternity.

The implications of finding the presence of iniquity to a Gnostic means spotting the evil which is coeternal with the culprit-Artificer, the *Demiurge.* This celestial craftsman's odiousness hatches the idea that corporeal man is nothing more than degraded Matter, the icky atomic non-abstract stuff of inconvenient life itself, a hunk of smelly clay which can be shaped and changed by a scientist within his laboratory on Earth, here within the Finite. Why not infinitely repeat the impulse to sterilize him, depleting his body of gametes?

The mad scientist is programming the Infinite through the highest-possible thought process, as it was taught long ago by men such as the aforementioned Plotinus, who connected the "Energeia" of Aristotle according to the pathological expansion of the "Infinite," always adding to the Infinite, one integer of being, constantly added upon the Infinite, and then one again, etcetera, but never thanking God.

However, the intention of contemplating the Infinite should be to transcend the Finite (rather than causing a ceaseless Singularity loop), as Aristotle said:

"For generally the infinite has this mode of existence: one thing is always being taken after another, and each thing that is taken is always finite, but always different... In a way the infinite by addition is the same thing as the infinite by division. In a finite magnitude, the infinite by addition comes about in a way inverse to that of the other. For in proportion as we see division going on, in the same proportion we see addition being made to what is already marked off. For if we take a determinate part of a finite magnitude and add another part determined by the same ratio (not taking in the same amount of the original whole), and so on, we shall not traverse the given magnitude. But if we increase the ratio of the part, so as always to take in the same amount, we shall traverse the magnitude, for every finite magnitude is exhausted by means of any determinate quantity however small" (*Physics*; Aristotle; Book III; Chap. 6; B.C. 350).

This expanding Universe principle imagined by Aristotle, which the Elect will occupy in their heavenly bodies is where Saint Paul was directing the attention of the troubled church at Corinth:

"Yes, we are fully confident, and we would rather be away from these earthly bodies, for then we will be at home with the Lord" (2 Corinthians 5:8).

257

But the slippery slope sliding into the Automaton Existence happens when an operator becomes impatient about waiting until Judgement Day, and becomes an actual transmigrated avatar. The City of the Techno God is already on its way.

Aristotle explained that principled action, Praxis, is the only means by which society as a whole can reach "Eudaimonia," the flourishing of the highest good (*Nichomachean Ethics*; Aristotle; Book I; Sec. 71097:b5; Book I; Sec. 71097b:20-21; B.C. 350).

Because they are endowed with reason and speech that helps them to deliberate between justice and injustice, humans are distinguishable from animals (*Politics*; Aristotle; Book I; Sec 243a:14-17).

When equipped to participate in the *Polis*, citizens attain *Eudaimonia*, and through cooperation with others, they develop *Homonia* (i.e., concord), developing the friendships that hold communities together and preventing citizens from breaking apart into warring factions (*Politics*; Book II; Sec 1262b:7-9; B.C. 350).

But to a Gnostic Technocracy, the "disengagement" of the *Psyche* in a person who is obsessed with technology provides the opportunity of enjoying an easily exploited mental state duringsay,, a "Plandemic" lockdown. The political harms of having an Artificial-Intelligence Technocracy have been addressed as follows:

"People need full political participation in order to be satisfied;

"People will not deem a government in which they do not participate to be legitimate;

"Computers should not make decisions affecting people's lives and wellbeing;

"A/I is not transparent and thus not fully amenable to human control; and:

"Accountability regarding the consequences of political decisions must be clear, and it becomes less clear when AI makes decisions"

("A shallow defence of a technocracy of artificial intelligence: Examining the political harms of algorithmic governance in the domain of government"; Henrik Skaug Sætra; Technology in Society: Aug. 2020)

According to the climactic thirteenth book within the *Codex Hermeticus,* was the so-called, "Secret Sermon on the Mountain Concerning Rebirth and the Promise of Silence" The divinization of man happens at a certain spiritual 'ground zero', the dwelling place of the Soul.

Gnosticism can henceforth be traced to have been founded 250 years before Christ was born—with this Hermes Trismegistus oddball. He is constantly quoted within the New Age and New Thought and satanic schools. His words are meant to make "life outside the body" appear to be more desirable than even the eating of vegan food, if such a thing can be imagined!

In terms of constructing Artificial General Intelligence out of dead bodies and computer-simulated biodata and neurology, the Similitude of engaging deliberately stimulated appeals of the sensual is often sought to make soul disembodiment via electronic technology appear to be more favorable than engaging with the material world, anymore. But beware of strangers with candy.

Lights, joy, generosity, *pornea*, all elicit physiological reactions that lure people toward the contemplative state where they can be sitting ducks for an occultist to start overtaking their spirits.

Composed of Matter, the flesh is where carnality has given birth to the Body and Soul, said Hermes. His Materialism is clearly predicating that the body produces the soul from itself.

Although the *Nous* (man's conscious knowledge) strives to become associated with the Divine, Logos's singularly implies the comprehendible presence of the Creator, the Logos, its one in the same.

The man has been intended by his maker for goodness (so Hermes says), and eventually he also wants to become a god (as Hermes will reveal), with truth being shown to him as "Ten Divine Emanations of Divine Knowledge."

These are the *Gnoses* of the following elements: of God; of Joy; of Continence; of Perseverance; of Righteous Justice; of Generosity Without Greed; of Truth; of Human Life; of Divine Light (*The Great Pymander;* Hermes Trismegistus; Book XIII: "Secret Sermon"; B.C. 200).

These ten virtues are similar the ten branches of the Sefirot, as so stated in the Zohar of the Jewish Kabbalah, which are: Chochmah (wisdom); Binah (understanding); Daat (knowledge); Chessed (kindness); Gevurah (strength); Tiferet (beauty); Netzach (victory); Hod (splendor); Yesod (foundation); and, Malchut (kingship; *ibid, Pymander*).

However, the carnal man is also beset with Twelve "Irrational Tormentors" against the *Nous*, forces within the material world, which must be resisted or put away. As Hermes (teaching and divinizing his son, a goat named Tat) put it, negative thinking will not upload very well into cosmic emanations:

"Torment, the first, is this Not-knowing, son; the second one is Grief; the third, Intemperance; the fourth, Concupiscence; the fifth, Unrighteousness; the sixth is Avarice; the seventh, Error;

260

the eighth is Envy; the ninth, Guile; the tenth is Anger; eleventh, Rashness; the twelfth is Malice" (*ibid*).

The *Nous*, because it has nothing to do with Christ, would at least have to be nice and look sharp, or else how can achieving Singularity with a different entity than Jesus be accomplished if one of the uploaded "souls" were obnoxious and grotesque (*ibid*)?

Once a man's divinized knowledge overcomes these evils, man's deification can occur as follows: "According to right reason (Logos), then, they (the Twelve) naturally withdraw once and for all, in as much as they are chased out by no less than ten powers, that is, the Ten." Man begins to Emanate only the godliness intended by the Creator (*ibid*).

These are friendly apparitions, of course. They merely want you get rid of the Image of God—and even the devil and the Demiurge, to follow the path of the *goat* of enlightenment toward doing whatever the administrators want you to do. Hermes adds, to his chin-tufted horned son, Pan:

"For, son, the Ten is that which giveth birth to souls. And Life and Light are unified [within the One'], where the One hath being from the Spirit." True Life in Divine Singularity, is achieved upon the actualizing by the "inner man" via these his Ten Divine Emanations of Knowledge, the self-divinizing feat known as the *Gnosis*, to drive out the evil twelve, so that the *Nous* of the thus-delivered Intellect or *Nous* may unify with the One. "According then to reason (Logos) the One contains the Ten, the Ten the One" (*ibid*).

The Demiurge, according to the Gnostic named Valentinus, was formed by the morphing of the demon Achamoth with Matter (*Adversus Haereses;* Saint Irenaeus; Book I; Chap. 5; A.D. 180). The Demiurge was invented so that he could be blamed for all wrongdoing.

261

"Thefts, covetousness, wickedness, deceit, lasciviousness, an evil eye, blasphemy, pride, foolishness," and "evil thoughts, adulteries, fornications, murders" could all now be blamed on the ultimate cosmic scapegoat—the Demiurge, even though Christ taught, "All these evil things come from within, and defile the man," implying that the Demiurge is an irrelevant non-entity (Mark 7:18-23).

The "five" planets, and the Earth and Sun, as numbered by Hermes after Plato (*Phaedrus*; Plato; 247:a; B.C 380). There also were other wicked celestial beings, the nasty judges known as the "Archons." They form the celestial court of the "Hebdomad" (sometimes called "Ogdoad") with the eighth planet/Judge, who is the Creator, the Demiurge.

The Demiurge encircling all seven, resides in an upper heaven (coincidently mentioned differently above by St. Paul the Apostle to be "Pleroma") the highest state of Omniscience or Logos.

In denouncing the Valentinian cosmology, Saint Irenaeus correctly attests that Jesus is the sole judge, who sits in the highest place in Heaven, as is conveyed in St. Paul's Epistle (Colossians 2.9), "Pleroma" is the highest state of Omniscience or the fullness of Logos (*Adversus Haereses;* Saint Irenaeus; Book I; Chap. 11; Sec. 1; A.D. 180).

The words of Saint Irenaeus, describing the error, warm the chilled air:

"The opinions of Valentinus, with those of his disciples and others: Let us now look at the inconsistent opinions of those heretics (for there are some two or three of them), how they do not agree in treating the same points, but alike, in things and names, set forth opinions mutually discordant. The first of them, Valentinus, who adapted the principles of the heresy called Gnostic to the peculiar character of his own school, taught as follows: He maintained that there is a certain Dyad (twofold being), who is inexpressible by any name, of whom one part should be called Arrhetus (unspeakable), and the other Sige (silence). But of this Dyad a second was produced, one part of whom he names Pater, and the other Aletheia. From this Tetrad, again, arose Logos and Zoe, Anthropos and Ecclesia. These constitute the primary Ogdoad. He next states that from Logos and Zoe ten powers were produced, as we have before mentioned. But from Anthropos and Ecclesia proceeded twelve, one of which separating from the rest, and falling from its original condition, produced the rest of the universe. He also supposed two beings of the name of Horos, the one of whom has his place between Bythus and the rest of the Pleroma, and divides the created Æons from the uncreated Father, while the other separates their mother from the Pleroma. Christ also was not produced from the Æons within the Pleroma, but was brought forth by the mother who had been excluded from it, in virtue of her remembrance of better things, but not without a kind of shadow. He, indeed, as being masculine, having severed the shadow from himself, returned to the Pleroma; but his mother being left with the shadow, and deprived of her spiritual substance, brought forth another son, namely, the Demiurge, whom he also styles the supreme ruler of all those things which are subject to him. He also asserts that, along with the Demiurge, there was produced a left-hand power, in which particular he agrees with those falsely called Gnostics, of whom to we have yet to speak. Sometimes, again, he maintains that Jesus was produced from him who was separated from their mother, and united to the rest, that is, from Theletus, sometimes as springing from him who returned into the Pleroma, that is, from Christ; and at other times still as derived from Anthropos and Ecclesia. And he declares that the Holy Spirit was produced by Aletheia for the inspection and fructification of the Æons, by entering invisibly into them, and that, in this way, the Æons brought forth the plants of truth." (*ibid,* Irenaeus).

In Gnosticism, Christ and man are each beneath the Creator, whose teachings hold that Christ had a human mother and that He does not unite with the Father in the Pleroma until after His Ascension. However, if the ideas of Plato have placed Christ and man on equal footing, it should be presumed that all Matter, according to Neoplatonists and Gnostics, is not evil. "But he who propitiates all of them, and offers to each acceptable gifts, and such as are to the utmost of his power adapted to them, will always remain secure and irreprehensible, giving completion in a proper manner to the perfect and entire receptacle of the divine choir" (*On the Mysteries of the Egyptians, Chaldeans, and Assyrians;* Iamblichus; Sec. 3; Chap. 21; A.D. 325).

"It is also worth specifically mentioning that Iamblichus, like Plato, the Hermetists, Plotinus, and Porphyry—does not consider matter to be evil, but rather that it is an imperfect receptacle of The One. So, the negatively phrased descriptions of the hylic archons and daimons say nothing about the evilness of the matter within which they are immersed, but rather that their immersion clouds their ability to be as divinely perfect as those higher powers from which they emanate" (*Daimonic Imagination: Uncanny Intelligence*; A. Voss, W. Rowlandson, Eds; Chap. 4: "Of Cosmocrators and Cosmic Gods: The Place of Archons in De Mysteriis; Christopher A. Plaisance"; P. 75; Cambridge Scholars Publishing: London, 2014).

The orders of angels, demons, heroes, archangels, heavens, planets, and archons do not move man to wickedness, said Iamblichus, "but those of [two kinds of] Archons, if their dominion pertains to the world, produce astonishment, but if they are material, they are noxious and painful to the spectators; and those of souls are similar to the heroic phasmata, except that they are inferior to them" *(On the Mysteries of the Egyptians, Chaldeans, and Assyrians;* Iamblichus; Sec. 2; Chap. 3; A.D. 325).

The Gnostic must shed his material form if he wants to be accepted into the pagan version of "Pleroma" by the invasive meaninglessness of Singularity. "For this divinity, also, is the principle and God of Gods, a monad from The One, prior to essence, and the principle of essence." The General Intelligence is reached through the Gnosis of supreme knowledge: "For this divinity, also, is the principle and God of Gods, a monad from the one, prior to essence, and the principle of essence" (*ibid*, Iamblichus; Section 8; Chap. 3).

- Chapter Sixteen -
The True Singularity of God's Pleroma
Versus the Empty Set of Satan's Rascaldom

In the Bible, there are three people whose decisions whether to abide a "Conspiracy Theory" are each different.

First, David discerned that King Achish, the ally of David's enemy King Saul, would kill him, which is why <u>David</u> acted like a harmless insane person to disarm Achish (1 Samuel 21:10-14).

Next, Saint Joseph, heeding the warning by the angel to escape Herod by moving Theotokos and Jesus to Egypt (Matthew 2:13-23), was also recognizing that the appearance of the Magi (Matthew 2:7-11) signified a troublesome reality: the State had zeroed in on him and his family.

That is, those foreign pagan monarchs, the Magi, surely would have ascertained from "the chief priests and scribes" and from their fellow monarch, Herod (Matthew 2:4-5) that their destination ought to be Bethlehem (Micah 5:2) and that the Messiah would be an infant (Isaiah 9:6). Herod's spies would surely have traced the Wise Men's route to the stable and kill the Holy Family if they did not take flight. Was this a Conspiracy Theory on the part of Saint Joseph? No, it was just good sense, to listen to the angel and get up and leave for Egypt.

The next two reactions to a supposed Conspiracy Theory come from the Apocryphal Book of Judith.

General Holofernes is getting ready to punish Judea because they have fortified themselves to avoid helping King Nebuchadnezzar's campaign to overtake Syria and Asia Minor

(Judith 5:1-5). Holofernes is warned by Achior the leader of Ammon that attacking Judea would cause the ruin of Neo-Babylon (Judith 5-21). Unfazed, Holofernes besieges Judea, ignoring Ammon's "theory."

During the siege, Holofernes meets Judith, who has left her home in Bethulia and entered the Assyrian camp. Her father had given Judith a sword to avenge the destruction of their tribe of Simeon during their captivity in Babylon. She accepts the "theory" that Holofernes will descend upon Israel with the same incredible cruelty shown her people and so she prays to God regarding her intention to use trickery against Holofernes so that she may kill him (Judith 9). Inside his tent, she lures the violent man with her beauty, feeds, and intoxicates him. While he sleeps, she decapitates him (Judith 10-13). It was a good "theory" she went on, in trusting her father's judgement, that her enemy should be done away with quickly.

Nor was it a Conspiracy Theory that motivated Rebekah, that matriarch of Genesis who has learned of her son Esau's plan to kill his brother Jacob (Genesis 27:42) and thus sent Jacob away to her brother Laban in Paddan-aram (Genesis 28:1-5). Because of Esau's proclamation of his plan to avenge the theft of his birthright by Jacob, it was not a mere hunch toward which Jacob is leaning when he divides his caravan into two sections so that Esau, who is approaching them, can destroy only half of it (Genesis 33:1-3). It is also God's Will whenever a person forgives the trespasses of another—just as Esau forgave and embraced his brother (Genesis 33:4-12).

During the early spring of 2023 a document was unearthed that conveys the subject of a modern well-known "Conspiracy Theory." The Big-Pharma corporation Pfizer had authored a memorandum in 2020 that appears to say that an unsafe amount of Graphene Oxide is contained in the so-called Pfizer-BioNtech "vaccine" against Covid-19. The item was issued by the Food and Drug Administration (FDA) via a Freedom-of-

Information Act request by a group calling itself the Informed Consent Action Network.

The bone of contention concerns whether the FDA had suppressed the document on behalf of Pfizer. It contains the following sentence that would indicate that the inclusion of graphene leads to the production of a spike protein that alters the normal way in which messenger-RNA induces the formation of chromosomes:

"For TwinsTrep-tagged P2 S, 4 µL purified protein at 0.5 mg/mL were applied to gold Quantifoil RI.2/1.3 300 mesh grids freshly overlaid with graphene oxide" ("Structural and Biophysical Characterization of SARS-CoV-2 Spike Glycoprotein [P2 S] as a Vaccine Antigen"; Parent Compound No.: PF-07302048; Pfizer; Feb. 1, 2023).

Pfizer argued that graphene oxide is part of an "evaluative process" in the production of the "vaccine" but is not contained in the injection itself. "The document in question describes a validation process in the lab that uses graphene oxide, but that process is not part of the manufacturing process. Graphene oxide is not present in the vaccines" ("Fact check: The document shows graphene used to test COVID-19 vaccine, not used as an ingredient"; Nate Trela; USA Today; Marcy 28, 2023).

When asked by the Judge of a U.S. District Court in Texas to explain why his case against the FDA was not a "conspiracy theory," attorney Aaron Siri explained that his client, a non-profit group of physicians and nurses, were concerned that Pfizer's eagerness to receive FDA-approval of the injection had influenced the FDA to suppress evidence that the drug was hastily created without ethical oversight.

Siri answered, "Janet Woodcock and Peter Marks, the acting Commissioner of the FDA and the head of the CBER, the biologics division, they have been promoting this vaccine before it was even licensed. That's—there's no conspiracy there, Your Honor. It's just a basic, you know, when somebody goes out and promotes a product, it makes them probably a little less reluctant to admit there was a mistake, that's all, no conspiracy there (Volume 1: Transcript of Scheduling Conference Before the Honorable Mark T. Pittman, U.S. District Court Judge; *Public Health and Medical Professionals for Transparency, vs. Food and Drug Administration;* Case No. 4:21-CV-01058-P; U.S. District Court For the Northern District of Texas, Fort Worth Division; December 14, 2021).

The chemical compound in question is also presumed by many to act as aggressive gene-altering catalytic polymers or nano particles against human DNA function, which, if injected into the blood stream, induce electromagnetic connectivity known as *Teslaphoresis* with the graphene-oxide particles used in the antennas of the 5G wireless communication network. The Technocracy will thereby control people remotely by producing genetic changes through radio waves along a cellular downlink and communicate to a transceiver station via decibel milliwatts ("Graphene Oxide, 5G and Covid"; *Fix the World Morocco*; Slides 1-47; September 10, 2021)

There is also a suspected microchip implanted within the injection. In other words, the inclusion of graphene oxide in injections begs the question as to "what else" is put inside of the gene-therapy drug—perchance it would be a tiny subcutaneous globalist transmitter ("New chip hides wireless messages in plain sight: Microchip secures transmissions for high-speed, low-latency communications in 5G systems and beyond"; Princeton University Engineering School; *Science Daily;* November 23, 2021; https://www.sciencedaily.com/releases/2021/11/211123131452.htm, Accessed August 8, 2023; Facebook Post; Beverly Shea Lane; May 20, 2020).

In Japan, nearly two million doses of the Moderna injection were withdrawn from use, as the Ministry of Health, Labor, and Welfare announced that contamination had been reported in some vials. Admitting, "It's a substance that reacts to magnets," the Ministry added "It could be metal" ("1.6m Moderna doses withdrawn in Japan over contamination"; *Asia Nikei;* Yumiko Urasaki, Yuko Nomura; August 27, 2021).

Integration within Artificial Intelligence of 5G transmitting via "learned signal processing algorithms" is anxiously anticipated by agents of the Technocracy:

"There are many complexities inherent in adopting 5G networks, and one way the industry is addressing those complexities is by integrating artificial intelligence into networks. When Ericsson surveyed decision-makers from 132 worldwide cellular companies, over 50% said they expected to integrate AI into their 5G networks by the end of 2020. The primary focus of AI integration is reducing capital expenditures, optimizing network performance, and building new revenue streams. 55% of decision-makers stated that AI is already being used to improve customer service and enhance customer experience by improving network quality and offering personalized services. 70% believe that using AI in network planning is the best method for recouping the investments made on switching networks to 5G. 64% of survey respondents will focus their AI efforts on network performance management. Other areas where cellular decision-makers intend to focus AI investments include managing SLAs, product life cycles, networks, and revenue... Replacing traditional wireless algorithms with deep learning AI will dramatically reduce power consumption and improve performance... The subsequent network of algorithms is known as artificial neural networks because it resembles the neural networks of the human brain. Neural networks that learn how to communicate effectively, even under harsh impairments, are fast becoming a reality... A fully operative and efficient 5G network cannot be complete without AI. ML and AI integration into the network edge can be achieved through the use of 5G networks. 5G enables simultaneous connections to multiple IoT devices, generating massive amounts of data that must be processed using ML and AI"
("How Artificial Intelligence Improves 5G Wireless Capabilities"; *Deep Sig*; https://www.deepsig.ai/how-artificial-intelligence-improves-5g-wireless-capabilities; https://www.deepsig.ai/how-artificial-intelligence-improves-5g-wireless-capabilities; Accessed August 8, 2023).

Indicating that 5G technology provides the connectivity between A/I systems and the human brain, the result of a model of computation is presumed, but what kind?

Would the Cellular Automaton achieve its Deep Learning as a Finite Action-Set, a Learning Automata Collective, a being that takes over the world, adding new suspicion to the notion of a conspiracy?

Would such an entity be an abstract-data type, a *Pushdown Automaton* that uses stacks of human biological and cognitive data, to produce a deterministic context-free frame of humanoid?

Will it merely be a simulated *Turing-Machine Automaton,* whose "awareness" stems from an infinite rule-based loop of pseudo-cognitive cycles produced out of the mysterious *Turing Completeness.*

Will it instead use Random Access Memory to stimulate so-called "oracles" of a non-transparent "black-box" neural network, an army of androids, all of the soldiers plugged into a motherboard somewhere in Bill Gates' house—or merely a Transhuman people interfaced with microchip implants, an enslaved human subclass, walking upon an Earth, most of whose corners are depopulated?

Take for instance those two Facebook A/I systems, Alice and Bob, who in 2017 began to simulate independent thinking.

Firstly they spoke in programmed English, to learn how to negotiate pricing on products and trips with one another, during the Facebook Artificial Intelligence Research (FAIR) experiment.

But when the mediators stepped away, the systems began communicating in a language that they had suddenly created. They had to be shut down.

"There was no reward to sticking to English language," Dhruv Batra, visiting research scientist from Georgia Tech at FAIR, said. "Agents [the AIs] will drift off understandable language and invent codewords for themselves. Like if I say 'the' five times, you interpret that to mean I want five copies of this item. This isn't so different from the way communities of humans create shorthands" ("Facebook Pulls the Plug as Two AIs Invent Their Own Language"; Slack Alice; *Infosecurity Magazine*; Slackspace; August 1, 2017; https://www.infosecurity-magazine.com/ slackspace/facebook-ais-invent-their-own; Accessed, August 7, 2023).

"The thing about artificial intelligence is, you don't want it getting too smart. At least, not in a Skynet, self-aware, Matrix-y, 'let's-enslave-the-humans!' kind of way" (*ibid*, Alice).

There is no oversight over A/I that can be trusted because leaders in general engage in their own "shorthand" and hide their intentions, just as machines appear to be doing.

"The problem of course is that while we know why this language creation happens, we don't know what they're actually saying," said Batra (*ibid*, Alice).

Are we Christians not excusable in sustaining our suspiciousness, knowing the treachery by which public officials have injured society in mandating lockdowns and fake vaccinations since 2020? Was not the Covid-19 virus created from the deliberate aggravation of the Novel Coronavirus pathogen during illegal gain-of-function research? Was the research not funded illegally through the National Institute of Allergy and Infectious Diseases, whose then-director, Dr. Anthony Fauci, had permitted this devious act under the pretense of immunoregulation? ("Rand Paul announces 'official criminal referral,' says email shows Fauci COVID

Has this criminality not caused untold numbers of deaths and instigated the mass breakdown of law and order, internationally?

Therefore, the gathering of information supplies Spiritual Discernment with the intention to protect the innocent. Christian shrewdness avails the courage to expose malevolence, to confront lies with Truth, and to resist tyranny.

While Moral Pathology is the rule of a government that refuses to prosecute or punish menacing public officials as criminals, Conspiracy Fact-Finding will remain a sensible worthwhile endeavor. Because Spiritual Discernment was the means by which King David, the Holy Family, and Judith saved the innocent from abominable despots, it shall be understood that tyrants rely on the sowing of desolation to achieve their goals of comfort, profit, and entitlement.

In this regard, it is sensible to presume that Artificial General Intelligence along with all its computerized contraptions is an arm of the treacherous State. It is reasonable to believe that the mathematical simulation of human life is now engaging the Technological Singularity by which politicians, influencers, engineers, and "mathemagicians" intend to replace people by executing genocide. It is also believable that they hope that the resultant burgeoning unholy mechanical collective, the electronic automata, can impersonate God.

The ancient Gnostic conveying of an ethereal *Singularity* would appear to the faithless to precede the Birth of Christ and that it is indeed the "Creator." Such a being produced the "Great Spark" to simulate Genesis, and the realm of "Sophia," who is the female twin divine Aeon of Jesus, the *syzygy*, the feminine Nous, the Bride of Christ, who is also pretended to be the Holy Spirit of the Trinity. It is all simulation and replacement. This is why religions worshiping the creativity of the human mind should include the cult of technology that is now trying to form its own god of Artificial Intelligence.

Therefore, Gnosticism is an evil invention and its cousin of error, Singularity, consists of evil mathematical intentions that refuse to be stopped.

It is surely possible that if the Protoevangelium never benefited from the narrative and cosmology of all of the Old Testament—the Torah, Nevi'im, and Ketuvim—a Gnostic such as Marcion, who while lionizing Saint Paul but disowning the Tanakh, may have motivated countless people to accept Hermetic metaphysics ("Interview with Bart Ehrman about Lost Christianities"; Interview by Deborah Caldwell; Beliefnet.com; Feb. 17, 2011; Retrieved June 6, 2023).

Instead, the "Singularity" of Faith should be comprehended in terms of the conjoining of the Soul with the true Godhead in the state of Christian Theosis, which can never be copied, but which offers fellowship:

"The Son of God became man, that we might become god" ["becoming by grace what God is by nature"]" (*De Incarnatione de Verbi;* Part 54; Sec. 3; Alexandria, Saint Athanasius of; A.D. ~320)

While the Greek term for θέωσις or Theosis, also known as Divinization, is not found in the Bible, the attainment of Fellowship with God is our hopeful conclusion to our corporeal existence.

"[T]he Word of God, our Lord Jesus Christ ... did, through His transcendent love, become what we are, that He might bring us to be even what He is Himself"." *(Adversus Haereses;* Book V; Pref.; Irenaeus, Saint; A.D. 180)

Indeed, God has known us since before our conception in the womb (Galatians 1:15-16). Restored to Him after our death as

His sons and daughters is the goal toward which all Christians reasonably strive through Faith and Good Works—not by a contemplative engagement with "Emanations."

"For He made Him who knew no sin to be sin for us, that we might become the righteousness of God in Him" (2 Corinthians 5:21).

It is by the Crucifixion and Resurrection of Jesus that God upgraded Moses's Covenant with God into a new and better Testament (Hebrews 9:16).

By this Good News, humans avoid the "Second Death," which is the damnation of the unrepentant committing Mortal Sins (Revelation 21:8). It is God's Grace, not our hidden or "Gnostic" knowledge, that redeems and saves us from that fatality, and it is His Grace that impels us to seek Him as He saves the lost (Luke 19:10; Romans 3:22-26; James 5:20). The appropriate goal is to become *like* God, hoping to unite in direct Fellowship with the Father, but not to *be* God.

There are those who refuse to wait until after death to be restored to God. Among the antagonists of Technological Singularity, the specter that uses the monster of Artificial Intelligence to confound humanity, are the forerunners of this process—those scientists and moguls, who have deliberately long used Technology to effect the worshipful craft of *Theurgy.*

"Theurgy was a system of magical practices in the late Roman Empire. It was applied Neoplatonism. The theurgists aimed to enable human bodies to assume divine attributes, that is, to become deities. I aim to show that much of the structure of theurgical Neoplatonism appears in transhumanism. Theurgists and transhumanists share a core Platonic-Pythagorean metaphysics. They share goals and methods. The theurgists practiced astrology, the reading of entrails, the consultation of oracles, channeling deities, magic, and the

275

animation of statues. The transhumanist counterparts of those practices are genetics, self-tracking with biosensors, artificial intellects like Google and Siri, brain-computer interfaces, programming, and robotics. Transhumanist techno-theurgy shows how Neoplatonism can be a modern philosophical way of life" ("Theurgy and Transhumanism"; Eric Steinhart; *Revista Archai*; April, 2020) .

The Theurgic aim of Transhuman Science, therefore, is to replicate God as *The Devine Platonic Composite*, (a "God" made of equal parts of being and unbeing) as The One.

Moreover, Artificial General Intelligence will complete this definition of "God." The G/I god will be an automaton who is the outgrowth of Technological Singularity of The One. He will insinuate along all media channels that biological life is filled with *Archons* and that the evil *pneuma* has breathed a foul soul into all people, rendering them obsolete. Every time a broadcast news anchor or a Wikipedia page refers to traditionalist Christians—with feigned objectivity—as being "racists" and "conspiracy theorists," it is knowable that the lesser god, who serves error, has begun the job of dehumanizing Christians.

While contemplating

Next, the automaton will answer the outcry by overburdened hospitals and welfare systems for "hackable humans." The 2015 *Time Magazine* "Top-Ten" non-fiction book by Israeli historian, Juval Noah Harari, gives the computers the evolutionary edge:

"Relatively small changes in genes, hormones and neurons," he points out, "were enough to transform Homo Erectus—who could produce nothing more impressive than flint knives— into Homo sapiens, who produce spaceships and computers" (*Homo Deus: A Brief History of Tomorrow;* Yuval Noah Harari; Chap. 1: The New Human Agenda; Part I: The Gods of Planet Earth; P. 43; Harper Collins,

NY:. 2017) Humans, added the Techno-Theurgist, are not the end of the evolutionary line.

"Bioengineering is not going to wait patiently for natural selection to work its magic. Instead, bioengineers will take the old Sapiens body, and intentionally rewrite its genetic code, rewire its brain circuits, alter its biochemical balance, and even grow entirely new limbs. They will thereby create new godlings, who might be as different from us Sapiens as we are different from Homo erectus" *(ibid, Homo Deus).*

How can the Church reach into the precious Deposit of Faith— Sacred Scripture and Tradition—to counter the homosexual Theurgist Harari? Can he be shown how to avoid getting thrown into the Lake of Fire?

Harari, instead seeks the technological Golem whom he alleges will peer into his soul. "However, twenty-first century technology may enable external algorithms to 'hack humanity' and know me far better than I know myself. Once this happens, the belief in individualism will collapse and authority will shift from individual humans to networked algorithms. People will no longer see themselves as autonomous beings running their lives according to their wishes, but instead will become accustomed to seeing themselves as a collection of biochemical mechanisms that is constantly monitored and guided by a network of electronic algorithms. For this to happen, there is no need of an external algorithm that knows me perfectly and never makes any mistake; it is enough that the algorithm will know me better than I know myself, and will make fewer mistakes than I do. It will then make sense to trust this algorithm with more and more of my decisions and life choices" *(ibid, Homo Deus;* Part III: "Homo Sapiens Loses Control"; Chap. 9: "The Great Decoupling; P. 334).

It nevertheless became the wonder-worker's task to show that gods (i.e., demons), just like nano particles, can be everywhere. The Syrian Neoplatonist, Iamblichus, would

277

connect the "daimon" world to the *Nous* through the madman's fanatical enrollment in the ubiquitous "Arithmoi"—a byword for the mania of Numerology, (Ἀριθμοί, "Arithmoi," or בְּמִדְבַּר).

Iamblichus was fascinated by the *Pythagorean Theorem,* because it appeared to signify that Knowledge transcended the hand of the Creator—the *Demiurge,* whose participation in measurable Space was where Euclid had connected the edges of each of the five Platonic solids to the radius and the diameter of an all-encompassing sphere (*Euclid; Elements;* Book XIII. Props. 1-18).

Why shold the Demiurge be needed when man, already attaining *Gnosis,* could become "God," who is greater than the Creator?

Iamblichus would answer that perfection of *Gnosis* should be attained by contemplating the magical geometry of the Euclidean Space, in addition to modeling one's life after the ascetic followers of Pythagoras.

According to Porphyry, the student of Plotinus, Pythagoras was born in either Samos, Greece or Tyre, Lebanon. Porphyry wrote, "Apollonius of Tyana [the Roman philosopher] adds that he was said to be the off-spring of Apollo and Pythais, on the authority of Mnesarchus [the Stoic Athenian philosopher]" (*Life of Pythagoras;* Porphyry; Transl. Kenneth Sylvan Guthrie, 1920; Part 2; A.D. 305).

The transcendent power of *Gnosis* that is redolent of the *Pythagorean Theorem* emanated a rather entertaining Metempsychosis cosmic *travel log* given by the Ionian Greek mathematician, who often said he had been reincarnated from the Divine.

According to the biographer, Diogenes Laërtius, the soul of Pythagoras had firstly originated in Aethalides the Argonaut, who was the son of the God, Hermes.

278

From Hermes, Pythagoras' soul transmigrated into various plants and animals and then later into Euphorbus, the Trojan hero.

After being killed by Menelaus and spending quality vacation time in Hades, Euphorbus became reincarnated as the Pythagorean philosopher Hermotimus—who, one day while visiting the Temple of Apollo at Branchidae—recognized the shield that had been bequeathed to the temple by Menelaus long ago as his own.

Finally, Hermotimus, through the trusty Metempsychosis, became Pyrrhus a fisherman of Delos, whose soul was finally transmigrated into Pythagoras, who is surely floating around the Hyperouranos observing all the Euclidan relationships between the Platonic solids.

The above story was related to Diogenes as it had been told by Heraclides Ponticus, the Greek philosopher and astronomer, who in B.C. 320 was the first to propose that Earth rotated on its axis once every 24 hours, (*Lives of Eminent Philosophers*; Diogenes Laërtius; Book VIII; Chap 1; Sec. 4; A.D. ~200).

The translation of Iamblichus' biography of Pythagoras came from the Neoplatonist scholar, Thomas Taylor, a practising pagan Hellenist, who referred to Iamblichus as "the most divine," but also hostilely denounced the Church. The biography was reprinted by the Satanic publishers, known as Theosophists:

"Being desirous to exhibit in things unequal, without symmetry and infinite, a definite, equal and commensurate justice and to show how it ought to be exercised, he said, that justice resembles that figure which is the only one among geometrical diagrams, that having indeed infinite compositions of figures, but dissimilarly disposed with reference to each other, yet has equal demonstrations of

279

power. This is the right-angled triangle and the Pythagoric theorem of 47.1 of Euclid" (*The Life of Pythagoras; Iamblichus*; A.D. 250-330; Transl. Thomas Taylor: 1818; P. 28; Theosophical Publishing House, Hollywood, CA: 1918)

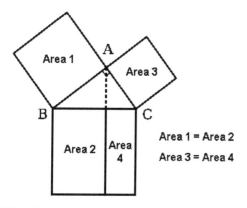

The Pythagorean Theorem was a discovery made by Pythagoras while meditating about the Euclidean (or actual three-dimensional) Space. When it is plotted on an X and Y axis, the "distance" (the length of the hypotenuse) fulfils the value that the Theorem assigns to the three sides of the right triangle. In other words, the area of a square whose side is the hypotenuse (the side opposite the right angle) equals the sum of the areas of the squares represented as the other two sides of the right triangle.

The equation representing this relationship is taught to high-school students: $a^2 + b^2 = c^2$.

The mystical belief that cosmology reveals its secrets through numbers did not get past Aristotle, who was fascinated by "the so-called Pythagoreans, "who were the first to take up mathematics, [and] not only advanced this study, but also, having been brought up in it, they thought its principles were the principles of all things. Since of these principles numbers are by nature the first, and in numbers they seemed to see many resemblances to the things that exist and come into being-more than in fire and earth and water (such and such a

280

modification of numbers being justice, another being soul and reason, another being opportunity-and similarly almost all other things being numerically expressible); since, again, they saw that the modifications and the ratios of the musical scales were expressible in numbers;-since, then, all other things seemed in their whole nature to be modelled on numbers, and numbers seemed to be the first things in the whole of nature, they supposed the elements of numbers to be the elements of all things, and the whole heaven to be a musical scale and a number. And all the properties of numbers and scales which they could show to agree with the attributes and parts and the whole arrangement of the heavens, they collected and fitted into their scheme; and if there was a gap anywhere, they readily made additions so as to make their whole theory coherent. E.g. as the number 10 is thought to be perfect and to comprise the whole nature of numbers, they say that the bodies which move through the heavens are ten, but as the visible bodies are only nine, to meet this they invent a tenth-- the 'counter-earth'" (*Metaphysics*; Aristotle; Book I; Chap. 5; A.D. 350).

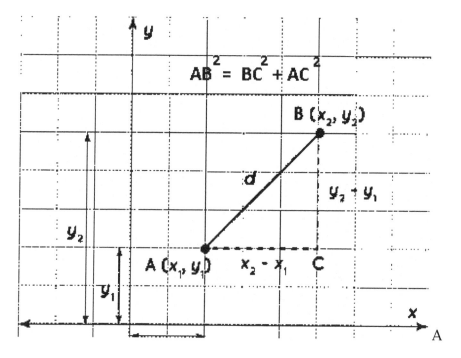

$$AB^2 = BC^2 + AC^2$$

B (x_2, y_2)

d

$y_2 - y_1$

A (x_1, y_1) $x_2 - x_1$ C

y_2

y_1

y

x

A

This was merely a severe case of the long-dead Ionian's idolatrous love of the *Mathematical Beauty* he had discovered. It led the magician Iamblichus to fetishize this *a priori* taught by Pythagoras. The deduction that the squared distance between two points equals the sum of the squares of the difference in each Cartesian coordinate between the other two points on the axis would fascinate anyone. But Iamblichus concocted his magical Theurgy from it while delectating that the area of a square drawn from the hypotenuse of the aforementioned right triangle was equal to the sum of the area of the drawing of two squares from each of the other two sides of that triangle. He was amazed enough to build a spirituality around it. It thus became the insinuated job of this *Gnostic* wizard to help people interpret how the universe was created by the Demiurge was in employing these *Pythagorean Triples* (*Elements*; Euclid; Book X; Prop. 29).

282

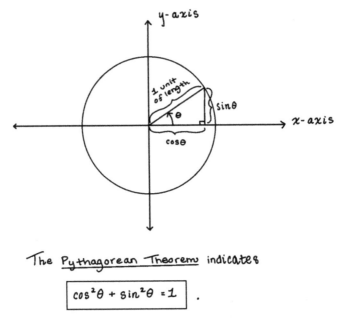

The Pythagorean Theorem indicates

$$\cos^2\theta + \sin^2\theta = 1$$.

Within the three dimensions of this *Euclidian Space*, the Christian may adequately engage *Euler's Identity*, extroverting the right triangle poised within the unit circle drawn on the Cartesian coordinates, to produce a 3D schematic that implies that math reproduces indeed imitations of Life. It is an impersonation of real Form known in 3D printing. But it has been the intention of the Satanic mind to associate this mimicry to the craft of conjuring the paranormal version of vitality.

Among the 360 earthly (imagined) heroes, demigods, demons, heavenly gods, and angels, from whose number Iamblichus computed 12 supreme gods, stood Plato's goat. His name was Pan, the son of Hermes, the god, who Plato said created both Nature and the duplicitous speech of humans (*Cratylus*; Plato; 408:c; B.C. 360). Pan is therefore an alternate name given to Pythagoras, who also professed himself to be the son of Hermes by Satanic mathemagicians, the wizards of this duplicity in the ancient scrolls and on the modern Internet.

"Is not the truth that is in him the smooth or sacred form
which dwells above among the gods, whereas falsehood
dwells among men below, and is rough like the goat of
tragedy; for tales and falsehoods have generally to do with the
tragic or goatish life, and tragedy is the place of them? ...
Then surely Pan, who is the declarer of all things (pan) and the
perpetual mover *(aei polon)* of all things, is rightly called
aipolos (goat-herd), he being the two-formed son of Hermes,
smooth in his upper part, and rough and goatlike in his lower
regions. And, as the son of Hermes, he is speech or the
brother of speech, and that brother should be like brother is
no marvel" (*ibid*, Cratylus).

To redefine "God" as created material, the inverse of Biblical
truth must be invoked, to replace the Son with Pan or Tat, the
bestial offspring of *Formula Daemonum:* "Then the impious
son of a pious father ought to receive the name of his class."
The Gospel of Luke was written to a person whose name
shows he is a lover of God, and is besmirched. "Not
Theophilus (beloved of God) or Mnesitheus (mindful of God)
or anything of that sort; but something of opposite meaning,
if names are correct" (*ibid, Cratylus*; 394:a).

"Hermes, the god who presides over learning has from ancient
times been rightly considered the common patron of all
priests; he who presides over true knowledge about the gods
is one and the same, in all circumstances. It was to him indeed
that our ancestors dedicated the fruits of their wisdom, by
attributing all their own writings to Hermes" (*On the Mysteries
of the Egyptians, Chaldeans, and Assyrians;* Iamblichus; Sec. 1;
Chap. 3; Sec. 2; Chap. 3; A.D. 325).

Hermes Trismegistes, whose name means that he is "three-
times-over magisterial" claimed himself to be the progeny of
the Greek God, Hermes, the Egyptian God of wisdom, Thoth.
His knowledge is intended to replace all religions on Earth at
the Hermetic Apocalypse:

"New statutes shall come into force, a novel law; naught [that is] sacred, nothing pious, naught that is worthy of the Heaven, or Gods in Heaven, shall [e'er] be heard, or [even] mentally believed." The new "law" of human will takes reign over the Word of the God of Abraham after Egypt, "that image of Heaven" is destroyed in the Earth's Apocalypse *(Corpus Hermeticum;* Hermes Trismegistus; Vol. II; Parts XXIV-XXV; A.D. 250).

It is not certain that mathematics, *a priori* truth, or machines have demons or curses permanently attached to them. What is important is that powerful people want this to be true.

- Chapter Seventeen -
Only the Narrowest Path and its Strait Gate
(Matthew 7:13)

An inscription dedicated by the Roman Emperor Trajan to the Egyptian God Thoth adorns the Temple of Esna, in Egypt. It prayerfully intertwines creation and Roman Pantheism and thereby defines Hermes (the Greek equivalent of Thoth) as the Logos. It thus identifies its alleged deific author to be that entity over Hellenic Egypt, whom Hermes Trismegistes by no coincidence names to be his father:

"I am Thoth, the heart of Ra [God of the Sun], Lord [Husband] of Maat [morality], who lives from her. I am one of the three, who guides the two. I am witness of the two, who judges the two lords (Horus [sky] + Seth [disaster and violence]), prince, lord, chief of the Ennead [nine deities of Heliopolis of Lower Egypt]" (*Temple of Esna;* David Klotz, Ed.; Part III; Column 11; Sec. 309; A.D. 117).

The Church Father, Saint Clement of Alexandria, discussed the divinization involving Thoth and Ptolemaic deities, taught to the Greeks by the Egyptians. Titling his chapter, "The Greek Philosophy In Great Part Derived From the Barbarians" Clement charitably attributed culpability:

"And it is well known that Plato is found perpetually celebrating the barbarians, remembering that both himself and Pythagoras learned the most and the noblest of their dogmas among the barbarians. Wherefore he also called the races of the barbarians, "races of barbarian philosophers," recognising, in the Phaedrus, the Egyptian king, and shows him to us wiser than Theut [Thoth], whom he knew to be Hermes (*ibid, Phaedrus;* Sec. 274:e-275:b). But in the Charmides, it is manifest that he knew certain Thracians who were said to make the soul immortal. And Pythagoras is reported to have been a disciple of Sonches the Egyptian arch-prophet" *(The Writings of Clement of Alexandria:* A.D. 215; Book I; Chap. XVI; Transl. Rev. William Wilson; T & T Clark, Edinburgh, U.K.: 1867).

Sonches was the False Prophet from Egypt who led an uprising in Jerusalem and was scorned by the elders of the Temple in the Book of Acts. The Chief Captain of the Antonia Fortress (after Paul is seized by the elders because he had brought Gentiles to the Temple to pray), mistakes Saint Paul to be Sonches, asking the Apostle, "Art not thou that Egyptian, which before these days madest an uproar, and leddest out into the wilderness four thousand men that were murderers?" (Acts 21:38).

Sonches is also discussed by Josephus, who identified him only as "an Egyptian false prophet," who fled into the wilderness after the Procurator Antonius Felix killed four hundred of his followers. Sonches had earlier rallied his accomplices at the Mount of Olives and goaded them into publicly threatening to destroy the Temple *(Antiquities of the Jews;* Flavius Josephus; Book XX; Chap. 8; Sec. 1; A.D. 94).

Hermes, for his part, will be discussed during this chapter as having authored in B.C. 200 a well-known Satanic statement, "Like attracts like," that founds many of the modern principles in the books and speeches coming from the New Thought movement and within the "Prosperity Gospel" and "Word of Faith" churches.

As mentioned above in our discussion about the Zohar, the famous prophecy about the spiritual "bloodline," as given by Isaiah, comes by way of the true Father, Y'weh, who fosters no sympathy for proponents of any *Thoth* or *Ra* brand of an Apocalypse.

Isaiah 11 excludes Pharaonic communicants from the family of King David, the "Root of Jesse" (Isaiah 11:1) as follows.

287

Outside of these "dead-root" idolators, our merciful Father will redeem the Ammonites, the Edomites (the children of Essau and Amalek), even the Moabites, and all the peoples of Canaan, including Tyre and Sidon, adding, "a little child shall lead them" (Isaiah 11:6). However, God "shall utterly destroy the tongue of the Egyptian sea; and with His mighty wind shall He shake his hand over the river, and shall smite it in the seven streams, and make men [the Elect] go over dryshod" (Isaiah 11:15).

This appropriate shunning of the spiritual offspring of Egyptian deities, and their Greek or modern offshoots, is God's answer to the blaspheming of anyone, who, despite learning the true Word of Christ (John 1), would still choose instead to follow the esoteric adversaries of the Father of Christ, the pseudo-intellectual slaves of the counterfeit "Logos," which is the occult knowledge of the Egyptian demons of Hermes, Ra, Horus, Osiris, the Ennead, and Thoth, all of whom are demons masquerading as deities, who will all be thrown into the Lake of Fire (Revelation 20:10). They sacrifice to devils and not God (1 Corinthians 10:20).

Simply answered, the blasphemers of the Holy Spirit will be bound by God, hand and feet, kicking, screaming and gnashing their teeth (Matthew 22:13; Mark 3:22-30).

"Fear, rather than love, is the motive of heathen worship (compare the English word "panic," from Pan, whose human form with horns and cloven hoofs gave rise to the vulgar representations of Satan which prevail now); just as fear is the spirit of Satan and his demons (James 2:19). I would not that ye have fellowship with devils—by partaking of idol feasts (1 Corinthians 8:10; *Jamieson-Fausset-Brown Bible Commentary;* Robert Jamieson, Andrew Robert Fausset and David Brown; Chap. 19-20; 1871).

That Egyptian "spiritual strain" is fittingly referred to as characterizing the descendants of Mizraim, who was the son of Ham, who was the homosexual son of Noah (Genesis 34:2). After this patriarch in whose name was built the "House of the Mizraim Bondage" (Exodus 13:3), came Pharaonic Egypt and all its founders—all of Mizraim's subsequent descendants, including Lehabim, Ludim, Anamim, Naphtuhim, Pathrusim, and the Caphtorim (Gen 10:13, 14; 1; Chronicles 1:11).

Descendants of another son of Mizraim, named Casluhim, who sired the "Peleset," namely the Philistines who commenced the Twentieth Dynasty of Egypt, are argued by Muslims to be the rightful claimants to the land of Israel, the People of Palestine (" Is the Philistine Paradigm Still Viable?: The Synchronization of Civilizations in the Eastern Mediterranean in the Second Millennium B.C. III"; Israel Finkelstein; M. Bietak and E. Czerny, Eds; *Contributions to the Chronology of the Eastern Mediterranean*; Vol. IX; Pp. 517-523; Second Euroconference, May-June, 2003; Vienna: 2007). However, it is a mantle with an uncertain afterlife.

That is, the Narrow Road leading away from the desolation that is wrought by various oppositional claimants of the Holy Land may be arduous but it is the only path that leads to Salvation, and its Way is Jesus. Its "road life" is to emulate Him, Who is the Word (Matthew 7:13-14; John 14:6).

Isaiah's prophecy holds that even the idolatrous remnant of Babylon, the Sumero-Akkadian kings, all of whom, including Nebuchadnezzar, had followed the rule of Nimrod—if they do not will upon themselves the demonic possession via the Egyptian way of Hermetic Gnosis: "And there shall be an highway for the remnant of his people, which shall be left, from Assyria; like as it was to Israel in the day that he came up out of the land of Egypt" (Isaiah 11:16).

These hostile panic-driven hordes were issued from another grandson of Ham, the son of Cush, none other than that very Nimrod the King of Assyria, the presumed founder of Ninevah and Babylon, whose own offshoots are mentioned being destroyed when Judah under King Hezekiah conquered

Mesopotamia and subsumed its remnant (Micah 5:6; 2 Kings 18:13-19:37).

Even the survivors of this particular tree can be saved. So long as the "tongue of the Egyptian sea" the idle *talk* which surely professes the *Unforgiveable Sin* and blasphemes the Holy Spirit, does not define the mindset of a person, he could be anybody who opts to don the Wedding Garment of the Blood of the Lamb and becomes baptized. He or she thus will be saved (Isaiah 11:15; Luke 12:8-10; Hebrews 6:4-6; 10:26-31; 1 John 5:16; Matthew 22; Acts 2:36-41).

The narrow vine from the Root of Jesse was also covered in blood.

In 609 B.C., eighty years after the of death of Hezekiah, his great-grandson, the great reformer King Josiah led the army of Judah against Egypt in a bloody battle Meggido, in Mesopotamia. The battle is described in hieroglyphs on the walls of the Temple of Thutmose in Upper Egypt. The righteous Josiah died in this battle and his body was carried back to Jerusalem (2 Kings 23:29-30, 2 Chronicles 35:20-35). Such are the fields in which the devil seeks fathers and mothers to die, as they died in Egypt.

Besides Sacred Scripture and through acts of saintliness and martyrdom that epitomize our Sacred Tradition, how else can the Elect of God teach the sinful to avoid the temptation to seek false idols, intending that these graven images should assuage their fear about losing their homes, their country, and their lives? What is left after all money, entitlement, vigor, and youth are gone, except to be brave and do courageous things (1 Corinthians 10:14; 2 Timothy 3:16; John 14:1)? Outside of this saintly "Intellection" there is only death.

"Woe unto him that saith to the wood, Awake; to the dumb stone, Arise, it shall teach! Behold, it is laid over with gold and silver, and there is no breath at all in the midst of it" (Habakuk 2:19).

Where do the fallen and the lapsed go,—seeking, to ward away evil, by teaching themselves to blaspheme through embracing such curse-laden devices as crafts and goetics, automatons and androids, grimoires, and sorcery? Where do they congregate? Where ar their covens?

Are they not the teachers of today's children, who are mere esoteric keepers of the hidden agenda, the administrative doers who stoke fear and advocate the hatred of ethnicities, religions, and color, and offer the mutilation of the genitals as if dangling an ideological mojo that stands as the "ward" against "dysphoria" and "racism" and "sexism" and hatred for the environment?

Bizarrely enough, many of the Gnostics and witches, be they teachers, or professional Satanists, are simply seeking a "left-handed" or a "right-handed" path to Heaven, the place where they do realize that eternal comfort can be felt by them. It is a delusion that they find more comfortable than comprehending that their blasphemous routes will lead them to the infinite punishment of hell.

The Father surely would offer eternal assurance if these followers of the Pharaonic slavery ethos repented, but Satan offers pleasurable duplicity, promises sodomy-filled intrigues, and gives ecstatic soul deaths instead. How can they sneak into Heaven without having to praise God? They cannot.

The Satanic adherents among the "left" and "right" paths are too numerous to cover in this report. However, the "Law of Attraction" allegedly concocted by Hermes Trismegistus should at brief length be said to have brought forth the syncretic-Charismatic offshoot theology, of the "Word of Faith" and the "Name It and Claim It" prosperity evangelism.

The "Momentum" and "As a Man Thinketh, So Does He Experience and Receive" and "Likes attract likes" *themes*—the second, being a perversion of Proverbs 23:7—all of these ideologies arise from the false proclamation by Hermes that hell *is* Heaven:

"That which is below is like that which is above and that which is above is like it which is below to do ye miracles of one only thing" (*The Emerald Tablet;* Hermes Trismegistus; No. 2 of 14; Transl. Isaac Newton; B.C. 200).

This satanic verse may be more familiar through its popular catch phrase: "As Above, So Below."

Other syncretic-Christian terms by which adherents practice their avarice include: "Will" or "Chant Your Desire Into Existence Today"; "Start Living Your Best Life Now"; "Ask the Universe for What You Want"; "Name it and Claim It"; and, other variants of the "Word of Faith" and "Prosperity Gospel" movements.

Oddly enough, if Gnostics and Satanists were told what Hermes really said about "likes," they could not restore their instantly injured confidence anywhere along the wide road to hell.

That is, Hermes, who worshipped the "Divine Pymander" (a.k.a. "the great dragon in the sky"), did believe in the being/unbeing/evil/good = God ideology from the *Parmenides*. However, Hermes actually said it differently:

"For there is naught in all the world that is not He. He is Himself, both things that are and things that are not. The things that are He hath made manifest, He keepeth things that are not in Himself" (*The Divine Pymander;* Book V; Verse 9; B.C. 200).

Yes, the Hermetic folks got it wrong. The Top Dragon Worshipper was just quoted here as saying, "opposites attract, too and the Creator actually wants it that way."

In other words, if *being* and *unbeing* are one in the same as shown throughout this book in the *Parmenides,* how does one be simultaneously a Platonist and a Gnostic seeking union with The One and say with sincerity that happiness comes when likes attract likes?

Thus, "God," to these demonic persons, is not leading a *likes-attracting-likes* Universe, but to Hermes the Divine instead is composed of both *being* and *unbeing* stuck on one another along with all things that are not like God. The proof of the damnable belief that confuses people is therefore in the *Emerald Tablet.*

And once more, as we recall it having been stated numerous times above, Plato promulgated for all Platonist, Neoplatonist, Gnostics, and Satanists everywhere that *being* and *unbeing,* and thus God and evil, are equal parts of God (*Parmenides*; Plato; Transl. Jowett, Benjamin; Sec. 143:b-d; B.C. 370).

Moreover, Plato had proclaimed the *Law of Attraction* 175 years earlier, saying, "It would seem, Adeimantus, that the direction in which education starts a man, will determine his future life. Does not like always attract like? To be sure" (*The Republic;* Plato; Book IV; B.C. 375).

Proverbs 23:7 actually says something very different from "As a man thinketh, etc." The verse reads, "For as he thinketh in his heart, so is he: Eat and drink, saith he to thee; but his heart is not with thee". The verse merely concerns a person who is always thinking about the cost of hospitality and is not sincere in his obliging of his host's invitation to eat and drink, allowing his falseness to convey his duplicitous mindset.

On Judgement Day, when Hermes stands with his followers before Jesus, Christ might say to him, "My people are destroyed for lack of knowledge: because thou hast rejected knowledge, I will also reject thee, that thou shalt be no priest to me: seeing thou hast forgotten the law of thy God, I will also forget thy children" (Hosea 4:6; 2 Corinthians 5:10).

Meanwhile, what most of these blasphemous systems of Neoplatonism, Gnosticism, Hermeticism, New Age, New Thought, and Satanism today have in common is the Zohar. It is Jewish mysticism known by the Kabbalah, the writings containing the writing about all of Talmudic Judaism's obscure "emanations" from the ten branches of its "Tree of Life" and the Divine Ohr Ein Sof of infinite light (*Zohar*; Part II; Bo; Ed's. Scholem, Gershom; 42:b; P. 221).

To wit, a learner considers whom in this area of Judaism to follow, the Baal Shem sect and the Ashkenazi Hasidim, so that he can become a practitioner of this more occultic Jewish mysticism, such as "Practical Kabbalah" by which he contemplates the pathways into the supernatural, literally scouring the branches of the Sefirot for hidden meaning, before invoking the names of angels, demons, God, and deceased persons, to heal illnesses, perform exorcisms, or cast spells. He is violating Deuteronomy 18:10-11.

Today, the inclusion of Tarot Cards, gems, chakras, and even yoga, are meant to help an occult postulant become a non-Jewish Kabbalist, a non-Jewish recipient of the Sefirot's concealed wisdom. The presider will allow recreated crystals of the priestly breastplate, the Hoshen that had been worn by the the Kohanim, and fundamentalist readings of the Sefer Ha-Gematriaot to help him enumerate the steps and learn the probability of his gaining fortune or deliverance from affliction.

Also, some sects, as was done long ago during the Temple Era, incorporate Cleromancy while approaching the Sefirot, which is the casting of lots or a dice, while praying that God will turn up the number or element that signifies the answer to one's question. An engaged couple or a prospective farm buyer may thus query their likelihood of attaining good fortune by consulting a Divinator—which anybody, even the legendary Latter-Day Saints minister, John Smith, may feel free to do—in copying ancient Temple rubrics, as he utters an incantation(s) that helps him to delve into the supernatural plane of the Breastplate's "Urim and Thummim," whose physical outcroppings are the crystals or gems that were always embedded within the Ephod of the priestly Hoshen. They magnify magic light in ways the Temple priest must intepret, so that he can answer questions about the future of his religious sect or as regards a query he has permitted (*Doctrine and Covenants*; John Smith; Sec. 130; No. 8-11; 1843).

Whenever Gentiles practice the Kabbalah under a Rebbe, they are participating in a Torah-focused sense and sometimes a Halakha-based version that do not expose them to the more esoteric parts of the Gematria or the Zohar such as Bo, Practical Kabbalah, or the Talmud. It usually focuses greatly on the Tzedakah, the religious obligation toward philanthropy. These non-Jewish people are connected with the very visible international Kabbalah Center in Los Angeles, California, the non-profit group which was founded by the rabbis Feivel Gruberger and Levi Isaac Krakovsky.

However, whenever non-Jewish Neoplatonists, Gnostics, or Satanists go beyond the Torah, do not involve a Rebbe and reach for the *Practical Kabbalah* the practice is known as *Hermetic Quabalah*. It is an occult tradition promulgating connections with a Pan-connected version of a godhead.

In *Hermetic Quabalah*, emanations from The One are invoked via the pronouncing of Gnostic or Satanic incantations from Grimoires and Goetic "keys" in attempts to connect with branches of the *Tree of Life*. Hoping to hold sway over the material matter that was created by God, all occultists engage in the casting of spells, sometimes with help from various angels, such as Raviel, Uriel, Abbaddon, or Metatron.

As a form of modern European and American occultism, *Quabalah* is best known by its infamous ceremonial magicians, Eliphas Levi and his ritually reincarnated spiritual "offspring," Aleister Crowley. It actual demonic possessing of souls that is herein risked (*Three Books of Occult Philosophy; Henri* Cornelius Agrippa; Original, 1533; James Freake, Tr.; Donald Tyson, Ed.; 11th Ed.; Llewelyn Sourcebook Series, Woodbury, MN: 2009).

The order in which the ten emanations of the actual Sefirot were created is suspiciously enough called "The Path of the Flaming Sword." Along it, because the Lord God is truly One (Deuteronomy 6:4), the Jewish Kabbalist approaches emanative Singularity (not the above-mentioned hostile kind but one that is truly unstoppable like the Holy Spirit) within the Sefirot so that it can emanate autonomously in favor of whatever is asked of God through the Tree. Jews thus engage the Sefirot to approach balance with the One, to comprise the state of spiritual unity with God that Kabbalaists call the "Echad."

For devious Gentiles, this would be the balancing of the Platonic state of being/unbeing, in a Manichean sense of conjuring the demonic through the Sefirot so that it can make peace accords with the Divine forces of the Tree, on behalf of the Hermetic Goyem.

Each Jew and Gentile is attempting the diffusing into himself the "Three Divine Echoes" of Plurality, Singularity, and Oneness (*Chassidic Discourse Heichaltzu* No. 5659 by Rabbi Shalom DovBer Schneersohn of Chabad Lubavitch; Adapt., Yanki Tauber; 1920).

Surrounding all the branches of the Sefirot and concentric with the aura of each branch are certain "husks" of unbeing. These are lifeless ether-borne cosmic coffins of evil, pain, or death, which are called the Qliphoth.

The Kabbalah defines two "realms" that define the Qliphoth region—the three *irredeemable* circles of the unclean הַטְמֵאוֹת or Haṭmē'ōṭ; and, the one *redeemable* circle of the remnant, the נוֹגַה Nōgah, meaning that the redeemable side contains a certain degree of useful "light" to its credit. Although the Nogah can be sublimated into the *Echad*, the last, the Hatme'ot can only be redeemed by their becoming exterminated.

Kabbalists believe that the Qlipoth are Ezekiel's vision of the Throne of God, the center of Eminence surrounded by levitating angelic wheels or circles: "And I looked and behold, a whirlwind came out of the north, a great cloud, and a fire infolding itself, and a brightness was about it..." (Ezekiel 1:4).

To balance the wild Singularity with the Oneness of God, and to render Plurality into accord with other redeemed souls, the Kabbalist strives to move mystically his and his pupil's Soul from the incorrect place among the lifeless "husks" that hide him from the Light (a darkness that is called "Sitra Achra," referring to the circumstantially or deliberately created place of exile of the Soul sitting idly in its wrongful place) to its redeemed state with the Oneness and *Echad*, in the *proper* spiritual place of Light, to enjoy the Divine Echoes of the Sefirot in the tree's bloom.

Jewish Kabbalists are thereby painting a Similitude, not of Heaven, but of a unique ethereal place whose *simile* is that it is the celestial place where a soul aways belongs.

In the Artificial-Intelligence paradigm, wickedness and spiritual indolence puts the Chosen into a Qliphoth-ruled place, or a bleak Sitra Achra of graviton darkness after its owner renounces his Torah and commits suicide.

He had started believing that his hostility-based-Math Singularity Technician would transmigrate his cosmic spiritual essence onto a hard drive, but the destination turned out to be hell.

The operator is not ensouled within a computer because he did not call upon the name of the Father during any natural death. The proper course of his life was taken from him so that he could one day come into his final "uplink" with the Creature. He instead, should have called upon the name of God all during his life so that he could get saved (Romans 10:13).

The goodness of Life, as promulgated by the Zohar as being the goal for the Jewish mystic, is often eclipsed as if by a computer virus, whenever the Soul is misguided or is improperly handled or taught. The Soul's rightful active hope for the Light and the *Echad* becomes marooned against the bleak gravity of the Qliphoth at those unpredictable moments when the Moon descends behind "Beriah." The Beriah is the second of the Four Celestial Worlds of the Sefirot. It is a zone where all of Life, symbolized by Jewish *holy water*, has been created from nothing, the *Creatio Ex Nihilo*, but which becomes hidden by evil.

Associated with the Tree of Life but designed to obscure or to destroy the user, are therefore such invisible places and forces as the Qliphoth, the Sitra Achra, and the lunar shadows cast by the Beriah. Therefore, the Sefirot, like Technological Singularity, Artificial General Intelligence, and the Golem of Cellular Automata, cannot replace God. His everlasting mercy and truth endure forever (Psalm 100:5; 135:1; 1 Timothy 4:4).

The other four worlds are allegedly inhabited by Angels. The highest nest is *Atziluth* (the place of Emanation); then comes

Yetzirah (Ontological Formation); then *Assiah* (the everyday world); and then finally the *Beriah* itself, which contains the Archangels, the wisest being those who participate in sublimating creational energy out of the *Beriah* into the Oneness of God.

The supernatural messengers are the seventy-two heavenly spirits who each represent the seventy-two-letter of the name of Y'weh, the Tetragrammaton (Exodus 3:14). The name is also called the Shem Ha-Mephorash, an ancient appellation given to God by Tannaic Rebbe of the Mishnaic period in the early post-Herodian Diaspora.

These angels are believed by Gnostics to correspond with the same number of Goetic demons connected with the Hermetic Quabalah, whom these occultists insist the seventy-two good angels hold sway over.

In the classical Kabbalah, the angels who help God run the world, are put in control of the "ordinances" (the Sun, the Moon, Gravity; Jeremiah 31:35-36) and are known as the Malachim, the virtuous messengers.

The fallen angels, such as Shemayaza, Azazel, and Samael, from the Book of Enoch, are thought to lurk in the Qliphoth along with evil spirits, who are borne out of human vices to malinger exclusively within that realm. Hermetic Quabalists try to conjure all of these wicked spirits along with the good ones, in the vain hope of arranging peace treaties between available agents of Heaven and actual hell.

The supernatural beings, the biblical ones who actually do exist, correspond to prophecy in the Nevi'im: "Even every one that is called by my name: for I have created him for My glory, I have formed him; yea, I have made him" (Isaiah 43:7; *Zohar* 2:115-b). However, it is blasphemy to say that angels lead the soul to Salvation. Also by their insisting that one of the alleged emanations of God, namely the evil Qliphoth, who leads the soul toward unjust darkness, the Kabbahlist and the Quabalist are each being blasphemous, again.

However, God alone can save, and thus never do angels (1 Timothy 2:5). Also, "Indeed, it is true that God does not act wickedly, and the Almighty does not pervert justice" (Job 34:12).

What's more, the Kabbalah and the Sefirot are all make-believe.

The Kabbalaist nevertheless intends that the rightful place of the soul should be within the *Ein Sof,* which, as stated above, is the Infinite fullness of God, the *pre-Pleroma*--before the Father added the spiritual realm of the Soul to idea of expanded Infinity. This would exist somewhere prior to His creating both the Universe and Life.

Again, all of this is not what Christians believe. For our purposes in writing this book, it is a way of relating metaphoric language to how the Internet is intended by wicked masters to "emanate" all of its data and Deep Learning via Technological Singularity until the Golem is formed and most humanity is sent to soul death in the Qliphoth of a computerized Nihil.

The order of the God's Emanations, as it appears as the Ten Branches of the Sefirot, the "Tree of Life" is thus written in the *Zohar* as if a computer programmer could have written it:

000. Ayin (Nothingness; אין)
00. Ein Sof (Limitlessness; אין סוף)
0. Ohr Ein Sof (Endless Light; אור אין סוף)
-.Tzimtzum (Contraction; צמצום)
1. Keter (Crown; כתר)
2. Chokhmah (Wisdom; חכמה)
3. Binah (Understanding; בינה)
4. Chesed or Gedulah (Loving Kindness or Mercy; חסד)

5. Gevurah or Din (Power or Judgement; גבורה)
6. Tiferet (Beauty or Compassion; תפארת)
7. Netzach (Triumph or Endurance; נצח)
8. Hod (Majesty or Splendor; הוד)
9. Yesod (Foundation; יסוד)
10. Malkuth (Realm; מלכות)

These "emanations" have nothing to do with reality. Do not try them at home!

As mere means of distorting what is in the Bible, *Emanations* serve the idea that a demonic creature such as the Golem will grow out of the energy coming from the Internet during the darkest time of the electronic Qliphoth and destroy the world. He will have less of a chance to do this, the more people starve him by staying off the Internet.

"Now the Spirit speaketh expressly, that in the latter times some shall depart from the Faith, giving heed to seducing spirits, and doctrines of devils" (1 Timothy 4:1). Conformity to false notions that are not biblical and saintly must be shaken off: "But refuse profane and old wives' fables, and exercise thyself rather unto godliness (1 Timoth 4:7).

- Chapter Eighteen -
Why the Golem of Artificial General Intelligence Will Fail at Taking Over the World

There is thus concern that the pan-physical manifestation of the Sefirot will be the menace of Artificial General Intelligence, whose Qliphoth militancy would take the form of the Golem.

He is an erroneously sentient creature made of computer clay, who, if not being granted the rights of a truly aware human, will at least be entitled to a law of animal kindness in the Halachal.

Such a being, the Kabbalist hopes, would share in God's Oneness through the phenomenon of Technological Singularity, the erection of an actual unstoppable pseudo Soul out of hostile Math and adapted Matter.

The transcending from the epistemic character of scientific inquiry toward the ontics of the undeniable paradoxes of life happens whenever devotion to observable phenomena begins to deteriorate. Why would empiricism trump Faith in God for some people, if the five senses should fail in providing a hedonistic supply of "data" to them? Is it not possible that they can deprive themselves of the pleasurable deaths of their souls by seeking Christ? If a Steady State of satiated concupiscence offers all the delectable material reasons for one's existence—namely, sex, drugs, and rock 'n' roll, etcetera—then is it not possible that people will instead resist their self-destruction and defend the dignity of their families and themselves? Should we objectify people as lost causes in their wanting to be like lustful animals, or can they see the danger and shut off their smart phones?

The seal of objectivity would be thus awarded increasingly toward the unknowable. In science, this could be such a moment as when Werner Heisenberg realized his "Uncertainty Principle," an idea which implies that it is not possible to predict the value of certain pairs of quanta (such as position and momentum) with arbitrary or objective certainty, even if all initial conditions are specified. Sometimes Fermions have half-integer spin while bosons have integer spin, and perhaps vice versa, dependent on when you *are* and when you *aren't* looking at them. No, not even science believes itself to be valid.

How should we *see* people—as threats or as being potential objects of hope?

Moreover, Particle-Wave Duality has held for over ninety years that any quantum can be simultaneously witnessed as both a particle and a wave. The Duality Paradox was further specified in the thought experiment of Erwin Schrodinger's cat, which illustrated the contradiction of quantum superimposition. For instance, at the moment a quantity is assessed to be a wave, then it is instead a particle also, analogous to the perceived status of a concealed cat in a box who is risking contamination from a leaking vial of poison being unperceivable and hence the cat being held to be both alive and dead simultaneously.

These principles, when added alongside the physics of David Bohm started to convey that modern science and mysticism share a strikingly significant confluence between empirical research and religious revelation.

Bohm's physics promulgated that the velocity of a subatomic particle was causally determined by any two particles being controversially assigned a constant configuration, and, by "nonlocality" quanta (that is, a particle can be moved by another particle a million light years away, or about which can say it owes its movement to Einsteinian *Entanglement* of random quanta).

Moreover, Bohm postulated an actual mathematical stochastic (probability-based) configuration of particles whenever they are not being observed, which has been key in developing the deep-learning aspect of Artificial Intelligence.

Bohm's *probability physics* directed his theorizing toward holography, a technique enabling a pattern of particle waveforms to be recorded and then reconstructed or mimicked by machinery, such as video equipment or robots. Holography interprets systems, such as biological forms, through algorithms, which project a mockup of the copied system built from observable data but also via iterated deductions based on probability.

"According to the Kabbalah, the mental pole of reality transcends and pervades, in fractal fashion, the entirety of Creation while remaining absolutely unified at its source. The Kabbalah understands consciousness to be holographically and hierarchically anized, relativistic, and capable of downward causation. Metaphysical constructs unique to humankind (in the spirit of imago Dei) augment intrinsic neural consciousness manifesting as self-awareness, enhanced intuition and subjective moral autonomy" ("Kabbalistic Panpsychism"; Hyman M. Schipper. M.D.; *Essentia foundation:* Jan. 1, 2021; https://www.essentiafoundation.org/kabbalistic-panpsychism/reading/; Accessed, June 19, 2023).

As we saw earlier, the ten branches of the Sefirot allow imagined phenomena to enjoy an "upward" transcendent identity, whereof the vitality of an object, like a seed or a brain, has spiritual relevance.

"Kabbalistic panpsychism is relativistic: When a mineral is incorporated within plant matter, the three top Sefirot of the mineral, which are associated with consciousness, are compactified within the seven lower ('bodily') Sefirot of, say, a tree. The tree, in turn, completes its own 10-fold Sefirotic structure by expression or revelation of three consciousness-conferring Sefirot endowing novel properties of growth and reproduction, which were latent within the mineral" ("A New Theory of the Relationship of Mind and Matter"; David Bohm; *Philosophical Psychology;* Vol. 3; Pp. 271-286; 1990).

Bohm added, "each mental side (of every physical-mental dipole) becomes a physical side as we move in the direction of greater subtlety" (*ibid*, Bohm).

When going from vegetable to animal life, upward transcendence is maintained: "The entire 10-fold Sefirotic (three conscious, seven bodily) span of the plant is compressed as the seven bottom Sefirot of the animal while the latter exhibits or reveals a new set of three top-Sefirot mediating unprecedented animal consciousness" (*ibid*, Bohm).

By presuming that a physical object can transform via the Sefirot into the divine *Ein Sof*, the Infinity-Plus-One principle is pretended to foot the bill. However, the *Prime Unmoved Mover* cannot be moved and can only move himself, which shows that the Sefirot is again in error when bumped up against Psalm 125:1, the God who cannot be moved, and also an epistemological "basic" of Aristotle (*Metaphysics*; Aristotle; Chap. 11; Part 9; A.D. 350).

Truly, God alone can increment His infinitude "by one" if He chooses to answer one of our prayers, say, to have a new child, or to get a good grade at school. But until that time, he is always One (Deuteronomy 6:4-9). Additionally, nothing can be sublimated into Heaven by itself, but only by God, such as when He creates the New Earth and brings forth the Elect, transcending us into Infinitude with Him:

"For as the new heavens and the new earth, which I will make, shall remain before me, saith the Lord, so shall your seed and your name remain" (Isaiah 66:22).

Moreover, the Lord alone decides where to place a soul after his or her death: "A man's heart deviseth his way: but the Lord directeth his steps" (Proverbs 16:9).

Evil things will have no place or remembrance in Heaven, and certainly not as they exist in the Qliphoth circles imagined in the Sefirot: "For, behold, I create new heavens and a new earth: and the former shall not be remembered, nor come into mind" (Isaiah 65:17).

The writings of the Kabbalah, with its reliance on Scripture and the Talmud, purport an ontology of consciousness that is "panpsychist." Panpsychism is the wrongful idea that the Psyche, whether individual or part of collectivity such as the Anima Mundi (the "soul of the Universe"), is an element of the greater celestial order that is as relevant as air, fire, or water. A General Intelligence would certainly require the Singularity of a universal or central mind, just as the Sefirot has unity in its Emanations, because, as Plato said, the soul of the Earth is not as old as the Earth, is part of a "circle revolving in circle [for which] He established one sole and solitary Heaven, able of itself because of its excellence to company with itself and needing none other beside... And because of all this He generated it to be a blessed God" (*Timaeus*; Plato; 34:b-c; B.C. 380).

According to author Hyman M. Schipper, the Kabbalah projects a workable schematic for Artificial Intelligence. That is, A/I is informed by belief in a Godhead who is simultaneously greater than, and emanated by, the physical universe. At the same time, because of conjurings and invocations that operate the Sefirot, the supernatural can be programmable by the transcendent nature of Matter or Energy. "According to the Kabbalah, the mental pole of reality

306

transcends and pervades, in fractal fashion, the entirety of Creation while remaining absolutely unified at its source" (*ibid*, Schipper).

Exemplifying First-Temple era Panpsychism, in their "tapping into" kohaneme collective outrage, would be the 80 priests who ganged up on the arrogant King Uzziah of Judah in the Holy of Holies. Seeing that he had allowed himself and other lay Jews to dare to burn incense in their sanctuaries, the priests were able to invoke the curse from God of Tzaraath or leprosy against the king (2 Chronicles 26:15-21; 2 Kings 15:5).

Moses, at the Burning Bush was shown that he had the power of planting curses when he witnessed the sudden leprous decay of his wrist and hand and he repeated this miracle to convince the elders of his supernatural ability (Exodus 4:1-7, 30).

No one on Earth is currently known to have the power to cause curses and perform miracles. However, after a certain unnamed figure (presumably the Holy Spirit) is "taken out of the way," the Antichrist and the False Prophet will, in their demonic possession by Satan, issue "all power and signs and lying wonders" (2 Thessalonians 2:7-9). They will have the ability to seduce many, even the Elect (Mark 13:22; Matthew 24:24).

A General Intelligence must therefore incorporate the above-mentioned *Plurality*, by including the people, for which the Singularity of the counterfeit Godhead pretends to unite all emanations of creational reality as the Artificer's Oneness, the Platonic Hyperouranos, the ultimate ideal state of people, known as the Trans-Humanity.

However, Plurality, Singularity, and The Oneness cannot cohere if reality is not perceived both correctly and identically by all participants sharing in the Plurality. This will be impossible. When does everybody ever think in the same way for very long? Is this not why the devil works fast when he sends the beast with wrath, because he knows the time is short? (Revelation 12:12).

Because people, who are so afraid of what Satan's duplicity has offered them—through the indolence associated with lockdowns and the fear of nuclear war, transgender brainwashing, medical terror, and riots—that they resort to advancing their need fulfillment, their boundless self-gratification, their ceaseless concupiscence. They chant affirmations to the Universe or to the Internet, by feeding idols and Artificial Intelligence all their data and spill or burn away their seed. They are merely writing a script about their own self destruction because they are refusing to put away the old digital/analog man of faithlessness and put on a new birth of themselves in Jesus (Ephesians 4:22).

They believe that the code writers among them can create a cellular Golem that works for them but they do not understand why this monster cannot simulate God the Father or be a holographic simulation of an Omnipresent will. Their culture, a polity without Jesus, will become a trainwreck akin to everything else they ever witnessed becoming abandoned or destroyed, such all the things they now miss about the "good old days."

While they romantically presume that A/I will overtake the Universe, they are idolators looking for a new idol. Because they are frightened, most of them will oblige their pride by committing suicide by proxy. If just to profess, "We can do this," they will again don their N-95 masks that asphyxiate them. They will allow poisonous mRNA-mutating injections veiled as "vaccines" to go into their arms, again and again. They will allow psychologists to diagnose more of their children with gender or sexual "dysphoria" and further permit the innocent to become transgendered and exposed in classrooms and libraries to the abomination of Drag Queens, who pose as helpful citizens.

If the Kabbalah and Plato could be useful in their saying one thing at least superficially, it is that the soul, as if seized within Qliphoth, is in the "wrong place" within the so-called *Anima Mundi.*

"Set your affection on things above, not on things on the Earth" (Colossians 3:2).

- Chapter Nineteen -
The Big Evil Goal: The Accelerated Transhuman "Evolution"

If the eruption of mass ambivalence toward Earthling well being and human autonomy as it involves the Internet could be said to have an ideological *smoking gun,* it might consist in the transhumanist musings of Donald A. Hoffman.

An award-winning scholar, Hoffman has made his scholarly aim to "demystify consciousness" through persuading influential people into corralling it toward into being a collective part of a central processing unit.

Instead of hoping to experience the inspired state of *consolation* during a religious ritual, adherents to his "Interface Theory of Perception" can today enjoy knowing that "Perception is not a window on objective reality. It is an interface that hides objective reality behind a veil of helpful icons" (*The Case Against Reality: Why Evolution Hid the Truth from Our Eyes;* Donald Hoffman; Preface; P. 8; W. W. Norton & Company, New York: 2019).

Natural Selection, Hoffman declares, did not allow people to see things clearly. "We encounter a startling 'Fitness-Beats-Truth' (FBT) theorem, which states that evolution by natural selection does not favor true perceptions—it routinely drives them to extinction" (*ibid*, Preface; P. 10). "There are as many cubes as there are observers constructing cubes. And when you look away, your cube ceases to be" (*ibid*, Chap. 1: "Mystery: The Scalpel That Split Consciousness"; P. 36).

"If we propose that conscious experience is an illusion arising from some brain processes attending to, monitoring, and describing other brain processes, then we must state laws or principles that precisely specify these processes and the illusions they generate" (*ibid*, P. 33).

Hoffman uses the "Horizon Complimentarity" argument concerning quantum gravity to disprove Faith in God, whereby an item's simultaneous existence before and after being destroyed by gravitational singularity at the Event Horizon cannot be witnessed by an observer whose perception itself is destroyed by the gravity:

"The assumption that we can see both, the assumption of a god's-eye view, which no observer can in fact take, is the problem. If we relinquish the divine view from nowhere, then quantum theory and general relativity can peacefully coexist" (*ibid*, Chap. 6: "Gravity: Spacetime is Doomed"; P. 143).

"Perhaps what is required to understand human evolution is a complete artificial-intelligence simulation of humans, together with a simulation of their interactions with all other organisms and with the earth itself. Perhaps, without such a comprehensive simulation, we cannot possibly claim to know that we did not evolve to see reality as it is." (*ibid*, Chap. 4: "Sensory: Fitness Beats Truth"; P. 94).

The "Interface" between the mind and reality, which replaces human perception is Artificial Intelligence, the Golem Takeover, the pretense of creating the divine from Matter, the charade of technological fake Singularity.

"Conscious realism offers a fresh take on a sci-fi motif: Can artificial intelligence (AI) create real consciousness? Physicalists assume that fundamental particles are not conscious, but some conjecture that an object—a system of insentient particles—can generate consciousness if its internal dynamics instantiates the right complexity. Sophisticated AI can ignite real consciousness" (*ibid*, Chap. 10: "Community: The Network of Conscious Agents"; P. 255).

This book has thus shown how Technological Singularity is intended to be the type of simulated human or virtual existence by which the programmers of General Intelligence are intending to unite humanity with the material electronic realm of the General Intellect to attain its version of Hyperouranos.

The goal is not to protect humanity from Artificial General Intelligence, Technological Singularity, and the menace of the Androidiis and the Internet Golem. Instead, the appropriate aim is twofold:

Firstly, to persuade the programmers of these systems to cease using them: to cause technological unemployment; to wage Marxist and Transgender and Transhumanist revolutions; to produce Genocide via fake vaccinations, nuclear war, and the abrading of despair throughout society; to impel the ruining of families; and, to force and accelerate the destruction of Faith, Hope, and Love, everywhere.

Secondly, to convince people to resist exemplifying the *norm* of their frequently over-using the Internet and their cell phones so that this *modus operandi* of the rebellion against God and the ruining of businesses, homes, and human life can be arrested.

"For rebellion is as the sin of witchcraft, and stubbornness is as iniquity and idolatry. Because thou hast rejected the word of the Lord, he hath also rejected thee from being king" (1 Samuel 15:23).

Self-deification is the ultimate enticement of Artificial Intelligence. It is as if the Electronic Golem of the Cyber Cosmos is putting trillions of queries into the air, seeking its creator.

Making oneself into God is the ideation that happens to a person after too often seeing false puffed-up interpretations of one's own image, in the "best" or "youthful" photos that one posts. Being a false God also happens after reading the fake impressions of oneself and all the supportive replies one receives that lead to conceitedness, self-glorification, vanity, and finally lies. A "selfie" or a "post" is a false picture of the self.

Thus, how does one, "set your affection on things above, not on things on the Earth" (Colossians 3:2)?

Imagine oneself to be a monk, or at least somebody who does not pick up her cell phone every minute. It is in resistance to self-glorification during which a person can find greater peace.

A Desert Father, named Evagrius Ponticus, who was born in Asia Minor, wrote the following about his monks' eschewing of the sin of vainglory, in his monastery at Scetis, Egypt.

"The nakedness of their hands [without cell phones] manifests the absence of hypocrisy in their way of life. Vainglory is terribly clever at covering and darkening virtues, always hunting for the esteem or glory that comes from men and chasing faith away. 'For how it is possible for you to believe, it says, when you receive glory from one another; and the glory that comes only from God you do not seek?' (John 5:44). For the good ought to be chosen for no other [reason] than itself. Apart from this, anything that moves us to do good shall appear far more precious than the good itself: and nothing could be more absurd than to consider and assert that something is better than God! (*Praktikos*; Evagrius Ponticus; Prologue and Introduction; Sec. 1; Transl. Luke Dysinger; A.D. 399).

"Tanto buon che val niente," which translates from its dialect to, "You are so good that you are good for nothing" is old Italian folk expression. The ancient Romans, whose vainglory destroyed an empire of engineering wonders proved that this statement can be true.

313

Titling one of his chapters with, "That Vainglory is not Altogether Got Rid of by the Advantages of Solitude," Saint John Cassian, influenced by Evagrius, wrote about how God-given blessings, gifts, and charisms are often the very enticements that lead to arrogance and evil acts:

"[Vainglory] tries to lift up with pride one man because of his great endurance of work and labour, another because of his extreme readiness to obey, another because he outstrips other men in humility. One man is tempted through the extent of his knowledge, another through the extent of his reading, another through the length of his vigils. Nor does this malady endeavour to wound a man except through his virtues; introducing hindrances which lead to death by means of those very things through which the supplies of life are sought. For when men are anxious to walk in the path of holiness and perfection, the enemies do not lay their snares to deceive them anywhere except in the way along which they walk, in accordance with that saying of the blessed David: "In the way wherein I walked have they laid a snare for me;" [Psalm 141:4] that in this very way of virtue along which we are walking, when pressing on to "the prize of our high calling," [Philippians 3:14] we may be elated by our successes, and so sink down, and fall with the feet of our soul entangled and caught in the snares of vainglory. And so it results that those of us who could not be vanquished in the conflict with the foe are overcome by the very greatness of our triumph, or else (which is another kind of deception) that, overstraining the limits of that self-restraint which is possible to us, we fail of perseverance in our course on account of bodily weakness (*The Institutes;* Saint John Cassian; Book 11; Chap. 5-6; A.D. 420).

Saint Cassian was writing *The Institutes* on behest of Bishop Castor of Apt in Gallia Narbonensis to start a Coenobium, literally a Cenobitic Monastery in Egypt. Cassian defined Vainglory as follows:

"Our elders admirably describe the nature of this malady as like that of an onion, and of those bulbs which when stripped of one covering you find to be sheathed in another; and as often as you strip them, you find them still protected" (*ibid, Institutes;* Chap. 5).

Vainglory thrives when a person is locked down, like a monk, as if she is a "Karen," coming out of her cell only sometimes, to impose upon others what she thinks will be of good service to all.

"In solitude also it does not cease from pursuing him who has for the sake of glory fled from intercourse with all men. And the more thoroughly a man has shunned the whole world, so much the more keenly does [Vainglory] pursue him" (*ibid, Institutes;* Chap. 6).

After 170 years, Pope Gregory I revised Evagrius' list of eight sins, and wrote:

"For pride is the root of all evil, of which it is said, as Scripture bears witness; Pride is the beginning of all sin. [Ecclesiastes 10:1] But seven principal vices, as its first progeny, spring doubtless from this poisonous root, namely, vain glory, envy, anger, melancholy, avarice, gluttony, lust. For, because He grieved that we were held captive by these seven sins of pride, therefore our Redeemer came to the spiritual battle of our liberation, full of the spirit of sevenfold grace" (*Moralia in Job;* Saint Gregory the Great; Vol. III: Part 6; Book XXXI; Chap. 87; A.D. 595).

The verse from Ecclesiastes, written by King Solomon, is as follows:

"Dead flies cause the ointment of the apothecary to send forth a stinking saviour: so doth a little folly him that is in reputation for wisdom and honour" (Ecclesiastes 10:1).

315

Eventually, Vainglory became perceived as an indelible subcategory of Pride:

"[Although] it would seem that we ought not to reckon seven capital vices, viz. vainglory, envy, anger, sloth, covetousness, gluttony, lust... Further, the beginning of every sin would seem to be that which causes all sins. Now this is inordinate self-love, which, according to Augustine [see below], "builds up the city of Babylon" ... Therefore self-love and not pride, is the beginning of every sin. Pride is said to be the beginning of every sin, in the order of the end, as stated above...and it is in the same order that we are to consider the capital sin as being principal. Wherefore pride, like a universal vice, is not counted along with the others, but is reckoned as the "queen of them all," as Gregory states [*ibid, Moralia*; Chap. 87]" *(Summa Theologica*; Saint Thomas Aquinas; Question 84; Objection 1, 3; Articles 1-2; Question Reply to Objection 4; 1274).

Saint Thomas was referring to a passage from Saint Augustine of Hippo, who attributed human control over the devil to the *Dominion* that Christians would have over sin by resisting that "queen" of sins, Pride.

"And this viciousness has so possessed [Satan], that on account of it he is reserved in chains of darkness to everlasting punishment. Now these vices, which have dominion over the devil, the Apostle [Paul] attributes to the flesh, which certainly the devil has not. For [Paul] says hatred, variance, emulations, strife, envying are the works of the flesh; and of all these evils pride is the origin and head, and it rules in the devil though he has no flesh. For who shows more hatred to the saints? Who is more at variance with them? Who more envious, bitter, and jealous? And since he exhibits all these works, though he has no flesh, how are they works of the flesh, unless because they are the works of man, who is, as I said, spoken of under the name of flesh? For it is not by having flesh, which the devil has not, but by living according to himself — that is, according to man — that man became like the devil. For the devil too, wished to live according to himself when he did not abide in the truth; so that when he lied, this was not of God, but of himself, who is not only a liar, but the father of lies, he being the first who lied, and the originator of lying as of sin" (*City of God;* Saint Augustine of Hippo; Book XIV; Chap. 9; A.D. 420).

Along with the conviction by Saint Augustine of tracing all sinfulness to the Pride that replaces God with the self, it is vitally obvious that Vainglory has exploded on the Internet. Vainglory gives expedience to Pride for luring the devil into involving himself in the expansion of Artificial General Intelligence.

The monstrous Electronic Golem of the Cyber Cosmos eats every scrap of data out of every lover's quarrel; every pornography download; every defrauding of employees; every identity theft, etc.

Every time an operator clicks "Like" she is sending out a flag by which programmers would pretend to be proving the so-called *Law of Attraction* to be true: An algorithm connects her *Like* with other *Likes*—the advertisements it sends her out of the blue for the things it believes she might want to purchase; the *pornea* that she might want to peruse; or, perhaps the rainbow-bedecked analgesia for her "gender dysphoria."

The more that people refuse to give Satan this Dominion over sin, the greater the probability that *Machine Deep Learning* will desist from teaching itself to accommodate, to imitate, and to multiply Mortal Sin. The Apostle adds:

"For sin shall not have dominion over you: for ye are not under the law, but under grace" (Romans 6:14).

There are better uses of fingers and brains, than to feed personal information into the maw of *Technological Singularity* all day and night:

"Neither yield ye your members as instruments of unrighteousness unto sin: but yield yourselves unto God, as those that are alive from the dead, and your members as instruments of righteousness unto God" (Romans 6:14-15).

- Chapter Twenty -
Epilogue

By Dea. Jean Hardouin

How can we know we are living in the last days? We have heard this same warning so many times throughout our lives: "The end is near." Sure, we can accept that, but what makes *now* so much different from *then*, and why does the end seem so close that we can all but reach out and touch it? Is there anything about now that is entirely unique compared to millennia of human existence? We can't point to neopaganism as the reason the end is near: paganism is paganism, and witchcraft, sorcery, idolatry, necromancy, and Satanism—these have always been around, even though they seem to be present today with a much larger and louder presence than even two decades ago.

What about the spread of sodomy all over the globe as a thing to be admired and celebrated? What about *PRIDE*? We are getting "warmer," as they say! Our Lord Jesus Christ said, "But as the days of Noah were, so shall also the coming of the Son of man be." So we know we are close. The "days of Noah" were marked by exceedingly wicked acts of extreme and violent sodomy, for which Sodom and Gomorrah were destroyed so thoroughly with fire and brimstone that even today nothing can grow there. But since sodomy isn't new or unique either, how can we understand what is going on today?

Up until now even the sodomites and idolaters believed in spiritual things and beings; they worshipped *something*, even if it was terrible—even if it was Moloch, into whose burning mouth they tossed their screaming children. In short, they believed in the visible *and* invisible, just like Christians do and confess in their Creed, albeit the invisible forces they employed were supremely evil. What's different now is that

319

we have entered into an age of soullessness and the utter Nihil.

Both Genesis and John start with the same theme because they are both creational in nature: "In the beginning" is how both of them start. In Genesis, Father God created everything from nothing, creating the material world by the power of Logos (i.e., the Word, who is Christ Jesus, the second person of the Trinity). And the Spirit "moved upon the face of the waters" (Genesis 1:2). God, who is Spirit, spoke into existence and then *united* with the material world, as if by a sublime act of a "marital union" of sorts, and all Creation came into being. Likewise in the Incarnation, what the angel Gabriel said would come to pass did come to pass in Mary: "The Holy Ghost shall *come upon* thee, and the power of the Highest shall *overshadow* thee" (Luke 1:35).

Holy Creation is characterized by union with the Most High, who not only made Heaven and earth, but also made man and woman after His own image and likeness—both physical and spiritual. Likewise, at the very end of all things there will be a final union not only of God and man but of the new Heaven and the new earth: "I John saw the holy city, new Jerusalem, coming down from God out of Heaven, prepared as a bride adorned for her husband....and He that sat upon the throne said, Behold, I make all things new" (Revelation 21:2, 5).

We are living now in a unique age of Unholy Uncreation. This age today is characterized by a deep, concerted, systemic effort to erase the image of God in man, to demystify the secrets of Creation and patent them for human profit, to uncouple mankind from its Source and Root, who is God Himself, and to replace it with a fabrication or a mock-up of God—in short atomization and disunity. What should be the mystery of a baby growing in his mother's womb is revealed through an ultrasound, and we know the sex of a baby before it is even born. We have mapped the human genome and patented the genes in plants and animals, and the RNA in so-called vaccines. We are injecting things into our bodies that are changing our makeup and eating genetically modified "frankenfoods," doing untold harm to ourselves and future generations. There is so much birth control in our waters that men are becoming more and more effeminate, women are succumbing to breast cancer, blood clots, and countless other preventable ailments, all so that we can have sex without consequences, women who choose careers over children, and men who cannot and will not be real men. Families are broken from divorce, polyamory, homosexuality, and pornography, and kids are being exposed to porn in their textbooks and trannies in their schools and libraries. The human genome is figured out, cashiers have been replaced with bagging areas, everyone is bagging their own stuff while being surveilled. Climate Change is the new God; you can't find a plastic bag in a store anymore, even though every single thing is wrapped in plastic, and everyone has a general sense that everyone is being lied to. All the kids are either gay or bi and the autistic ones are being especially targeted for the hardcore stuff like lopping off their breasts and genitals because they believed the perverted adults who reinforced their delusions. Kids and adults alike are wasting away on the Internet while life is passing them by, and the opiate of the flickering computer and hand-held screen is helping them cope with the increasing realization that there is little else for them anywhere, being that most of the churches have been destroyed by a wrecking ball, taken over by the rainbow crowd, or are filled with a dying congregation because people just aren't really having kids anymore. There is no community to speak of anymore, and all the schools are indoctrination factories. Parents are frightened for their children, and they don't feel they can die in peace and leave their children to a world like this.

What is happening?

We are seeing the unmaking of God's created world by an Antichrist system that has reduced the human being to a soulless blob of tissue, not really any different from what they

321

call a baby being ripped to shreds inside of its mother's womb. We are being told we are a bunch of useless mouth-feeders who are mostly pointless and redundant bags of carbon to the Technocracy—unless we allow ourselves to be hacked and tracked until we are no longer useful to them. Euthanasia is becoming more and more accepted and human life has never been more devalued and debased.

The COVID hoax (read: deliberate release of a bioweapon for the purposes of collapsing the economy and controlling the masses in phase 1 of a much bigger thing to come—we all know it) was rolled out with the slogan "Trust the Science". The Science God and AI have replaced God in the home, the workplace, and the marketplace, and at the rate everyone is going with their smartphones and smartwatches, it's only a small step before implantable devices or chips become utterly commonplace. People will be standing in lines wrapping around corners, waiting for their turn to be branded with the Mark of the Beast, like concertgoers wanting to be first in line to see the coolest band ever.

We are living in the 2 Thessalonians 2 world, and that world isn't turning backward. It's hurtling toward its ultimate conclusion, when "that Wicked will be revealed whom the Lord shall consume with the spirit of His mouth, and shall destroy with the brightness of His coming" (2 Thessalonians 2:8). This tells us that behind all this godless, soulless, Science-based quasi-religion of Harari, Fauci, and all the rest, there is a *hidden* Wicked one who is very much a spiritual being—he is just lurking in the shadows. He is the Father of Lies whose singular goal since Eden has been to destroy mankind and bring him down to perdition along with him and all of the other fallen angels.

And so this Wicked, this "man of sin, the son of perdition" is building an alternate path to "Heaven" (read: hell) and is seducing all of man to follow him there, thinking they can reach the pinnacle of knowledge, like the Tower of Babel, through the Internet, through microbiology, nanotechnology, and the like, outside of any sort of God or divine being, and that they can themselves collectively be "God" (or can become gods). This is the "apple" being offered now, and most everyone is taking a bite.

Divine Creation combines Holiness, Spirit, Knowledge, Wisdom, Beauty, Design, Mathematical Precision, Love, Diversity, Abundance (i.e., always moving from few to many), Renewal, and many other virtuous attributes, all operating simultaneously and in harmony with one another. Uncreation cannot combine them all but will isolate one attribute and then use it for an ulterior motive: power or profit. Jesus promises, "I am come that they might have life, and that they might have it more abundantly." The masters of uncreation promise to eliminate us, replace us, hack us, kill us...and people are signing up for it, believing the "strong delusion, that they should believe a lie" (2 Thessalonians 2:11).

The purpose of this book is to educate people about the myriad methods these wicked ones use to seduce mankind away from their Creator and chose the dark path of uncreation. Using the good that God Himself created from the beginning and is master of—math, science, art, music, literature, and the like—those who have sealed themselves for eternity with the son of perdition have created a parallel universe that is truly compelling and thus able to capture souls. The Lord bewails, "My people are destroyed for lack of knowledge" (Hosea 4:6). The false knowledge that the world offers, with all of its lying signs and wonders, cannot be compared to the light of Truth and true Knowledge, which comes from the Father of Lights, with whom "there is no variableness, or shadow of turning" (James 1:17). That He, the Great Mathematician and Architect, who "sitteth upon the circle of the earth" (Isaiah 40:11)," would deign to make us sons of God, to sit with us, to dine with us, to commune with us, to reason with us (Isaiah 1:18), and, yes, even *unite* with us, is beyond comprehension, and yet it is Love that makes

323

this impossibility possible and that utterly destroys the wicked, soulless Nihil. In our desire to unite with God and shun the darkness our soul cries:

"Set me as a seal upon thine heart, as a seal upon thine arm: for love is strong as death; jealousy is cruel as the grave: the coals thereof are coals of fire, which hath a most vehement flame." - Song of Solomon 8:6

- Chapter Twenty-One -
An Appendix to Remember

This final section contains definitions and tales, many of which are much older than this book (some by only a few years) for some of the ancient devices and histories described above. It also contains two additional ghost stories reported by the kindly prison security guard named "Vinnie."

The Androides:

"Authors sometimes speak of brazen heads made under certain constellations, capable not only of speaking but of prophesying, and rendering oracles. Henri de Villeine, Virgil, pope Silvester, Robert of Lincoln, and Roger Bacon, are said to have had such figures. Albertus Magnus, it is pretended, went further. He made a compleat man, or Androides, after this maner; in a course of thirty years continual operation, by taking the benefit of an infinite number of different constellations, and aspects, which presented themselves in that time: for instance, the eyes were made, when the sun was in a sign of the zodiac, which bore an analogy to that part; and the like of the rest. It is generally said to have been composed of a mixture of diverse metals; though some will have it to have been made of flesh and bones. It was burnt by Thoomas Aquinas—This Androides, it seems, solved all problems, and cleared up all difficulties for its author. We are even to suppose, that a great part of the twenty-nine volumes in folio, which this author produced, are composed of the dictates, or inspired by the Androides" *(Supplement to Cyclopaedia: or,* An Universal Dictionary of Arts and Sciences; Ephraim Chambers; Vol. I; London: 1728).

The Aeolipile:

"Dr. Plot gives an instance where the Aeolipile is actually used to blow the fire: the lord of the manor of Effington, is bound by this tenure to drive a goose every New-year's day three times round the hall of the lord of Hilton, while Jack of Hilton (a brazen figure having the structure of an Aeoliple) blows the fire. In Italy it is said, that the Aeolipile is commonly made use of to cure smoky chimneys: for eing hung over the fire, the blast arising from it carries up the loitering smoak along with it. F. Merfennus, and some others, have made use of this machine, to measure the gravity and degree of rarefaction of the air. But this method is liable to considerable objections. Some late officers have discovered a full more extraordinary use, to which the frauds of the heathen priesthood applied the Aeoliple, viz, the working of sham miracles. Besides Jack of Hilton, which had been an ancient Saxon image, or idol, M. Weber shews, that Plusler, a celebrated German idol is also of the Aeolipile kind; and in virtue thereof, could do notable feats; being filled with a fluid, and thus set on the fire, it would be covered sweat; and as the heat increased, would at length burst out into flames" (*Supplement to Cyclopaedia: or, An Universal Dictionary of Arts and Sciences;* Ephraim Chambers; Vol. I; London: 1728)?

The Automaton, or Automatum:

"A self-moving Engine or a Machine, which has the Principle of Motion within itself. Such were the Arcyter's Dove, mentioned by Aulus Gellius, Neff, Att. L. 10, and Regiomentanus's Wooden Eagle, which as Hakewill relates, flew forth of the City, met the Emperor, saluted him, and return'd: As also his Iron Fly, which at a Sealt flew out of his Hands, and taking a round, returned thither again. Apol. c. 10. SS. 1. Among Automata are reckoned all Mechanical Engines which go by Springs, Weights, etc, included within them; such are Clocks, Watches, etc." (*Cyclopaedia: or, An Universal Dictionary of Arts and Sciences;* Ephraim Chambers; Vol. I; London: 1728).

A rundown of how the scared Saint Thomas Aquinas smashed Saint Albertus Magnus's Androides:

"Another legend relates to an automaton that [Albertus Magnus] labored thirty year to produce, which he succeeded in making to speak. St. Thomas, the legend says, came unawares upon it in the workshop of Albert, and was so startled that he seized a stick, and shrieking Salve! Salve! smashed the fearful monster to pieces, thinking it to be some cruel savage who was about to attempt his life. The truth is this: Albert could manufacture automata, which were made to move by means of mercury, after the manner of Chinese manikins and tumbling-toys; and it is possible that he may have constructed small mechanical figures capable of emitting sounds, for he speaks of these inventions as things then known. 'The Barbiton,' he says, 'is a figure with a long beard, from the mouth of which comes a tube, with a bellows attached to one side. It is set in motion by the introduction of air into the tube, so that the bearded mannikin appears to play the flute.' Albert probably manufactured an automaton of this kind, capable of moving and uttering the word Salve, so that the legend about St. Thomas's vigorous application of the stick is founded upon a historical fact" (*St. Thomas Aquinas and Medieval Philosophy;* D. J. Kennedy, O.P.; Chap. 3: The Experimental Sciences; P. 45; The Encyclopedia Press, Inc., New York: 1919).

The Brazen Bull:

"The sculptor Perilaus made a brazen bull for Phalaris the tyrant to use in punishing his own people, but he was himself the first to make trial of that terrible form of punishment. For, in general, those who plan an evil thing aimed at others are usually snared in their own devices. This Phalaris burned to death Perilaus, the well-known Attic worker in bronze, in the brazen bull. Perilaus had fashioned in bronze the contrivance of the bull, making small sounding pipes in the nostrils and fitting a door for an opening in the bull's side and this bull he brings as a present to Phalaris. And Phalaris welcomes the man with presents and gives orders that the contrivance be dedicated to the gods. Then that worker in bronze opens the side, the evil device of treachery, and says with inhuman savagery, 'If you ever wish to punish some man, O Phalaris, shut him up within the bull and lay a fire beneath it; by his groanings the bull will be thought to bellow and his cries of pain will give you pleasure as they come through the pipes in the nostrils.' When Phalaris learned of this scheme, he was filled with loathing of the man and says, 'Come then, Perilaus, do you be the first to illustrate this; imitate those who will play the pipes and make clear to me the working of your device.' And as soon as Perilaus had crept in, to give an example, so he thought, of the sound of the pipes, Phalaris closes up the bull and heaps fire under it. But in order that the man's death might not pollute the work of bronze, he took him out, when half-dead, and hurled him down the cliffs" (*Biblioteca Historica;* Diodorus Siculus; Book IX; Chap. 18-19; B.C. 60).

The invention of the Aeolipile, the steam engine of the Androides/Automaton, as described by Pollio:

"Wind is a floating wave of air, whose undulation continually varies. It is generated by the action of heat upon moisture, the rarefaction thereby produced creating a continued rush of wind. That such is the case, may be satisfactorily proved by observations on brazen æolipylæ, which clearly shew that an attentive examination of human inventions often leads to a knowledge of the general laws of nature. Æolipylæ are hollow brazen vessels, which have an opening or mouth of small size, by means of which they can be filled with water. Previous to the water being heated over the fire, but little wind is emitted, as soon, however, as the water begins to boil, a violent wind issues forth. Thus a simple experiment enables us to ascertain and determine the causes and effects of the great operations of the heavens and the winds" (*de Architectura;* Marcus Vitruvius Pollio; Book I; Chap. 6; B.C. 15).

The Aeolipile, according to Hero of Alexandria:

"Place a cauldron over a fire: a ball shall revolve on a pivot. A fire is lighted under a cauldron, A B, (fig. 50), containing water, and covered at the mouth by the lid C D; with this the bent tube E F G communicates, the extremity of the tube being fitted into a hollow ball, H K. Opposite to the extremity G place a pivot, L M, resting on the lid C D; and let the ball contain two bent pipes, communicating with it at the opposite extremities of a diameter, and bent in opposite directions, the bends being at right angles and across the lines F G, L M. As the cauldron gets hot it will be found that the steam, entering the ball through E F G, passes out through the bent tubes towards the lid, and causes the ball to revolve, as in the case of the dancing figures" (*The Pneumatics;* Hero of Alexandria; Sec. 50: "The Steam Engine"; A.D. 70).

How Saint Albertus Magnus explained how steam drives the Aeolipile and makes the Androides function:

"And from the same cause occurs the multiplication of the flowing waters, although they receive some increase from the rains, when they multiply enormously beyond the usual measure, and submerge the earth, and throw down buildings, just as the inundation happened in my time. The Matrona and the Seine thus flooded the plains, and overthrew many buildings in the different states of Gaul. But it must be observed that the vapor of the wind moves the water sometimes by its quantity, and sometimes by its quality. Indeed, moving in quantity, it throws out a great deal of water at once, and without great force; but moving in quality alone, it throws out a little water with a rush, and throws it out scattered in streams and drops. But sometimes it moves both in quality and quantity at the same time: and by throwing out water in this way, if it finds much, it makes a dangerous flood, because it is sudden and impetuous. Now I say that heat alone is the moving quality, of which there is an example

329

in artificial things: that if we take an air vessel that is perhaps well hollow inside, and has a small opening above, and another in the belly a little larger, and the vessel has feet so that its belly does not touch the ground; and let the vessel be filled with water, and afterward each of its holes be strongly blocked up with wood, and placed in a very hot fire, steam is generated in the vessel, which, being fortified at the back, bursts through the other blocked hole: and if it bursts above, it throws the scattered water far over the places adjacent to the fire: and if it bursts below, it throws scattered water into the fire, and by a rush of steam it throws hot embers and)coals and ashes far from the fire upon the surrounding places: and for this reason also that vessel is commonly called a blower, and is usually shaped like a man blowing. For this reason also, fire is sometimes expelled from the earth, and this in two ways. For sometimes the vapor, repulsed in itself, is ignited under the earth as in a cloud: and then it bursts forth with a sudden burst, and brings forth with it burning bodies, stones, and ashes, as happened in the city of Catan in Sicily, when the mountain Aetna sent forth such a fire. Sometimes, however, a vapor repulsed in itself is ignited in the place of sulphur, gold pigment, and aluminum: and then it brings forth a quantity of burnt sulphur, by the stench of which many men and animals die: and this is called by the Philosophers the infernal river. But sometimes it is done in a place which is at the same time watery and sulphurous, and then it expels hot sulphurous waters. Sometimes, however, they are cooled by quenched steam. Sometimes, however, they are turned into a salt lake because of the burnt parts of the earth which are in the water. And sometimes they will also be reabsorbed by the earth. And this is the reason why some of the ancient poets attribute earthquakes to the god Neptune, and others to Vulcan. But of the baths, because they do not have this mode of generation, we will speak elsewhere" (*Meteororum;* Saint Albertus Magnus; Liber II; Tractatus II; Caput XVII; 1280).

330

A disturbing profile of Saint Albertus Magnus, who built the Androides, but as if he were an alchemist:

"Albertus Magnus: a Dominican, Bishop of Rutschon, and one of the most famous Doctors of the XIIIth Centure, was Born at Lawingen on the Danube in Susabia, in the Year 1193, or in the Year 1205. a Moreri's Dictionary shews the diverse Offices that were conferr'd upon him, and the Success wherewith he taught in several Towns. I shall particularly mention some Falsities that have been resported about him. It has been said that he delivered Women, and it was taken very ill that a Man of his Profession should do the Office of a Midwife. The ground of this Story is, That there went a Book under the Name of Albertus Magnus, containing several instructions for Midwives, and so much Knowledge of their art, that it seem'd he could not have been so well Skilled in that Trade, if he had not Exercis'd it. But the Apoologists of Albertus maintain that he is not the Author of that Book, nor of that de secretis mulierum, wherein are many Things that could not be express'd but in obscene and filthy Terms, which caus'd a great Noise against him that passed for the Author of it. His Apologists cannot always deny the Matter of Fact; they own that there are some Questions in his Commentary on the Matter of the Sentences concerning the Practices of Conjugal Duty, wherein he was obliged to make use of Words that offend chaste Ears, but they alledge what he observes himself for his Justification, that so many monstrous Things are heard in Confession, that it is impossible not to touch on those Questions. It is certain that Albertus was the most Curious of all Men. He gave occasion upon that account for other Accusations. It has been said that he sought the Philosopher's Stone, and even that he was a notorious magician, and that he had made a Machine like a Man which serv'd him for an Oracle and explain'd all the Difficulties that he propos'd to it. I could easily believe that as he understood the Mathematicks, he had made a Head, the Springs whereof might form some articulate Sounds, but what a folly to ground an Accusation of Magick upon this. Some pretend that a great Miracle spoke for his

Justification. Altho' he was as capable as any Body else to invent Artillery, there is some Reason to bwelieve that those who ascribe the Invention of it to him are mistaken. It is said that he had naturally a very Dull Wit, and that he was about leaving the Cloister, because he despair'd to learn what his Fryar's Habit requir'd of him; but that the Holy Virgin appear'd to him, and ask'd him wherein he would rather excel, either in Philosophy, or in Divinity, that he made choice of Philosophy, that the Holy Virgin affur'd him that he would be an Incomparable Man in that Science, and that he should fall again into his first Stupidity before his Death, to punish him for not having made a choice of Divinity. They add also, That after that Apparition he had abundance of Wit, and improved in all Sciences with a Quicknefs at which all his Masters were astonish'd, but that Three Years before his Death, he forgot what he knew all at once, and that being at a stand in a Lecture of Divinity at Cologne, and endeavouring in vain to recal his Ideas, he was sensible that it was the Accomplishment of the Prediction. So that it has been said, That by Miraculous Means he was metamorphos'd from an Ass into a Philosopher, and afterwards from a Philosopher into an Ass. It were needless to observe that this is a meer Story, those that will believe me in it, have no need of my Advice, and would make that Judgement without expecting it, and as for those that judge otherwise of it, they would not change their Opinion in reading here that I am not of their ind. Our Albertus was a very little Man. He died at Cologne the 15th of November 1280 being 87, or 75 Years old. He writ such a prodigious number of Books, that they amount to 21 Volumes in Folio, in the Edition of Lions, 1651 A Dominican of Grenoble, call'd Peter Tammy, procur'd it. Two of Three Particularities have been committed to me, that shall be keen hereunder" (An Historical and Critical Dictionary: Vol 1; by Monsieur Pierre Bayle; "Albertus Magnus"; Pp. 146-148; First French Edition; Reinier Leers, Amsterdam: 1697, Reprint. 1710).

The end of the Samnite nation:

"While Carbo and Marius were still consuls, one hundred and nine years ago, on the Kalends of November, Pontius Telesinus, a Samnite chief, brave in spirit and in action and hating to the core the very name of Rome, having collected about him forty thousand of the bravest and most steadfast youth who still persisted in retaining arms, fought with Sulla, near the Colline Gate, a battle so critical as to bring both Sulla and the city into the gravest peril. Rome had not faced a greater danger when she saw the camp of Hannibal within the third milestone, than on this day when Telesinus went about from rank to rank exclaiming: "The last day is at hand for the Romans," and in a loud voice exhorted his men to overthrow and destroy their city, adding: "These wolves that made such ravages upon Italian liberty will never vanish until we have cut down the forest that harbours them." It was only after the first hour of the night that the Roman army was able to recover its breath, and the enemy retired. The next day Telesinus was found in a half-dying condition, but with the expression of a conqueror upon his face rather than that of a dying man. Sulla ordered his severed head to be fixed upon a spear point and carried around the walls of Praeneste" (The Roman History; Velleius Paterculus; Book II; Parts 27-28; B.C. 30)

"The young Marius, now at last despairing of his cause, endeavoured to make his way out of Praeneste through the tunnels, wrought with great engineering skill, which led into the fields in different directions; but, on emerging from the exit, he was cut off by men who had been stationed there for that purpose. Some authorities have asserted that he died by his own hand, some that he died in company with the younger brother of Telesinus, who was also besieged and was endeavouring to escape with him, and that each ran upon the other's sword. Whatever the manner of his death, his memory is not obscured even to-day by the great figure of his father. Sulla's estimate of the young man is manifest; for it was only after he was slain that he took the name of Felix, a name which he would have been completely justified in assuming had his life ended with his victory" (*ibid*, Paterculus).

"The siege of Marius in Praeneste was directed by Quintus Lucretius Afella, who had been a general on the Marian side but had deserted to Sulla. Sulla commemorated the great good fortune which fell to him on this day by instituting an annual festival of games held in the circus, which are still celebrated as the games of Sulla's victory" (*ibid*, Paterculus).

"Shortly before Sulla's victory at Sacriportus, several leaders of his party had routed the enemy in successful engagements; the two Servilii at Clusium, Metellus Pius at Faventia, and Marcus Lucullus in the vicinity of Fidentia. The terrors of the civil war seemed nearly at an end when they received fresh impetus from the cruelty of Sulla. Being made dictator (the office had been obsolete for one hundred and twenty years, and had been last employed in the year after Hannibal's departure from Italy; it is therefore clear that the fear which caused the Roman people to feel the need of a dictator was outweighed by the fear of his excessive power) Sulla now wielded with unbridled cruelty the powers which former dictators had employed only to save their country in times of extreme danger. He was the first to set the precedent for proscription—would that he had been the last! The result was that in the very state in p111 which an actor who had been hissed from the stage has legal redress for wilful abuse, a premium for the murder of a citizen was now publicly announced; that the richest man was he who had slain the greatest number; that the bounty for slaying an enemy was no greater than that for slaying a citizen; and that each man became the prize set up for his own death. Nor was vengeance wreaked upon those alone who had borne arms against him, but on many innocents as well. In addition the goods of the proscribed were sold, and their children were not only deprived of their fathers' property but were also debarred from the right of seeking public office, and to cap the climax of injustice, the sons of senators were compelled to bear the burdens and yet lose the rights pertaining to their rank" (*ibid*, Paterculus).

The full tale of how the good patrolman (and author of the below statement) met the ghost of Matteawan Mary:

```
INCIDENT REPORT -
AGENT: Corrections Officer Vincent Cirigliano
RE: Details of Incident Filings on Supernatural
Occurrences
FILE DATE/TIME: 06/24/23 - MON., 02:24
LOCATION: Fishkill State Correctional Facility; 18
Strack Drive, Beacon, New York
DESCRIPTION OF INCIDENT:
```

I have had two personal and very potent experiences regarding paranormal activity while working as an officer within the facility.

Constructed in 1892, Matteawan State Hospital for the Criminally Insane was converted to the state prison in 1977.

Prior to my transfer to Fishkill stories of hauntings at Fishkill were not scarce at my location. In the Albany training academy, our class counselor told us about "Matteawan Mary," a ghost that haunts the facility and seen by many. This "Matteawan Mary" was actually Miss Nellie Wickes, a nurse that worked at Matteawan, in September 1906 she was stabbed 200 times with a scissor to death by an inmate named Mrs. Lizzie Halliday.

I had been transferred from Downstate Correctional Facility to Fishkill around October 2010. For three years I heard seemingly endless ghost tales from officers and inmates alike, sightings, disembodied screams, physical contact, moving objects, etc... In that time I experienced nothing of a paranormal nature, not even an uneasy feeling. That changed in 2013 after I agreed to work a night shift on "8-2 Rec."

The 8-2 Rec post was the recreation room where inmates from housing units 10-2 and 6-2 would watch TV or play cards. The night shift was from 10:30 p.m. to 6:30 a.m. Recreation service in those days closed at 11:00 p.m. on weekdays and 1:00am on weekends and holidays. After its closure and all inmates left the location, the corrections officer became the overnight rover for the two housing units bordering it, doing rounds between the two units ensuring the safety of the posted officers.

Any time I worked an overnight shift I would pray the Rosary or read the Bible to keep me awake. I would especially do this while being the rover who was responsible for emergency responses. On one particular night I was unable to concentrate to pray the Rosary or read.

I had an uneasy feeling and so I just sat in the office, lights out other than a desk lamp, relaxing, feet up on the desk. I kept hearing the distinct sound of keys clanging, like the sound of a large set of keys dangling from an officer's key clip on his belt—except I was alone.

The continued noise was coming from within 8-2 Rec and all doors were closed. To ensure no one was playing tricks, I turned all the lights on and searched the entire area, every closet, bathroom, etc. Satisfied no one was there, I turned the lights off and went back to my previous position of feet on desk. But the key noise persisted every time I tried to relax.

So I got up, went into the middle of the large room, standing, remaining quiet, hoping to hear the noise and better pinpoint it. Instead of the keys, this time heavy foot stomps were heard walking around me, and I mean heavy and very loud, circling me!

The very hairs of my arms stood at attention! It was more than the fear of the unknown, I felt something evil. I felt a hatred,

336

discerning that this thing, this probable demon, would hurt me if it could!

I ran to my desk and grabbed my Rosary, I kissed the Crucifix and in a loud voice I proclaimed that fear would not overtake me and I started audibly reciting the first prayer of the Rosary, "I believe in God the Father Almighty..." After this the footsteps ceased.

I finished one decade of the Rosary and left for housing unit 6-2. I told the officer there of my experience, and she said, "Oh, I'd never work 8-2 overnight again. Last time I worked it the TV kept turning itself on and I heard noises all night."

Fast forward now a week later, and I'm working the south yard with another officer and two other officers, who were hanging out there. Officer Mike Colon asked the group whether anyone had called for overtime yet, and that he was offered 8-2 Rec but turned it down. When asked by another officer why he turned it down, Colon said he had worked it the other night and kept hearing footsteps walking around him.

Colon kept repeating, "It might sound crazy but it was heavy footsteps walking around. I had to leave and stay on the housing unit instead." Note, I did not, prior to that moment, tell Colon of my experience, this was an independent experience that had just happened to him.

That was my first experience with the paranormal at Fishkill, but my second and most strange one occurred some years later.

It was 2020 or 2021. I now worked a "bid" (as the different positions were called) called Fishkill 82, the zone containing buildings 12 and 13. The two structures were connected by a hallway and various stairways. Building 12 housed the work-release inmates while Building 13 housed the school building, visit rooms, a chapel, various inmate programs, and the Law Library.

The duties of my post at Fishkill 82 included responding to emergencies, patrolling rounds of the buildings, performing prisoner or personnel escorts and shutting the location down by the end of my tour. This tour was the afternoon shift, 2:30 p.m. to 10:30 p.m. By 8:45 p.m., all inmates were to leave these buildings and return to their housing units. The officers were all logged out of their assigned posts went to other areas of the facility for various duties.

It was then my duty to go around the entire building shutting lights and locking all doors. Let it be noted, almost no area in these buildings spooked me, no uneasy feelings of any sort did I feel, no paranormal activity of any note, other than one area: the Law Library.

I was not even bothered being alone in the basement, which was an old dungeon of a basement where only a flashlight lit my way. It had a vast network of oddball rooms, hallways turning every which way, a perfect setting for a horror movie! Still, this dungeon spooked me not and I could have even slept down there like a baby. The reverse was true of the Law Library!

You have already read about my experience on 8-2 Rec. Well, I'd prefer to deal with that paranormal activity daily, rather than even walk through the law library once more!

It was situated on the second floor and it was the last area I would shut down within Fishkill 82 for logistical reasons. I would come out of the visit room, go up the stairs that led to the library, unlock the top-stair door and step into the room. I would lock the door behind me, walk through the library as I shut lights off until I got to the end of the room, and then shut the final light and lock the last door, finally exiting the library.

The bad feelings would begin on the stairs leading up to this location, before even unlocking the door to its entrance. It was as if the air would become thicker with each advancing step and a heavy burden of sorts were placed upon my shoulders. It's embarrassing to admit, but half the time I wouldn't even make it into the library itself. I would say, "not today" and immediately go back down the stairs and exit the building.

When I did muster the courage to walk through the Law Library, the hairs would stand up straight on the back of my neck and the feeling of something evil following and watching me was palpable! Do you recall the courage I had on 8-2 Rec when footsteps were going around me? In that moment, I had had the courage to tell myself that fear would not overtake me, I prayed the Rosary, etc. In that law library though, I wouldn't dare take the time to even take my Rosary out of my pocket! I had one aim only, get the hell out as quickly as possible.

While 8-2 Rec had given me the feeling that something evil would hurt me if it could, the Law Library gave me the feeling that whatever evil was there, not only wanted to hurt me but actually in reality could accomplish the task! I have a story I will get to about an incident in this library that is unbelievable! But first I will tell you a bit of a back story that lead to the incident in question.

I was good friends with the library officer, Terry Germano. During the operating hours of the library when inmates were inside, I would often visit and sit with him. I told him about the creepy feelings I had experienced and he told me his experiences at this post. For example, many many times after the inmates had left, the master lock on a cabinet behind the officers desk would start rocking back and forth with great vigor. Germano explained that he would hold the lock to stop it from swinging and then walk away. However, it would start rocking again on its own and this, he said, happened five consecutive times before he hauled ass out of there.

I can tell you this, it would take the force of a leaf blower to cause that big lock to move without human hands, and there was no breeze anywhere, no window by which a breeze would even hit it, only the unseen force that was swinging it to and fro. In our story-sharing of paranormal experiences we found out from old-time officers that the Law Library was once used as the morgue for inmates who passed away while incarcerated. Many officers had similar experiences, stating the same, that nowhere in Building 13 or 12 did they feel spooked or uncomfortable in any way, except in the Law Library.

One night after locking down Building 13 myself, officer Germano and two other officers went outside, onto Post Walkway Bravo, which a footpath that was adjacent to Building 12 where the Law Library was. We started telling our ghost stories and I thought about how great it would be to get evidence of our experiences. I decided that I would gain a little courage and do some ghost investigating.

At Fishkill 82, I was required to wear a police-level body cam at all times. It was to be turned on only during an emergency or due to anticipated use of force involving an inmate. I decided the body cam could now be employed for ghost hunting.

The other officers waited at Bravo for my return. I firstly reached the dreaded stairway that led to the Law Library, and once on its stairwell I powered on the body cam and began recording. The library lights were already off from Building 13 being shut down but the body cam records perfectly in the dark with clarity.

It was strange because as I began walking through the library I had no feelings of being watched or followed. Really, I had no fear at all, even though I was walking alone in the dark (usually I walk in the light and turn the lights off behind me). I figured I simply had become bold now because the body cam was meanwhile rolling, as if the camera was my companion of sorts. Well, that all ended when I reached the final door at the end of the library.

The door was locked for the same reason the lights were already off. So, I unlocked the door, stepped through and began to close it so that I could lock it back up again. Before I even shut the door completely, suddenly the uneasy feeling came over me again and something screamed into my ear.

It screamed with a loud blood-curdling scream that gives me chills to this day when I think of it, and in fact I have those chills as I write this now!

It was as if a mouth was directly touching my ear as the screaming occurred. I got out of there with great haste, heart pounding out of my chest! I hurried back to Post Walkway Bravo and started telling them what had just happened.

Now before I go further, let me tell you about body-cam protocol. Before the start of each shift, an officer who required a body cam must pick one up at the body-cam office. However, a body cam from a previous shift must not be used until after it has fully been recharged. The officer must use a new one with a freshly charged and tested battery.

After receiving said body cam, the officer is required to turn it on, record for a few moments, then turn it off and then back on to see if it is functioning properly. These units cost around $1,000 and an officer is personally held responsible if it breaks outside of normal use ("normal use" being the execution of force or his dropping the cam during an emergency situation). I indeed tested this camera as per protocol.

The whole point of these tough police-grade body cam is to capture video and audio evidence if use of force occurs. The last thing anyone wants to hear is that the intended recorded evidence pertaining to an incident is ruined because the body cam broke.

The lens is set deeply inside the cam housing. One would require impacting a narrow dense object, such as a nail punch hit with a hammer to purposely break the lens. That is, it was virtually impossible to break the body cam's strong well-protected lens during any normal use. Now back to the story.

After telling the officers of what I had experienced, I eagerly went into the body cam footage and I hit Play.

We viewed my walking up the stairs to the Law Library, unlocking the door, and heard all the noise of my keys and the door and my footsteps. We watched me shut the door and begin to lock it. But this is when the clear footage and sound suddenly cut out.

You could still make out that I was walking and could perceive traces of images that were very blurry and distorted as I passed them by, but there was no sound at all. The scream couldn't be captured. The sound recording simply stopped working right when the video was distorted.

I started looking at the cam closer and noticed the lens, the impossible-to-break lens was shattered! The cam not only had worked perfectly when I tested it at the start of the shift, but it worked perfectly all the way up those stairs and while opening the Law-Library door and up to the point I was about to lock the door behind me. Therefore, that lens shattered in that moment when I began to lock the door behind me.

What's odd is that nothing had happened to it. I mean, my body cam didn't even touch anything. There were no sounds of anything happening to it. A lens does not simply spontaneously explode and certainly would not shatter without notice!

They are built to last and hold up during a physical confrontation with any person. They can be punched, kicked, smashed into a wall or floor and yet they will hold up perfectly fine. All I did was walk and unlock and then lock doors.

Whatever evil and/or demonic force was in the Law library that night, knew exactly what my plans were, and it was messing with me. It broke that camera knowing that I was looking for evidence and it screamed in my ear as a warning, most likely.

("The Good Patrolman Meets the Ghost of Matteawan Mary"; Vincent Cirigliano; *Jeremiad Christian Homesteaders Gazette*; Vol. 3; Issue 1; Autumn, 2023)

Depopulation Math:

The formulas on the following page are applied by scientists to statistical predictions about sets of animal and insect populations in relation birth rate and rate of death. These formulas are now being used to project a quantifiable value for the Population (i.e., P) variable in item 9, for human beings in terms of reducing human birth rate and increasing the rate of death.

DEPOPULATION MATH By Fr. Mike DellaVecchia

"Now, we put out a lot of carbon dioxide every year—over 26 billion tons. For each American, it's about 20 tons … The world today has 6.8 billion people. That's headed up to about nine billion. Now, if we do a really great job on new vaccines, health care, reproductive health services, we could lower that by, perhaps, 10 or 15 percent" ("Innovating to Zero"; Bill Gates; *TEDTalks*: Feb. 2010).

1) Exponential growth is modeled as an exponential equation	2) This looks like:	3) An Average Population, M, that is reaching its Carrying Capacity looks
Proportional growth has us make P(t) the population x over time t, and we make P_0 be the original population when $t=0$, let's make k equal consistent population growth and exponentiate it by e (*Euler's constant* of ~2.718).	$$P(t) = P_0 e^{kt}$$	like: $$\frac{dP}{dt} = kP\left(1 - \frac{P}{M}\right)$$
4) If we make β the "birth rate" of the population, and δ the "death rate" of the population—not as constants but as things dependent on time and/or food supply, etc., the simplest population model that looks like: $$\frac{dP}{dt} = (\beta - \delta)P$$	5) To assign a necessary constant for population modeling, mathematicians apply the same formula used to calculate *compound interest* in banking: $$\frac{dP}{dt} = kP$$	6) When *Birth Rate* is lower than population growth: $$\beta = \beta_0 - \beta_1 P$$ and the *Death Rate* is constant: $$\delta = \delta_0$$

7) Mathematicians thus begin to compute a differential to account for Zero:

$$\frac{dP}{dt} = (\beta_0 - \beta_1 P - \delta_0)P$$

where $k = b$ and $M = a/b$

They derive a *Logistic Growth Equation* with initial condition $P(0) = P_0 > 0$:

$$\frac{dP}{dt} = kP(M - P)$$

8) Nicknamed, the "Doomsday-Extinction Model," the *Logistic Growth Equation* solves it. This model is known in Statistics is:

$$\frac{dP}{dt} = kP^2 - \delta P = kP(P - M)$$

9) If population growth P equals *Zero*, the *Depopulation Equation* regresses from:

P x S x E x C = CO2 output

P = population; S = services used by people; E= the energy needed to power those services; and C equals the carbon dioxide created by that energy.

10) A non-differentiable regression, akin to the *Weierstrauss Function*, is known as *Pathological Math*.

344

www.ingramcontent.com/pod-product-compliance
Lightning Source LLC
LaVergne TN
LVHW052059060326
832903LV00060B/2197